God Told Me to Hate You!

An Evangelical Minister's

Escape from the Clerical Closet

By: Rev. Tom Muzzio *(resigned)*

Territorial Enterprise Foundation
P.O. Box 16
Virginia City, NV 89440

ISBN: 0-9969628-1-6
ISBN-13: 978-0-9969628-1-0

Library of Congress Control
Number: 2015912431

Cover photo: Westboro Baptist
Church

Edited by Edith Zdunich

Table of Contents

PROLOGUE: AN ISLAND SOMEWHERE

"They ought to take them all out and put them on an island somewhere!" declared Dr. Al Crawford, his jowls quivering. He wasn't really a doctor of any kind, but had an "honorary doctorate" from some obscure little Bible institute in southern India. We all called him Doc, nevertheless, because he liked the sound of it. A real fossil, he was basically harmless—a relic of a bygone era—a crusty, old–school missionary who genuinely wanted to bring salvation and "civilization" to the darker-skinned peoples of the Earth.

"Yeah," piped up one of the younger guys. "They can't reproduce, so hopefully they will just die out."

"Well, gentlemen, this is just another sign of the times," said one of the other ministers thoughtfully. "This just indicates to me more clearly that Jesus could come at any time!" They all hoped that it would be soon.

We had been passing around the latest issue of Asian TIME magazine, featuring an extensive cover story on gay rights. As usual, for the sake of sensationalism, prominently featured right up front in a photo montage were the now famous *Sisters of Perpetual Indulgence*—gay guys in nun drag, complete with beads, sequins, and high heels. I thought it was a hoot, but it was apparent to me that everybody else was taking it all very seriously.

Of course, I had a different perspective than the other ministers who were sitting around the living room in my large flat in Hong Kong, with French doors wide open to the beautiful harbor below, millions of lights glowing in the twilight. We had met for our monthly prayer meeting. And since my place was the biggest, I usually hosted these events where the women all got together in the kitchen and talked of weddings and babies, while the men sat around in the living room drinking coffee and talking of politics and airfares. By this point in my ministry, I already knew that I was no longer a part of saving-the-teeming-millions stuff. However, having a family and career, and always receiving a great deal of respect for my talents and accomplishments in the Gospel business, I was as yet unsure how I was going to actually manage my escape.

Suffice it to say that I finally succeeded. Now, as I look back and recount the events and emotions of my life as a Fundamentalist Evangelical Christian, I both laugh and cry. I have found that Fundamentalism is like flypaper for me. No matter how hard I try to shake it, I can't quite get free of it. I receive emails daily from Fundies who have one of two agendas. The first are old friends who really do love me (and hate my sin). And the others are old enemies who hate me (and hate my sin). The first are genuinely concerned for my eternal soul, and the second gleefully relish the idea of me burning in the dreaded lake of fire. My ex-wife said to me in amazement that even after rejecting everything about Fundamentalism—its doctrines, practices, and all of its miscellaneous trappings—I was still a Fundamentalist at heart. Even though I had gone from being a Fundamentalist believer to a Fundamentalist nonbeliever, I was just as adamant and dogmatic as ever about how I approached religion. I used to preach: "It's either all or nothing at all!" . . . And, actually, I can't help it—I still buy that. It was once all, and now it is nothing at all.

Regarding name-calling: I am still fundamentalist enough to want to use certain terminology. To me, the word "Christian" means a born-again, Bible-believing, Fundamentalist *Protestant* Christian. If I want to speak about Roman Catholics, Mormons, the Moonies, or the Jehovah's Witnesses, I always refer to them specifically as *non*-Christians. And above all, I always refer to liberal Protestant denominations by their specific church affiliations. We referred to them as "Christians in name only." In other words, a Christian *is* a fundamentalist—period. How is that for dogmatic?

There is a general understanding that Fundamentalist Christians and Roman Catholics are quite different. Catholics talk to God, while God talks to Protestants. In no place is this more obvious than Pentecostal churches, where even the most unsophisticated can get a "word of knowledge" directly from the mouth of the Almighty himself.

Years ago, I was preaching in an Assembly of God church in Springfield, Oregon, and, during the course of the sermon, I mentioned that I had a phobia about something which I presently don't even recall. But the part

I remember fondly is what happened after the service, during the period when the acolytes swarm down upon the visiting speaker, usually asking for a special prayer or blessing from one of God's truly anointed. On this particular evening, a well-meaning, portly woman in a white faux fur coat and matching boots pushed her way up to me. She looked like a polar bear, and the ensemble just wouldn't have been complete without the matching white coffee-table-sized family Bible that she carried conspicuously near her heart. She came up to share a word that the Lord had given directly to her for me during my sermon.

"Brother Muzzio," she exclaimed breathily, "God gave me a word of knowledge while you were preaching, and he told me to tell you that you should have no phobias. Phobias are of the devil. In fact, while you were preaching I saw the letter "F" appear on your tongue! That was clearly a sign that God doesn't want you to have any more fobias!" I admit that I was a bit skeptical. Either God needed an editor or spell-check. But what could I say? God told her!

THE CHOICE

To jump or not to jump? That is the question.

The express train was racing at high speed down the tracks on the main line between Wu Han and Chang Sha in the flat plains of central China, when it suddenly lurched violently. Luggage from overhead came cascading down on us as the iron wheels shrieked against the rails with the sound of a metal saw. The passengers who were riding forward flew into those of us riding backward in the six-person compartment. It took what seemed like forever to finally make a full stop.

The five Chinese guys that I had only met within the hour when I boarded in Wu Han, had been in that compartment for hours since Beijing where the train had begun its long haul to its destination, Guangzhou. We had become fast friends, sharing snacks that they had wisely brought along for the twenty-five-hour trek, and tea from one of those thermos bottles that are so ubiquitous in China. We all jumped up at once, slid the compartment door open, and rushed into the narrow aisle that was full of people and luggage in total disarray. The sliding window was already down, as it was May, and the warm spring air came wafting in along with all those familiar smells of rural China.

"What's happening?" everyone was shouting at each other. At this point no one had a clue, but we knew that something was definitely wrong. Across a field of blooming yellow rapeseed plants was a small village like any other found in their tens of thousands throughout the ancient Middle Kingdom. Villagers were coming out to see what was going on. I am sure they were quite accustomed to the trains of the Chinese Rail Service regularly zooming past their oblivious sleepy village. But this afternoon it had stopped with enough noise to raise the dead.

They were walking single file along one of those narrow footpaths just wide enough for one person to allow another to pass sideways. Then some of the men in front began to run. At that moment we heard the sound of running feet crunching on the gravel siding below, and suddenly the train's conductor appeared with several other official-looking men in uniforms. They stopped directly beneath our open window. All I could see was the tops of their stiff, round, military-style hats and uniformed shoulders with epaulets containing the red insignia of the People's Rail Service. They had run from the engine all the way back to our carriage, which was second from the end.

They were in a state of panic, shouting to each other, totally ignoring the passengers who were yelling to us what was wrong. It was hard to make much of anything when everybody was yelling and screaming at the same time. But we finally began getting the drift. "She just jumped right out in front of the train," the engineer shouted. "I hardly even saw her," shouted the other. And the others all yelled their agreement. By then the first of the male villagers had arrived, and the rest began running up to the train as well. By the time the women began arriving, there were at least thirty peasants on the scene. They all began shouting as well, and the cacophony grew.

Finally we got it. A woman from the village had been hit by the train, and her remains were right under our very car. Of course, from our vantage point, we could see nothing. But the railroad officials were now shouting at the villagers: "It had to be suicide! She just jumped right out in front of us. We didn't even see her!" I could tell that the peasants, always leery of men in official uniforms of any kind, appeared skeptical. "Look," one of the uniformed men shouted at the crowd, "She must have jumped onto the tracks on purpose! Ai Ya!, anyone could have seen this train coming a mile away!" Of course, we all knew that they were right. On that straight stretch of track, an approaching train could easily be seen and heard from far away.

That discourse lasted only briefly followed by the next obvious question: "Well, what are we to do now?" I guess one of the officials had already anticipated that and had started to run back up to the engine to radio for help, and for instructions from a superior of the rail line. Very seldom do officials take any initiative in a totalitarian society like China's. It's easier and safer to ask a higher-up and wait for a comeback. Often it has to filter up through layers of bureaucracy or at least wait until someone in real authority (meaning the Communist Party) gives the word.

Everyone was still chattering like a flock of geese when they suddenly noticed me. "Look, a foreigner! A Ghost!" For a moment the old woman under the train was forgotten as all eyes were on me. I thought: How amazing! This day is really weird. And likely tongues will be wagging for weeks in the village about how the "Foreign Devil" must certainly be behind all this mischief and mayhem. Old superstitions die hard in those myriad small rural villages in mainland China. Despite years of the ruling Communist Party's attempts to eradicate all superstition (including all religion), it is just a thin veneer over centuries of tradition. And in little nameless villages like the one across the field, traditions trump most of the party's efforts to change things in the countryside.

Before speculation had resumed as to whether or not the dreaded foreigner had in any way cursed the woman, the train, or whatever, a man in his fifties pushed through the crowd. Everyone deferred and parted to let him through. He addressed the train's conductor directly. "I am So and So, the Village Leader." He said matter-of-factly. I was never quite sure how somebody got to be a village leader. By a democratic vote? Hardly. Consensus? I doubt it. Somehow I figured that he was a Communist Party member. It is so often assumed in the West that everyone in China is a communist. This is untrue. The Party is not something one just decides to join. It is considered an honor to be selected in childhood to become a *Young Pioneer* and begin years of political indoctrination and training to become one of the elite four percent of the population that will be entitled to the privileges due party members, who get to ride roughshod over the other ninety-six percent of the population. This was just a clear case in point.

He then barked an order: "Get her out from under there!" Immediately several villagers and the rail officials sprang into action and climbed under the carriage to pull her out. She was so twisted and gnarled as to almost be unrecognizable as a person. I'll say that I haven't seen anyone as badly dismembered and deformed since bomb victims during the war in Viet Nam. As they searched along the length of the train for missing limbs, the villagers wrapped her in a black plastic sheet used to cover plants in the early spring. Then they carried her away toward the village. The village leader and the railway personnel began walking up toward the front of the train. Obviously, they needed to compare notes and get their story straight. There would likely be an inquiry, and no one wanted to be the one left without a chair when the music stopped. We took our seats again and the suppositions flew. Unlike earlier in our trip, before the incident, when I was being bombarded with questions from the guys who admitted that none had ever even spoken to a Westerner before, I was no longer the subject of fascination. We had all been through a very wrenching experience, and I guess I had become just one of the guys at that point. We all discussed the tragedy and analyzed every angle until long after dark. After we stopped briefly in Chang Sha, the city where Chairman Mao Tse Tung was born, we all fell silent, anticipating the eleven remaining hours aboard before reaching

Canton. I tried to sleep, but it was impossible. The others dozed. Alone at last with my thoughts, accompanied by the rocking of the train and the sound of the iron wheels on the tracks, I put the awful experience of the day out of my thoughts. I had just returned from several days with friends in Wu Han, and it had been a delightful experience and a time of soul-searching and confession as well. I recalled our time together fondly.

* * * * *

Dominique and Renate were the quintessential Will and Grace, years ahead of their time. I had known them and traveled with them for a few years already, as they came to Hong Kong together, whenever they could get permission from the honchos at the University of Wu Han, to escape the drudgery of life in the People's Republic. The Universities in China were rarely administered at a very high level by educators. The top dogs were always party hacks who were more concerned with maintaining order and the status quo than in education. And then there were the secret police spying and reporting back to somewhere.

Dominique and I had met in Hong Kong and immediately become friends. It helped that we knew a lot of the same people. The next time he arrived in the Crown Colony, he had Renate in tow. We also hit it off immediately. Dominique taught French and French literature at the University. He was a gay man serving his "sentence" in China to make enough money to return to France someday to be with Christian, his lover of many years, who was working for the French Department of Culture in Morocco at the time. They made far more money this way by a long shot than they would have teaching in France. He explained to me that they both had to suffer living in undesirable places to make enough to afford life in a "fashionable" neighborhood near the heart of Paris later on.

Renate was a German teacher from Vienna. Her situation was similar, as money was the only thing that kept her in China as well. She was crazy about Dominique, and they hung out together all the time—the closest of friends. As they were inseparable, everybody just assumed that they were an item. None of the thirty or so foreign teachers in the Language Department doubted that they were sleeping together. That would have been against the rules, but the administration assumed the same thing, turning a blind eye. Even the Gung An Bao (the secret police) had reported the same. When Dominique told me this, we both rolled on the floor laughing.

I had sent Dominique a telegram from Hong Kong telling him that my big boss and his wife were visiting from the States and wanted to go into Mainland China. I would escort them and two other American colleagues of mine from Hong Kong. Then, I would leave them in Shanghai, and fly onward to Wu Han. The flight would have been unremarkable if it were not for the folding chairs in the aisle to accommodate more passengers—sans seat belts!

I arrived at the seedy airport in Wu Han. No Dominique. Well, damn . . . now what? I figured I would just stand in the hotel line, get a room, and figure things out from there. Then, out of the blue, there he was, his cute little French face beaming! We hugged in a rather Gaulic way—which in itself is seen as weird and very strange in China. Then we grabbed a cab and headed for his place. "I just learned this morning that you were coming!" he said, to my surprise. "I sent the telegram two weeks ago!" I said incredulously. "Yes, I saw that when they gave it to me today, but they said that they withheld it because your upcoming visit might negatively impact my teaching." We both had a laugh, as we knew full well that that was bologna. It's a control thing.

But the good news was that not only had they given him a freebie leave of seven days, but that they had given Renate one as well! Go figure. We had a ball. I met all the other teachers, first eating at the French-speaking table, then the German. The two English-speaking tables were keen to meet and talk as well as were the Italians. Everyone was impressed that Dominique had not only managed to have a visitor from the "outside," but that he got a seven-day leave . . . and not only that—Renate got one too! Word travels fast. How did he do it, people asked. He was really enjoying this, and just replied obliquely, if demurely.

We ran all over Wu Han and the surrounding countryside, visiting all the sights and experiencing way more freedom than any of us had thought possible. No doubt, the Gung An Bao were watching; but their cover must have been pretty good since we didn't see them at all. We rode all over in buses and cabs, speaking German just to frustrate the English-speaking cab driver who no doubt was assigned to keep tabs on us by you know who. If we needed a cab, the University would quickly call for one, complete with the eyes and ears of the powers that be.

Most of the time we just rode bicycles supplied by the University. It was great and we all got very much better-acquainted if that was possible. In my case, it certainly was. We had each talked about intimate details of our lives, childhoods, thoughts, hopes, dreams, and disappointments. I couldn't believe how much we were able to talk about ourselves and our previous adventures together in Tibet, Xinjiang, and other off-the-wall parts of China that few foreigners had yet visited at the time. I still remember Renate's great remark: "Gott sei dank, (thank God) we got there before the Coke machines!"

We were so used to being bugged inside buildings that, like everyone in China, we never spoke too freely unless we knew that we were out of range of the secret police. However, we managed to overcome that in parks and other public places. Finally, I was about to explode. Really wanting to talk on a deeper level about the inner conflicts in my life, I suggested renting a boat to go out on a local lake. I had learned this trick from a Chinese friend in Hang Zhou. He had told me that it was a way to escape the government's tentacles since they couldn't hear you if you spoke softly. We did. I had not known friends to be so open and sympathetic in ages. So I shared my secret. (Although Dominic had visited my office in Hong Kong one night late after all the staff had long gone, he really did not know what I did there and had never asked.)

When I said that I wanted to tell them my real secret they spoke in unison: "You work for the CIA!" Actually, I did have a friend in the American consulate in Hong Kong who always "informally interviewed" me over lunch whenever I was back from a trip to China. But I explained, "CIA? No, worse . . . I am a clergyman." They looked puzzled. "And not just that. I am a missionary!" They still did not register a real response—just a sort of "go on . . ." I was sure that they were picturing the typical 19th century cartoon image of the missionary wearing a pith helmet, sweating and bubbling in a large black stew pot surrounded by natives in loin cloths with spears, who were anticipating a fresh meal.

I knew, of course, that Europeans have a totally different idea of what a missionary is. Having lived in Europe for years, I already knew that the French had an image of the Black Robes, French Catholic missionaries who had penetrated deep into the wilds of Canada in the late 18th century. Their stories about the ruthlessness of the native tribes were legendary. The German image was that of Albert Schweitzer. In any case, my two friends had absolutely no clue about American religious culture, so I began to explain.

I had been born into a Post-World War II world in the United States. It was a very secular world where it was unsurprising that the notion of a God or Jesus was rarely mentioned in my family as I grew up. In college I had converted to Christianity, and I had been on a journey ever since that had taken me all over the world, through all sorts of changes, self-reinventions, and metamorphoses. At first I had been like a sponge, enthusiastically learning all about my newfound faith. As time went by, I felt "called" by God into the ministry and to overseas missionary service. All of this had ultimately led me to China where I had become involved in what I had begun to consider illegal, unethical, and deceptive behavior.

They had heard of Pat Robertson, Jerry Falwell, and Jim and Tammy Faye Bakker, as well as some others. But it was all a strange and weird American thing to them. They encouraged me to tell my story. So I did, and by the time they saw me off at the Wu Han railway station the following day, my head was spinning, as I had not confided my true and inner feelings to anyone in years. I had a lot to think about on the long trip back to home in Hong Kong.

What was I doing here? I had become a missionary to bring the Gospel of Christ to people like the old woman they had just pulled out from under the train a few hours earlier. And yet, there she had been—dead as a doornail . . . and now, supposedly burning in a Christian hell—a lake of fire designated for those who have not accepted Jesus Christ as their personal Lord and Savior.

In earlier times I would have blocked out issues like these from my mind. I reconsidered the question most often posed to Christians by non-Christians: "How can your loving God condemn those who have never even heard the message of the Gospel?" How indeed?

Even then, on the train gliding down the tracks in the darkness, I wondered whether or not I really believed any of it anymore. By the time I stepped off the train onto the hard concrete platform in Guang Zhou in the muggy, early morning light, to wait another three hours alone for the connection to Hong Kong, I knew this chapter of my life was over. Now what? I had time to think back on how it had all begun.

NATURE OR NURTURE?

How many times do we have to ask that?

Since this is a memoir and not an autobiography, I don't feel the need to slavishly follow the calendar or otherwise create a rigid time line in recounting things as I remember them. Looking back over the years, and listening to the Christian Fundamentalists' endless preachings, I have concluded that I was a real dope for ever falling for their line. But I did. Nevertheless, before I "accepted Jesus Christ into my heart as my personal Lord and savior," I was an atheist. "How can a little kid be an atheist?" one might ask. Well, I suppose you could say that I was "agnostic" from birth, as it sounds so much more benign to the sensibilities of many who fear the word *atheist*—especially as it may apply to young children. Okay, I was agnostic. In other words, I didn't know anything of the Christian god, his son Jesus the Christ, Mother Mary, the heavenly host, or that really super bad guy, Satan. I honestly had never heard of any of them in any detail or with any explanation at all about them until a certain incident happened in 1955. It rocked my life completely.

I grew up in a rather idyllic environment, with two loving parents, four wonderful grandparents close at hand, and an assortment of aunts, uncles, and cousins all living within close proximity of the city of Portland, Oregon, in the cool green Pacific Northwest. I had an elder brother whom I loved dearly. We were like a little version of Mutt and Jeff. We played in our large yard, in the surrounding fields and forests, horse pastures, and just about anywhere else within earshot of my Mom's calling voice. What a cool way to be a little kid! Then, when Warren turned six he started school. I had to entertain myself until that big yellow school bus rumbled its way down our unpaved rural road and dropped him off right at our mailbox. I waited for him faithfully every day. When he was seven and I was five, he came home from school in the usual way and we headed out to play together as always. He told Mom that he didn't feel well, but insisted that he was fine. He wanted to go and watch some carpenters who were working on our small horse barn. That night he died.

For years I never knew of the circumstances, as I was in a kind of shock. I was sent to live with my grandparents temporarily while my parents grieved and took care of my younger sister who was just a toddler at the time. Years later, whenever I had reason to mention this—especially to my religious friends—they would suck in air and exclaim that it was such an early childhood loss that "turned me gay." A trauma like that had certainly triggered something in my little brain that made me want to replace my dear brother with "men." Of course, at five I was hardly thinking of oral sex or frottage at the time, but I actually bought into that possibility for a spell when I was a "new Christian" some years later.

Oddly enough, my father also pointed to that loss years earlier as an explanation for why I felt compelled to "get into religion." Obviously, everybody felt for my loss, but then used that event and experience to espouse their own particular point of view on the subject of religion and sexual orientation. I still think both points of view are stupid. I didn't "go gay" due to a childhood trauma. Likewise, I did not "go into religion" as a sort of replacement therapy. I was born gay, and I have always been attracted to guys; and have always had a "best friend" in school and college, the military and beyond. So what? I was always dripping with self-confidence and had a natural cheerful disposition to which I credit my Mom's lucky genes. I always said that she was "born on a sunny day."

Dad was a different story. His midwinter birthday sort of reflected his dour personality. He did, I guess, have a sort of sense of humor. Well, he always thought his jokes were funny. Never "laugh out loud" funny— his yarns. You had to get with his program to understand them. He taught high school at the all-male academy, Benson Polytechnic, which I likewise attended. We drove in to school each morning and back again like clockwork in the afternoon. It was then that we bonded. I had long ago learned that he was a bigot. In later years, my sister, Birdi, and I laughed, saying that he was not prejudiced, as he hated all minorities equally. He was truly intolerant. He hated all blacks, Hispanics of all descriptions, all Asians, and all women, whom he called "dames." He would say the most horrible things about women in front of my mom. She simply ignored him. I learned to do that later as well. He never noticed. He hated all foreigners whether they were living in the U.S. or even in their own countries. He hated all Europeans, especially the Swedes, as "they voted against us in the UN every chance they got!" Latin Americans and Africans didn't even count.

If he had lived long enough to learn the neocon term "mud people" he would have loved it. Asians were all dogs, especially *The Japs.* Channel surfing, I realize that I know something about Republicans. I grew up in a family full of, not just Republicans, but rip-roarin' Republicans—and not the religious wacko-birds, who I came to know as time went by, but more "country club Republicans." Heck, I was about ten before I realized that "damndemocrat" wasn't all one word! Of course, he would have looked down his nose at most of the "Mrs. Robinson" Republicans, preferring to pontificate to me alone, and to his students who needed his approval and his liberal grades. He managed every year to make little conservatives out of several of his students who vied for his attention and approval. I wonder how many of them stuck with the bizarre political theories and wacked-out attitudes that he daily perpetrated on those otherwise very brilliant students under his year-to-year tutelage.

* * * * *

Benson High School was unique for its time. Unlike the neighborhood schools that form the city's various school districts, where a young person would simply go from grade school into the nearest high school in their part of town, Benson required an application. And they never let us forget that we were there to study and not play around. "If you don't cut the mustard here, you can always go back to your neighborhood schools!" was the constant threat. Most of us took it seriously and did get a fine education (as far as the American educational system might allow). Dad had the brightest students in the school—juniors and seniors with a scientific bent. He taught a two-year course of study called "radio electronics." It was the era of the transistor—after the vacuum tube and before the silicon chip. Today it would more likely be called computer science, but back then it was definitely the cutting edge; and most of his students went on to great universities and later into lucrative careers. He loved his students, and reveled in their successes. But he was still a jerk when it came to any socially-related subject like history, social studies, religion, or politics. He was a devotee of Ayn Rand and her ilk. And I struggled to break free for years . . . until I did!

But lest I give the impression that my dad's self-centered ways "made me gay," I hasten to point out that he systematically turned me into a carbon copy of himself over time. I bought into all his Right-wing, jingoistic bullshit for many years during my childhood. And I can only imagine what an insufferable little snot I must have been during those formative years. I was always the "smartest kid in the class" and I knew it. I felt superior but had the good sense not to show it too much. Maybe it was my mom's natural charm that informed me to be kind and polite to everybody—even if I thought they were "lowbrow" (as Dad would call just about everybody everywhere all the time). I did have a humane streak, and it defined me more and more as I became an adolescent and then gradually a young adult.

My father did, however, give me one gift when I was fifteen that really helped me shape the course of my life, altering its trajectory forever. He always saw me as his ultimate project—a mini version of himself, able to do things that he never could, nor ever had the opportunity to. One afternoon while riding back home after school, Dad kind of surprised me. He stated in the form of a mild lament that most of his students were "wasting their time" in high school. "All of those guys could easily be in college right now and doing fine." Then the shocker: "Of course, you could too." It is such a waste that the school system forces all students of the same age to go through school at the same pace despite the inequities of their I.Q.s! Gosh. I hadn't even thought of it like that. But he had been thinking that way for years.

"How would you like to skip the rest of high school and go right to college after school ends this spring?" he asked flatly. I don't recall much of what happened next, other than that I was sitting in class at Lewis & Clark College a month or so later for Summer Session. Apparently they had a category called "special student," which was a catchall category for certain foreign students and others who didn't fit into any particular mold, but who otherwise qualified academically to attend school there (and could afford the tuition). How he pulled it off I will never know. But Dad had graduated from that small yet snobby university with its park-like campus overlooking the city of Portland, and he still had friends in the faculty and administration.

Well, I took a full load of difficult classes like Poli Sci., International Affairs, and U.S. History. And to pump up my grades and enthusiasm, I took several art courses. I loved them all and finished the first two terms with a 4.0, quietly registering for fall term as a regular student without drawing any undue attention to myself. Computers would catch stuff like that these days; but I just registered, paid the money, and showed up for class the first day, never looking back.

I studied like mad and was a great student, perhaps due to the fact that I had no real social life. Being obviously younger than my classmates, I never really got acquainted with anyone, save for the occasional friendly conversation or shared work project. I learned to subordinate my snooty self-centeredness and cultivated my inner Mom. I took over our 1959 Ford pickup, driving to school every day and living at home. Mostly I just studied and lived a rather insular life. I didn't regret missing out on the high school prom or leaving behind friends and the fun fun fun life of a baby boom teenager in the 1960s. The times were indeed a changin'. And I was, as usual, simply ahead of my age and time.

My father had lived through the Great Depression of the 1930s, and the experience really defined his whole life and mentality. He never felt like he had enough, and strove endlessly to gain more and more of everything. He was a penny-pinching miser of the first order; and when he began paying my exorbitant tuition at school, I was indeed shocked. I began realizing that it was an investment on his part. It was not just that he was going to prove his point that most of the top performers in high school could handle college level work after their sophomore year, but that I personally was going to validate that postulate for him. On top of that, he had already figured out my whole future for me, including what classes I should take and what courses of study—what curricula—I should embark upon immediately. After all, he figured, since he was paying for it, I would simply have to comply. And I did—at first, that is.

My dad's theory—his hypothesis—was open-ended enough to allow me a lot of latitude regarding what courses I would need to take. He didn't much care *what* path I pursued . . . as long as it made a lot of money in the end. I was good at everything I had ever tried (save math), but since I had been quite infatuated with my high school biology teacher, Father Dearest rather locked in on the idea that I should plan on Pre-Med as option A. Of course, I loved English, foreign languages, literature and history, so a walk down the legal isle was not out of the question either.

Lawyers make big bucks as well. The main point was that an education had one goal only: the accumulation of wealth. Certain professions clearly paid higher salaries and afforded more opportunities to gather wealth that could be invested to make more wealth. He was a sincere devotee of the likes of the "Robber Barons" of the 19th century in America. The Andrew Carnegies, John D. Rockefellers, and J.P. Morgans of the world were his true heroes. He so wanted to be like them, but having settled for the humble life of a school teacher, he felt totally cheated. Well, if he wasn't ever going to be really rich, then—by God—his kid was going to. And that was final.

My artistic abilities had always impressed him, and were the cause of a great deal of bragging to his friends. His elder brother was an architect, and my dad was jealous of that all his life. When I was young and showed promise of natural innate art talent, he felt somehow vindicated. He may not have been gifted with skill in music or art, but by god, he could produce someone who was. That would be me. Art to him was like a parlor trick—one of those things that super intelligent people just happen to be able to do out of their hip pocket. Well, my son, the big time rich doctor is also an accomplished painter. I figured out that fantasy of his clear back in grade school. Art is not a possible career choice. It is a backup to impress people at cocktail parties. "Artists starve." But it is a handy aside to impress people—especially perfect strangers. He embarrassed me endlessly with his boasting about the talented artist that his loins had produced. I saw it as a kind of divine gift. And that attitude played well in Evangelical circles, as I was to soon learn.

China was in the throes of the Great Proletariat Cultural Revolution at the same time that I was considering career moves. I read about it in one of my classes in cultural anthropology or some other such course that I was taking on the sly. If my dad knew that I was wasting his precious money on such frivolity, he would have "blown his top." That was a popular expression of his time, but "freaked out" would have been more appropriate for the mid-sixties, I guess. Anyway, I took to intercepting the mail from school—including report cards—that were sent directly to our mailbox by the college. I was aware of my vulnerability financially, and doing such things was risky. As with all such criminal activities, sooner or later I was bound to get busted. But I kept pressing my luck, studying what I liked and not what he liked. It was not really a battle of the wills, as I had long before learned to yield to his will—even if I was only play-acting. Then, the plot thickened when

I decided that what I really wanted to study at the time was Chinese. Well, Lewis and Clark didn't teach Mandarin. But Portland State did. I quietly and surreptitiously enrolled myself as a transfer student and began my career as a double agent.

Most gay young men of the time were already adroit at playing a role. For the most part, we had learned much earlier on in grade school (or certainly in high school) to "play it straight." Pretending to "like girls" was second nature to me by then, so it wasn't much of a stretch pretending to be studying at the library at Lewis and Clark while driving a few miles into downtown Portland to attend my Chinese classes. Even at that time, PSU was the biggest university in Oregon—larger in student population than either Oregon State (where my parents had graduated years earlier) or that dreaded bastion of liberalism, the University of Oregon in Eugene. I was still under my father's influence enough politically at the time as to actually have believed that the U of O was nothing more than a "hippy college" that was full of damndemocrats, communists, socialists, unsavory foreigners, and other undesirables of various descriptions.

Actually, this anti-liberal bias that I had learned as a child, stood me in good stead in the years that lay ahead in the Fundamentalist Christian movement, where such attitudes are not only enshrined but demanded. Being a Right-wing stooge was an easy role to play despite the fact that certain more open-minded traits were beginning to spring forth from the cold earth of my psyche even at that time. But I just kept my mouth shut around home and railed against those dreadful "red" Chinese at the dinner table, much to the delight of my old man. I dedicated my entire life at the time to study, so getting a job to support myself and my useless, self-indulgent studies was impossible. I was living on an intellectual gravy train, and I knew it. I also knew that it wouldn't last, so I enjoyed the ride. And it lasted a couple of years. In that entire university with over twenty-thousand-plus students at the time, there were exactly four of us who were studying Chinese. It was so unpopular that there was a constant rumor that the course would be dropped, and Dr. Kuo, the only professor of the language would have to find work at a local Chinese restaurant or take up teaching something else.

Actually, he too was totally aware of the precariousness of teaching a course the school administration found suspect. I learned later that he'd always been under quiet surveillance by police and governmental organizations for "un-American" activities. He also taught a class in the history of China, which I audited, not daring to risk being caught walking that close to the "red" line.

I never talked about my life as a double agent to anybody. I concealed my interest in all things Chinese from my folks and my few friends at Lewis and Clark. And, of course, I hid my homosexual interests from everybody all the time. It was second nature. I was never "found out." I just quietly lived a life of unquenchable desire for meaningful sex, never acting on those forbidden impulses. Then I met Glenn.

We sat side by side in a drawing class and hit it off right away. He was outgoing and seemingly carefree. He always had time to stop and smell the roses (and all other plant life as well). He was always full of new and interesting discoveries, and I fell in love with him in an unusual way. I guess it was kind of like male-bonding before the term was even invented. We are still close friends today despite the years and the distance. There was something different about him; and I picked up on it, but couldn't quite put my finger on it. We studied together in the school library—a building that I loved. It had wonderful private little study areas radiating out from the hub where the card catalogs stood. Long before internet searches, this was the primary source of information for research on just about any topic one could imagine. It was magic, and it played a big part in my life as I began discovering new things "out there" that I had never known nor yet encountered.

Glenn was an unabashed Christian. I was still content to maintain my ignorance of all religion at the time, but was intrigued with his outlook on life. He did seem to have something special. Was he just lucky like my mom to have been born on a sunny day, or did he draw his happiness from a different source—one that I had not run up against thus far in my limited life? I wasn't sure. We became friends and hung out together all the time, both in class and just dinging around town, going to art shows, museums, protests, and pretty much anything, as he was always aware of some new thing that we needed to check out. That was the mid-sixties and despite all the turmoil of the time, we sort of floated on a quiet sea of our own when everyone else around us seemed to be in such a frenzy all the time. Politics and religion had never interested me much before then, but like most young college students, I was rapidly becoming aware of the world and events swirling around me. It was fun and exciting, and Glenn made it all the more interesting and challenging every day.

Still wrapped up in my father's Right-wing jingoism and intolerance, I slid, nevertheless, almost effortlessly into a far more accommodating posture toward just about everything and everybody around me. I concealed all that when at home, not seeing any point in rocking the boat. It was a bit thrilling to constantly step over the line, discovering so many things on my own without having to see everything through the prism of my dad's point of view—his multiple prejudices, and biases. It was exhilarating and daring—at least to me.

Glenn was quite an accomplished "witness" as I soon found out. I had never been the target of a religious pitch before, but by the time Glenn finally got around to presenting the message of Christ to me, I was open and wanted to hear more. It was called the Gospel. And although I was as familiar with the term as the next guy, I had no idea at all what it was all about. Like a lot of new ideas and concepts that were washing over me like an incoming tide in those early college years, I guess I was just ready to hear what the "good news" was all about. I wasn't interested in arguing, as I really had no point of view, experience, or honest interest in religion in general. And Glenn's love and enthusiasm for his "life in Christ" prompted me to just shut up and listen. So I did just that.

The plan of salvation was simple and made sense if one was to believe it. Since it could not be proved one way or the other, I made what is referred to as "Pascal's Wager." It states that as a result of my choosing to proclaim Christianity, accept Jesus as Lord and savior, and ask him to forgive my sins and come into my heart; he will save my soul, forgive all the sins that I have ever committed, and give me eternal life with him up in Heaven someday when I die. Otherwise I could go straight hell. I chose the former, as it sounded way better, given that it was not based on anything but a "leap of faith." So I leapt. Oddly enough, I had a tremendous sense of peace about the whole thing. I felt a kind of adrenalin rush or something that I later called a divine directive from the Almighty. I had a kind of out of body experience, as I looked at everything differently. My life had to have meaning, purpose. This was it. My interests in the arts, languages, philosophy, and history all dovetailed with my current reading for my college classes. I got what is referred to in the God biz as a "calling." It seemed so real, so logical, so metaphysical. I announced to Glenn that I had been talking to God and that He had called me to take the Gospel to China, to which he just smiled, shook his head, and just said "Wow." He didn't say, "Oh, haven't you heard that China is closed?" He believed me. How cool was that? I ramped up my studies . . . but this time with feeling!

Well, then I finally got busted. I knew it was inevitable, and that the intellectual gravy train wouldn't last forever. And with my newfound faith, shaky though it was, I was ready to launch out into the deep—and let the shoreline go. My dad was furious, but not for the reason that I had anticipated. He wasn't pissed off that I had secretly gone behind his back to study at Portland State University, but that I was studying Chinese at PSU. What? What kind of a stupid thing to study is that? "Don't you know that they are commies? . . . Reds?" He ran out of pejoratives. Those were the worst words he could think of during his tirade. I was totally aware of what was going on inside China at that time. It was in the throes of the Great Proletariat Cultural Revolution. They were marching, chanting the words of Chairman Mao, and burning books, temples, and churches. So what? I mused: God has called me to take the Gospel to China, and that is exactly what I intend to do. Looking back, it was rather out of character for me to be so decisive in the face of surely being cut off from further funding of my profligate studies, based on a mere whim! :-)

"Well," he ranted, proclaiming with a snort "Don't expect any further help from us!" Like I hadn't expected that. Come on. I loved his next line, as I fully expected it as well: "You have no choice!" . . . Trump. Ah, but I did have a choice, and I had already researched it. I had been to the U.S. Army recruiter—just a short walk from the PSU campus in downtown Portland. I had talked to the sergeant in charge of enlisting young guys like me to fill the ranks of those heading off to fight in Southeast Asia. I had even taken all the military aptitude tests, and mentioned my Chinese study at the local university. That didn't impress him as much as all of my scores did. He suggested Officer Candidate School (OCS). . . . Can you fathom a Chinese-speaking artist and latent homosexual leading a squad of men through jungles, over hills, and through swamps to kill Viet Cong? The image repulsed me in a dark-humored kind of way. I declined interest. But I indicated that I would join up if I could be guaranteed further study of Mandarin at the Defense Language Institute in Monterrey, California after basic training. So, that pending, when my dad said that I had no choice, I said flatly . . . "I always have a choice."

What could he say? He had bragged for years of his "illustrious" army career during World War II, which he spent in Hawaii. How could he say anything but "I think this is a big mistake" . . . then adding, "Not joining the army, that is—which is noble and great. But Chinese? What good will that ever do you? I mean *ever*?" Ever? Spoiler alert: He lived to eat those very words (with chopsticks).

IN THE COMBAT ZONE

If you memorize twenty verses of scripture you can snow anybody!

The helicopter was kicking up a cloud of red dust as it touched down in that landing zone in the Central Highlands of Viet Nam. A row of heavy black plastic body bags was lined up for removal. I took off my loose-fitting fatigue shirt and wrapped my cameras with it against the flying dust that can get into the lenses and camera mechanisms. I came over to help lift the bodies onto the chopper. Some of the bags were not even zipped up yet—the pallid white faces of the young soldiers faced heavenward. I was used to seeing the dead in that horrible war by this time—the white guys with faces like paper and the black guys as gray as ash.

I resisted the temptation to pray for their souls. By this time in my spiritual journey I had become all too aware that their eternal fate was of their own making, and that nothing I could do at this point would make any difference as to whether or not they were saved or damned. Which of these guys had accepted Jesus into his heart sometime back in a worship service in his home church somewhere in the American heartland, and which others had been out whoring around in the local town the night before? I couldn't tell. They were all dead, and I would never have a chance to "witness" to any of them. I prayed for their families instead. It was all I could think to do. I felt then, as I often did in circumstances like this, that I should talk to God about it. Later, when I would return to Saigon, I would talk about it with my new friend, Ernie who also worked in the headquarters.

I had only been "in country" a few days when I met him. He had been assigned to show me around and help me get settled in. A short time earlier, I had been "discovered" by the military as having what they referred to as a RUA (a rare or unusual ability). Artists, to my surprise, were given special treatment, as were photographers and others that came with skills that the military could use immediately without costly special training. I always joked that I was in the same category as the air-conditioner repairmen and tuba players. Being assigned to the graphic arts department was fine with me. I bonded right away with Ernie (who worked in the communications center), as well as I did with the other artists, photographers, and photo-lab technicians working in G/A (as we called it).

It wasn't a secret handshake or a magic password that gave him away as a born-again Christian, but when he took me to the mess hall for the first and bowed his head to say grace before eating, I knew. He was delighted to learn of my newfound faith and commitment to Christ. Figuring out quickly that I was a "new convert" and eager to learn, he set out to get me started on my religious education. I was enthusiastic. This was my first encounter with "organized religion." Ernie, lacking Glen's free-spirited nature, was a dedicated, knowledgeable, and well-schooled "mature Christian."

"Have you read the Bible?" he asked right then and there. "Of course," I answered confidently, having read through the New Testament once in a modern, easy-to-understand translation. But, as we got better acquainted, it became glaringly apparent to me in the days and weeks that followed that he really meant: "Do you know the Bible?" By that point, I already recognized what he meant, and that I did not know much at all about "the Word of God." I wanted that to change. I was keen to learn all I could. Soon I began a systematic Bible study course that he gave me, published by an Evangelical organization called *The Navigators*. A comprehensive series, it consisted of a ten-workbook set outlining the basic core beliefs of the faith, which I came to learn are called "doctrines." The course was not easy, as it required an intense amount of reading and becoming familiar with new terms and ideas, as well as a lot of memorization of scripture verses.

"If you learn only twenty verses of scripture you can snow anybody," he confided. "People are always spouting what they think is from the Bible, and for the most part they rarely know what they are talking about. Unless you know better than they do you can be buffaloed by fools. By memorizing scripture you will always know more than they do, and it will always stand you in good stead when sharing your faith or debating nonbelievers, as well as answering their questions or debunking their ridiculous fallacies."

As both an illustrator and combat photographer, I spent about an equal amount of time in the nice, dark, air-conditioned photo lab as I did in the hot, humid jungles of Viet Nam with what seemed like tons of camera gear. While running hundreds of film rolls in the lab, or while taking a break somewhere in the field, I always had my Navigator Bible studies with me in my backpack and I took every spare moment to work on my spiritual education and memorization. I learned fast, and soon had gained a rudimentary grasp of key Christian doctrines and hundreds of scripture verses by heart. I was high on Jesus and feeling my faith growing stronger when one day I was griping to my supervisor about all the weight I was carrying around while in the field.

"I feel like a donkey, carrying all these cameras, film, lenses and stuff. It's just too heavy in all this heat; and on top of that, carrying an M-16 (rifle) to boot!" "Well," he replied offhandedly, "You can carry a .45 (pistol) instead, I guess." I had qualified with a .45 and knew how short their range of accuracy was. So I just said, "Look, if the Viet Cong ever get close enough for me to need a .45, I'll be dead already anyway! I am a Christian and I will trust God to take care of me!" An old time backslider from Baptistbama, he knew it was hopeless to argue with this young whippersnapper intent on taking his life in his own hands to prove that his god would protect him from stray bullets and other sundry mortars, rockets, landmines, and the like. So I never carried a gun again, and made it through the war without a scratch!

* * * * *

One of the first doctrines that I encountered right away is one that our Fundamentalist friends base their lives on. I had never heard the term before, but it is a foundational element of most Christian theology. It is known as Biblical *inerrancy*. In simple terms, it means: "without errors." The Bible is perfect and complete as is, and contains no mistakes or contradictions. I joked in later years that it just "fell down out of the sky in perfect 1611 Old English."

I got tired of the spell-check program not recognizing this key word that is essential in understanding where Fundamentalists are coming from, so I added it to my computer's vocabulary, as we should add it to ours because it is worth fighting over for our Fundie friends. They can be real mean if they think for one minute that you are being disrespectful of their holy scriptures. How often have I heard their chant (which I really like to think of as a mantra) "God doesn't make mistakes! Don't try to understand the Bible. Just read it and believe it!"

Ernie was a Fundamentalist in most ways, but was not a Bible thumper. He had a serious knowledge of the "Word" (short for "word of God"). And I suspected that he wasn't really telling me of his own doubts about the veracity of the Old and New Testaments. He confided a lot of that to me years later when I was in the ministry and was more adroit at parrying Fundamentalists' arguments. He was what I came to call a "real believer" as opposed to the moniker "true believer," which has a rather pejorative connotation for those who have the courage to doubt. However, in those days of "simple childlike faith" that Christians talk of so fondly, I kept my questions to myself regarding the subject matter that I was dealing with on a Bible 101 basis.

In addition to my relationship with the Navigators, and by means of their other associations in the Evangelical world, I came to be introduced to the Christian Servicemen's Center in Cholon, the Chinese section of Saigon. This was a wonderful place, as it was a bit of Americana right in the heart of a war zone. It was a place of prayer, Bible study, and fellowship—a term I figured at the time was an exclusive Christian possession. I learned later that nonbelievers could have fellowship as well. The center is still in my mind as an example of what born-again Christians do best. It was a very convivial environment where one could escape the crass sexual jokes and the endless swearing and profanity of the Army "heathens" as we called them. I preferred Ernie's word, "pagans," which in years to come would become more associated with Wiccans of northern European root, as opposed to the Biblical pagans of the New Testament who were pantheistic Greeks, Romans, and other Mediterranean peoples who worshiped multiple Gods.

The Bible rants and raves against the "pagans" and various worshipers of "false gods;" so in my mind, a pagan was just about the worst thing a Christian could call a non-Christian. The Servicemen's Center housed a small bookstore that I loved. I augmented my Navigator study regimen with an increasing number of other Christian books on all manner of doctrines and teachings of "The Church." It was at this point that I came squarely up against a second doctrine of the faith which was non-negotiable. Catholics, Mormons and other groups refer to themselves as the *true* church in much the same way that Native Americans and many other of the world's inhabitants call themselves "The People," implying that all others are not really human, or are some strange devils or ghosts, as in the case of the Chinese. "The Church" (spelled in capitals) refers exclusively to Protestant Evangelical Christian believers, and *no others*.

This was the first encounter I had with the absolute exclusivity of the born-again believers, and I learned the lesson well. So well, in fact, that to this day, even in my atheism, I still use the term "Christian" when talking of Evangelicals, and "Non-Christian" when referring to all others. At first I really felt that it might be a bit much to be so totally exclusive, but was convinced by others at the Servicemen's Center that it would be unfair to the souls of the "eternally lost" unless we faced the fact that until they accepted Jesus into their hearts and as their personal Lord and Savior as I had done back on that spring afternoon in the college library, I would be withholding valuable information that could make a difference as to whether or not they would spend eternity with Jesus and me up in Heaven or in a "literal burning hell." Despite the sinking feeling of recognition that all my Catholic friends were damned, I took even more to heart the Biblical challenge to "Go into all the world and preach the Gospel to every creature." Known by Evangelical Christians as "The Great Commission." If I didn't warn them, who would? And in a war zone, where any of us could be killed at any moment, the warning seemed even more urgent to me.

From the small, but well-stocked bookstore, I bought just about everything they offered for sale. After all, what else did I have to spend my money on? Smokes, alcohol, hookers? That was not at all who I was or who I aspired to be. It was very important to set a stellar example for the pagans. In the Gospel of Matthew it challenges the believer to: **"Let your light so shine before men that they may see your good works and glorify your father in heaven."** We called it "living the life," and it involved being holy and never being hypocritical or phony in any way.

I bought a serious-looking book that I figured was over my head, but was intrigued by what I learned was called "apologetics." A funny way to say that this is the study of explaining seeming Biblical errors or boo-boos, the book systematically pointed out hundreds of contradictions and all manner of downright mistakes, and proceeded to explain them away. Oddly enough, the book raised more doubts in my mind than it answered questions that I had. Years would pass before I had the courage to crack it open again, but I kept it in my personal library and still have it. It is a great read. I was accustomed to highlighting texts that I was reading in yellow dayglow marker. I marked a passage in the forward to try to keep myself from having misleading thoughts . . . *"To all professing Christians, the authority of the Lord Jesus Christ is final and supreme. If in any of His views or teachings as set forth in the New Testament He was guilty of error or mistake, He cannot be our divine Savior, and all Christianity is a delusion or a hoax."* I had already memorized a similar verse that Saint Paul wrote to the Corinthians . . . **"And if Christ has not been raised, our preaching is useless and so is your faith. For if the dead are not raised, then Christ has not been raised either. And if Christ has not been raised, your faith is futile; and you are still in your sins."** (I Cor. 15:14-17.)

Your faith is futile. That is a scary thought to our Fundamentalist friends. In other words, if the Bible is fallible, their faith is pointless. Life is meaningless. In their black-and-white world, either the Bible is one hundred percent error-free and perfect as is, or they may as well throw the whole thing away and go out and trash around, live in sin, and whore it up. Although I tried to see it this way, I wasn't sure. The notion of inerrancy is indeed the bedrock of their faith, as it certainly was mine.

But does the faith really depend on a mistake-free "word of God?" My experience in my years in the ministry is that although most modern Christian Evangelicals and Fundamentalists living in the early 21st Century claim to adhere to every word of the Bible. Even in the face of overwhelming evidence to the contrary, most have their doubts; but it would shake faith and confidence so severely to admit this that they just fake along, claiming that it is one of the "mysteries of God."

Later, when I was ordained and in the "full-time ministry," I often sat for hours with ministerial colleagues of mine and discussed Biblical issues and problems. Among ourselves, and out of earshot of laymen and other "pew-sitters," we often practiced a form of theological discourse that we referred to as the theology of ig-nor-ance. (Notice the accent on the middle syllable.) In other words, if it seems like a contradiction or an out-and-out error, it really isn't because it *can't* be. The Bible is without errors, so it is our fault for being so stupid and obtuse that we cannot understand it. It is not that the Bible contains bloopers, but that we just aren't smart enough to figure them out. So we will just ignore them for now, as we will understand it all "by and by" . . . when we die.

Whereas the clergy can employ the theology of ignorance, the average Christian in the pew can always fall back on the *by and by theory.* In other words, God will explain it all to them after they die when they go to live in Heaven with him for eternity. By that reasoning, they are simply excused from trying to understand anything confusing or challenging. This system really works well for the poorly educated or simpleminded as it allows them to buy the most far-fetched lunacy regarding science, medicine, history, and sociology; and to maintain their cultural and social prejudices intact as Biblical. But at this point I had not encountered the downside of Fundamentalism . . . yet.

I did, however, encounter a fork in my journey on the Christian Yellow Brick Road at about this time. I really thought I was making a lot of spiritual progress when I fell into a declivity along the way. I met two great Christian guys at the Servicemen's Center, and we fell into a fascinating conversation. I liked them immediately. We were discussing "things of the spirit" when they posed a puzzling question: "Are you filled with the Holy Spirit?" Unsure, I not only did not want to expose my ignorance, but also didn't want to deny that there may be something more than plain old vanilla salvation. They refined their question: "Do you believe in the gifts of the spirit?" I was sunk. I really did not know what they were talking about, but I faked along. "Sure," I said, "I believe in the gifts of the spirit," having read something about that in the book of Colossians. They were almost ecstatic. "You mean you know about the 'Baptism in the Holy Spirit'?" they pressed. Unable to determine an appropriate answer, I replied that I had heard about it and was interested in learning more.

That was enough. Without further ado, they swept me out of the Center to another Servicemen's Center—an alternative one fairly close to Tan Son Nhut Air Force Base. I was about to learn the difference between Evangelicals, Fundamentalists, and Pentecostals. The following Sunday evening, the three of us rolled into the Pentecostal Servicemen's Center, soaking wet from running down a muddy side street in a tropical monsoon downpour. The service had already begun. I was in total shock from the first moment we walked through the iron gates into the courtyard where a few land-rover-like vehicles were parked. There was a hubbub pouring out of the open, barred windows. "What in the world?" I thought. We came in the back door, totally unnoticed by any one of the fifty or so G.I.s and Vietnamese who were singing at full steam, clapping and carrying on in a most outrageous manner.

This was so unlike the regular Protestant Servicemen's Center where I had participated in the Sunday evening service the week before—sedate, prayerful, and dignified. This place was wild! It had a large electric organ and an upright piano. "An organ and a piano together at the same time?" I thought. How strange! I would, as time went by, find it un-Pentecostal like to have a worship service without these two key elements. But there was more! Guitars, both electric and acoustic, were accompanied by a trumpet, a violin, and something I would have never imagined—a marimba!

"Make a joyful noise unto the Lord!" extolled the somewhat portly elderly American preacher from the pulpit. "Sing unto the Lord a new song!" A joyful noise indeed, I thought. Wow, if last week's service was a streetcar; this one is a freight train! "Praise God for our musicians here tonight!" he proclaimed. "And for those of you who cannot play a musical instrument, use your ten-fingered instruments and rejoice in the Lord!" Everyone began clapping in time as the band played on. The rhythmic clapping, I learned, was a hallmark of Pentecostal worship. Hours later and still drenched, this time with sweat, we made our way back through the streets of Saigon. The heat, humidity, enthusiasm, and energy had exhausted me, but in a most wonderful, exhilarating way. This was my first experience in the Pentecostal world, a world that would become my own shortly thereafter.

I thought back on the events of the evening. It was loud, fast, long . . . but fun. However, there was one element that I was unprepared for—the speaking in tongues. The theological term is glossolalia. It is defined by Webster's dictionary as *profuse and often emotionally charged speech that mimics coherent speech but is usually unintelligible to the listener and that is uttered in some states of religious ecstasy and in some schizophrenic states.* I could see the difference between this and conventional Protestant worship on my first night out. I loved the hand-clapping and the arm-waving and exuberant singing, but the ecstatic shouting and even singing spontaneously in an unintelligible language floored me. Of course, I had read in the Book of Acts chapter two about the "mighty wind and tongues of fire" that the apostles experienced on the day of Pentecost after the death and resurrection of Jesus. But I had already been taught that all this had passed away. I sensed an oncoming storm. I was right.

I had promised to attend the Sunday evening service at the other Center the following week, as a friend from *up county* was in Saigon en route back to the States. Since I would likely never see him again, it was very special. I walked into the center, feeling an icy chill in the air. "Where were you last week?" asked the Baptist minister who ran the center. "I went with John and Dan to the Pentecostal Servicemen's Center" I replied truthfully. "Did you learn to speak in tongues?" he queried rather dryly. "Well, I did hear quite a lot of that." I answered kind of sheepishly like I had done something wrong. "You should really stay away from those people!" he said matter-of-factly. "There is a lot of false doctrine going on over there, you know." I will have to confess to a feeling of shock. "Aren't we all Christians?" I thought to myself, but, in my bewilderment, decided to say nothing.

We sang conventional hymns accompanied by one very out-of-tune upright piano with a bullet hole in the side. It reminded me that we were in a war zone. Little did I realize that I had already entered a spiritual minefield. The sermon was about the evils of this world and the forces of darkness lurking around every corner ready to attack and ambush every unsuspecting Christian soldier. He went on and on about smoking and drinking, and made a big point about avoiding licentious Vietnamese women, as many were really prostitutes in disguise. "Cleanse your minds and purify your hearts!" he admonished us. "Avoid unhealthy and unholy places like the pool halls and movie houses!" he bellowed. "God demands righteousness and purity! Search your hearts so that you may be holy. Any of us could die tonight. A rocket could hit this building at any moment. Is your heart right with Christ?" I was scared. I was certain of my salvation, but was not familiar with this fatalistic message—one that would become very familiar in coming months and years.

Ernie was getting short, as we said. That meant that he was getting ready to finish his term in Viet Nam and would shortly be reassigned by the Army to somewhere else on the Planet. I would likely never see him again. I was sad, confused, and perplexed. He sensed it. We sat under a lighted bulletin board complete with swarming mosquitoes and sundry other indeterminate species of winged insects. He laid out the differences that divide Protestants. I needed to know and understand this before he left.

"We are all Christians," he pointed out. "We all share a common theology that defines us as different from, say, Catholics, Mormons, and other so-called Christians, who are all damned as we know." Then he taught me an important phrase. "These are Christians *in name only.*" I swiped at the annoying insects as I pondered the import of this. He went on. . . "There are hundreds of false religions around the world—Islam, Hinduism, Buddhism, to name a few—and political systems that are really false religions in disguise, like the Communism that we are fighting against right here in Viet Nam." This all made sense. I knew this already. Then he said something that I had sort of suspected, but had not thought through in depth. "Just belonging to a Protestant church does not make one a real born-again Christian, although there are some true Christians within the 'Liberal Protestant churches' who may be saved. Among these *liberal* churches is my own. I am proud to be Lutheran. And my church's pedigree goes all the way back to Martin Luther. But alas, many in my church are Christians in name only." Then he singled out the Methodists, Presbyterians, and, above all, the Anglicans, known in America as Episcopalians. "Although there are good, saved, born-again believers in all these churches, they are the exceptions rather than the rule."

"So then, how do we know who's who?" I asked, waiting for the defining answer. "It doesn't matter what Protestant church you attend or are a signed, sealed member of; we who are truly born-again are all the only true Christians, and we are called *Evangelicals.*" He went on. . . "The word Evangelical is a sort of umbrella concept. It is not an organization with filing cabinets and letterhead, but a sort of fraternity of believers who all have the basic doctrines of the faith in common. You are learning about these in the course that you are studying. By the way, how are you doing?" "I'm on book nine!" I said proudly. The ubiquitous crickets provided a kind of white noise in the background as he continued to answer the burning question in my mind. What are the differences between the two servicemen's centers?

I listened with rapt attention as he continued. "Under the general banner of Evangelicalism there are two main groups who are in agreement on almost everything, except one obvious thing that you found out for yourself recently. That is what is called "the Baptism in the Holy Spirit." He further explained, "It is considered a second experience beyond salvation, and the proof that one has had this experience is evidenced by speaking in tongues. Their message is more experiential and demonstrative as you observed last week. They are the "Pentecostals" and are true Evangelicals, but they think they have more than other Evangelicals, which can make them a bit much to take now and then. But we who have not had their experience don't put them down. We just say . . . my salvation alone is good enough for me."

"And the other group are the Baptists?" I volunteered. "Yep," he quipped, telling me a fun Baptist joke from a very Lutheran perspective. "Their message is far harsher and more dictatorial in nature than the Pentecostals —more austere and judgmental. They aren't the only church in this category that we refer to as the *Fundamentalists,* but are by far the biggest!" Everything about them is a bit more legalistic and "by the book" than the Pentecostals, who they consider a bit over the top with all that shouting and carrying on. But in the end they can hug, call each other "Brothers in Christ," and live as sort of scrapping siblings under the same roof in the family of Evangelicals. "So, that's all there is to it, huh?" I mused thoughtfully. "Well, there is a lot more to it than just that. But for now in your process, that should serve you well," he said with a grin.

I took him to meet his out-of-country flight a few days later and felt a genuine sadness. Years later I reflected back, wishing that it could all be as simple as it seemed then as I watched him get on that military plane and fly away. I was really on my own now.

FINDING MY OWN WAY

Living the life 201

My last month or so in Viet Nam was actually kind of fun as I had become a celebrity of sorts around the headquarters. I was—believe it or not—respected for being a Christian in a very non-Christian environment. I was in the business of "living the life" as we called it: being a witness for Christ by living an unambiguous life as an example. I had to earn that respect by not being hypocritical or phony in any transparent way. I was the only "real" born-again Christian in my unit, and when I was getting "short"—that is, nearing the end of my hitch in Nam—I was tasked to train the new photographers and lab technicians that would replace me in due time.

My first assignment was to train a rather obnoxious guy named James Herren from Kenosha, Wisconsin. He resented being in Viet Nam, as his last assignment had been in our agency's super headquarters in Washington D.C. where they had all state-of-the-art lab equipment. He trashed our primitive "jungle" equipment and techniques, and longed to be back with his girlfriend about whom he bragged endlessly. We all heard constantly that she was a great "lay." I did my best to witness to him, but he was absolutely not interested. I prayed for him. Apparently I didn't pray hard enough, as during my last upcountry trip to Da Nang, I returned to find that he had been arrested for drug possession and nobody had seen him since. I was dumbfounded. "You mean, he had drugs right here in the photo lab?" I asked incredulously. As the senior guy in the department by then, I realized immediately that I might somehow be a co-conspirator—or whatever. But everybody just laughed and said: "Tom, you are such a goody two-shoes Christian . . . Nobody would ever think that you would do drugs, let alone be dumb enough to bring them into a secure area!" I felt reassured that all my witnessing had at least made a positive impression as to my character :-)

His replacement was from Wacko, Texas—or Plano, or somewhere in the Bible Belt. Named Jerry Hill, he came from a "Pentecostal Holiness" background. I was totally beside myself with enthusiasm. "Just think of it . . ." I mused, "having another born-again believer right here in the Graphic Arts Department! I envisioned us studying the "Word" together while running Ektachrome. Fat chance. He was the backslider of the century.

I had met a few wandering Baptist sheep by this time in my religious career—and an occasional "Jack Mormon" as well—but a real unholy roller? I was crushed. But the next time I was at the Servicemen's Center, I shared the news as a prayer request. I had already picked up that anything even remotely gossipy could be couched as a prayer request. LOL. So we all prayed that I would break through his hard shell and lead him back the Lord. The opportunity to do so came rather sooner than I expected. He was not a particularly skilled lab technician yet, so I taught him how to run various kinds of film. When he was ready to go on his own, I sat back and monitored, letting him do his thing with the chemicals.

I had always enjoyed my quiet times while being "dark" in the darkroom— imagine that! I always used that time to do personal Bible study and memorization. By this time I had memorized almost 500 of the scripture verses assigned by the Navigator's program I was just then completing. Nobody could come into the darkroom when I had the red light on, lest it wreck the film or photographic paper. In fact, I was locked in from the inside. It was a sort of spiritual retreat away from the "pagan world" of the U.S. Military. Of course, it was one of the all-time favorite places for the guys working at the U.S. Military Intelligence spy headquarters in Saigon to escape and play hooky from work—referred to as "skating." In fact when I was not dark, I had a nonstop collection of gold bricks who were looking for a nice place to skate for a while. The Graphics Department was the most popular skating rink in the headquarters since we always had various interesting projects underway. And, as smoking bans inside buildings were years away in the future at the time, the air in the whole place was blue with cigarette smoke, except the darkroom where it was strictly forbidden due to the need to keep the environment free of smoke, ash, and all that stuff that sticks to wet film and photo paper. We did try to make it as dust-free as possible, but I had more spiritual reasons for enforcing the ban. Of course, few visitors failed to notice the photo lab was the only place in the headquarters or the company barracks where one was absolutely alone and free to jack off. Of course, I never took advantage of that perk. LOL.

Jerry was running a large order of colored slides from an Awards and Decorations ceremony that I had shot earlier in the day. So, we had over an hour to kill. I made my move, asking about his upbringing in a Pentecostal church. He was aware of my role as the Holy Joe of the complex, called "White Birch" in code, as it was painted white. It was a reinforced concrete, bunker-like building with no windows and only one door. They say that it could withstand a direct rocket hit. I was not sure, but did feel quite secure in its confines.

Jerry was really an affable fellow, and seemed to have no grudge against God or his wild and woolly Church of God childhood and teen years. But he had grown weary and skeptical throughout his adolescence. In fact, there was quite a family story to tell. He explained why he had "fallen away from the Lord." It wasn't that he didn't believe any more, but that following Jesus was just too hard. Besides, he had seen some of the weirdest stuff as a kid growing up in the Fundamentalist South that had more or less convinced him that most of his family and a goodly number of his neighbors were kooks. Part of his family was seriously into the snake-handling thing from Mark 16:17-18: "**In my name they will drive out demons; they will speak in new tongues; they will pick up snakes with their hands; and when they drink deadly poison, it will not hurt them at all; they will place their hands on sick people, and they will get well.**" Apparently Aunt Patsy and Uncle Fred would actually get into the "pit" with the vipers and preach up a storm. Well, the snakes were okay with that. But anyone who watches the Jeff Corwin Experience on the *Animal Planet* Channel knows not to move too fast around snakes. Well, one night someone set a Bible on the altar rail next to the snake's enclosure, and in a moment of ecstatic worship, knocked the Bible off into the pit with a thud, startling the snakes into a frenzy. After Fred was released from the hospital, Jerry decided that being a Fundamentalist was just too weird . . . not to mention, dangerous.

Admittedly, I didn't succeed in getting him back into good graces with the Lord, as my new assignment orders came down the next day and I was off on my way to Frankfurt, Germany—the then-headquarters of U.S. Army Europe. I was thrilled. In fact, a good friend from Oregon who worked in the personnel office—responsible for filling slots in the military—had wangled that assignment for me for about twenty-four rolls of Kodachrome.

I arrived in Frankfurt on a warm autumn afternoon, and fell in love with the city immediately . . . and planned to make it *meine Heimatstadt* (my hometown). And I did. My job in the military there was a lot like in Saigon, but without the war droning on in the background all the time. Our mission was to hold back the Russian hordes from the East. I worked on the sixth floor of the massive Nazi-era I.G. Farben Building. It was the only structure, save for the Dom (Cathedral), left standing in the city of Frankfurt after the war. Hear tell, Eisenhower instructed that it not be bombed, so it could become the headquarters of the Allied occupation of Germany thereafter. I took pictures at A and D ceremonies as usual, did charts and graphs and maps endlessly, and—above all—cartoons for various important military functions like the Officers' Wives Club, the PWOC (Protestant Women of the Chapel), and the NCO Bowling League. It was just like a regular nine-to-five day job as an all-purpose artistic handyman. I loved it.

The Graphic Arts Department was way in the back, so we got way fewer "skaters" than we did in White Birch. But we did have something unique at the time that most folks in the modern workforce take for granted. We had a copy machine! What is that? It was the size of an overstuffed La-Z-Boy chair, and only authorized personnel with specialized training could operate it . . . and only with an approved work order at that. It was a beast and only a few of us were even allowed to touch it. It didn't like me from the very beginning. And that was when I first realized that I have very bad karma with machines. But I coddled it, cajoled it, and petted it daily. It finally warmed up to me enough to let me make copies on it. It was magic to the entire headquarters, including the spooks who worked two floors up in the NSA. They had to come down to our department to get top secret documents copied, as no one else in the vast USAEUR complex had personnel with high enough security clearances to even look at those hush-hush items.

I have always said that large corporations, the military industrial complex, and—as I learned later—religious organizations, all run on a sea of paper. Sooner or later everything has to be synthesized into graphs, charts, briefings, slide presentations, brochures, and all manner of visual aids. Everything has to be funneled through the hands of artists in one form or another. I always loved being at the neck of the funnel. Of course, I didn't become a "pain in the neck" until much later. LOL.

On the religion front, things got off to a rocky start. I attempted to reestablish a relationship with the Navigators, but found that I was kind of shocked at how hierarchical their organization was. It was quite a military-style group, with a severe command structure. I had been told by many of my old Nav. buddies to be sure to look up a certain Joe Stone, who would be able to help me get plugged into a group of "on fire" guys in Germany. He was kind but abrupt. He basically told me to connect with a certain Terry Furth who was the "Team Leader" in Frankfurt. I did so. Terry was your basic military school product. He was compact, athletic, and self-confident. I could imagine why he was a Navigator team leader. Men tend to follow guys like that into combat. I learned that out in the field in Viet Nam.

Terry and I didn't hit it off. I failed to show up for football day at a local soccer pitch in Sachsenhausen. (I went off on my own to take in an exhibit of Edward Keinholz at a local art museum.) Did I mention that all team contact sports bore me to the nth degree? Well, not asking permission to miss the "scrimmage" (or scrum, or whatever), I was being insubordinate. He "invited" me to a meeting at a coffee shop near downtown for a man-to-man talk. He knew that I was fresh from a war zone, so he could imagine that I was used to doing things in a less structured way. I emphasize "imagined" as he had never even been in the military, let alone in combat. But he (with his military bearing) could gather why I might not be accustomed to taking orders from a weekend warrior like him. He began to work me from a counseling approach, asking personal questions about my family background, childhood, and religious upbringing. I filled in the blanks, but as a casual aside mentioned that I had attend Pentecostal services during my stint in Viet Nam. He was nonplussed. "Do you mean that you speak in tongues?" he asked incredulously. Well, the chasm widened. My relationship with Evangelical Fundamentalism more or less ended at that point. I had chosen wild-eyed, fanatical Pentecostalism over rational and organized Christianity as he saw it. As we left our session, I felt liberated. I was an orphan in the Christian universe, but I was a happy one. I found the nearest Assemblies of God meeting the next day and never looked back.

Talk about a welcome! I was embraced (literally) with open arms. Pentecostals are very huggy types, and I genuinely enjoyed embracing all those soldier bodies on a regular basis. It was the closest I would come to genuine male-to-male sexuality for years to come, but it felt good. As luck would have it, I fell in love/lust at my first prayer meeting. His name was Dave Loyal and he was an NSA technician who worked two floors up from me on the 8th floor of the I.G. Farben building. That was so cool. But what was even better was that we lived in the same barracks, which used to be a high school during the Nazi Zeit. It was a rather unimpressive seven-story edifice located at the corner of Bremerstrasse and Eschenheimer Landstrasse. My window on the third floor looked out onto that major intersection. I used to gaze down watching the traffic lights change in the wee hours—even when the streets were totally empty. I prayed for strength and temperance despite my desire for that hot guy sleeping quietly and unknowingly upstairs on the fifth floor.

We became friends, but he was the first "biological Pentecostal" that I had dealt with on a day-to-day basis. Whereas Ernie was what I later came to call a "biological Lutheran" (one born into a Lutheran family), Dave had been born into Pentecostalism, so to speak. He was no convert. Maybe his pregnant mom singing and dancing in the spirit at the Tulsa First Assembly of God immunized him from demonstrative religious displays in later life. Or maybe compulsory Sunday school attendance when he would have rather been out playing baseball—or too many snakes, or something—had made him kind of cool and aloof toward church stuff in general. He was definitely not "on fire" for God as I so definitely was at the time. I tried my best to "challenge" him to a deeper walk with the Lord and all that, but he was quite content to watch me spin and spin constantly as I sought to preach the Word of power, both with my oral witnessing and my exemplary life! (-: I never gave up, but just being around him was enough. He was to-die-for cute.

I'd arrived a few months early to fill my slot in the graphic arts department, replacing a particularly obnoxious jerk from North Carolina who was a total bigot. I had met others like him already in the army, of course, so I wasn't shocked—just turned off. Not only was he blatantly racist, sexist, and homophobic; but he actually called himself a Christian! Oddly enough, I came to understand over my years in the ministry that he was really more indicative of American Christianity than I was!

The master sergeant in charge of all of the Document Services Department (another backslidden Southern Baptist from North Carolina) was primarily a print shop man himself. He loved all the noise and din of printing presses chunkin' and chunkin' along in discordant cadence. The cacophony rattled my brain, but I sang Pentecostal choruses to the rhythm of my machine, whom I named Lewis (after C.S. Lewis, my hero at the time). My bad karma with machinery, a lifelong curse, showed its ugly head during my two month fill-in as a pressman—waiting for the bigot from Boonesville to rotate out and leave the military. Lewis put up with my mechanical ineptitude, but would cough and sputter, jam up, or throw paper out the wrong end frequently to test my patience (a Christian virtue that I am often so lacking around anthropomorphs of his kind). But I learned a hell of a lot about printing at that time, which stood me in very good stead in the years ahead in the ministry. I just didn't know it then. Of course, later I would give God all the credit for allowing me the privilege of working those two glorious months in the ink mill asylum.

Then I was discovered . . . by the Church, that is. Hitherto I had been kind of known as an "on fire" super witnesser and Bible-memorizing machine. I was a novelty to Dave and the other Pentecostals who had grown up "in the Way" as church kids, preacher's kids (PKs), or missionary kids (MKs). Our group, that met every Sunday at the 97th General Military Hospital chapel, was drawn from soldiers and airmen from all around the greater Frankfurt area, and was headed by a real honest-to-God American "appointed" Assemblies of God missionary. I was impressed—not knowing that I would be one of those myself one day. This fellow, Dick Fulmer, was totally unlike his Navigators counterpart, Joe Stone. Dick and his wife Jean were the perfect example of what Christians should be like—at least according to the Bible, that is. Not only were they kind, outgoing, and caring; but they actually noticed and paid attention to me personally. I was obviously not a typical pew-sitter. It was clear that I was not a church-born and bred A/G kid from the Pacific Northwest. I was a rip-snortin', scripture-quotin', Bible-totin' convert. And they loved it. And they loved me. And they let it show. It was cool.

They learned that I worked as an artist/illustrator in the Graphic Arts Department in the massive I.G. Farben building, with access to all manner of printing and promotional materials—and was willing to appropriate such at any time for the glory of the Lord. Hallelujah! Heck, I figured, I am designing fliers and doing cartoons for Captain Joe Blow's "Hail and Farewell" party at the Officer's Club all the time. Why not do some stuff like that for the Lord? I saw no conflict. Still don't.

I was beginning to understand the idea that I had a "natural renewable resource." I could take a blank piece of paper and create something from nothing. It is an artist thing. The military industrial complex uses guys like myself to create from scratch all kinds of educational and promotional materials; so why waste talent—or limit it—to killing people or making them rich? I was moonlighting then for an American advertising agency (with their European headquarters in Frankfurt) that paid me to use my talents to sell things to people. Why not use that same talent to inform the lost about the Gospel of Christ, and to preach the Christian message of love and peace to the perishing? Still works for me, to tell the truth.

I became sort of a mini celebrity among the clergy at that time—a graphic artist (and now printer) willing to do art work or printing projects with military equipment and materials for free. Word spread. I was getting near the end of my illustrious military career when I met a fine fellow who was the honcho of an organization that I knew of called Teen Challenge. I had read the famous book entitled *The Cross and the Switchblade*, written by a quirky Pennsylvania preacher named David Wilkerson. "Brother Dave" had been called of God to leave the idyllic farms and churches of rural Pennsylvania, and minister to the wild and woolly street gangs of New York City. I knew his story, having read it out in the jungles of Viet Nam; and knew that of one of his most famous early converts, Nicky Cruz—a notoriously dangerous Puerto Rican gang leader—had been miraculously saved, filled with the spirit, and was now a big-time preacher. Like the Fulmers, Howard and Pat Foltz were real and authentic Christians. They had been called to join Dave and his brother, Don Wilkerson, to begin an "outreach" ministry in Europe called

GOD TOLD ME TO HATE YOU

Continental Teen Challenge. I loved them and did my best to help them in any way possible with art and graphics projects. As I said, religious organizations, like the military and the commercial world, run (or float) on a sea of paper and ink! It proved to be truer than I ever imagined. I loved working with these "laborers in Christ's vineyard," if only in a supporting role.

As my time in Europe and the military was coming to an end, both the Fulmers and Foltz's made an effort to tune me in to the nuts and bolts of getting involved in what is called "full-time ministry." I was receiving on all channels. As a convert, I learned that I had no "home church." Also, despite my Navigator training and massive catalog of memorized scripture verses, I really had no formal religious education or training in doctrine and stuff like that. Sure, there are some who are called to just drop everything and buy a plane ticket to a foreign country to start preaching. But if I were truly called to missionary service, I needed to begin doing certain things right away on my release from the Army. First of all, I needed to finish my secular education, which was almost done due to my taking extension courses during my entire military enlistment. Then I needed a *bona fide* religious education from an acknowledged institution so that I could seek "ordination" as a minister with a real denomination that actually sends out "full-time" career missionaries who dedicate their entire lives to the service of the Lord. I got it.

CONTINENTAL TEEN CHALLENGE

Learning the Ministerial Ropes

Leaving the military was fine by me. I was tired of it despite all the fun of my last year of service, spent in Augsburg where our headquarters had moved. Also, I was revved up to charge forward to my next life goal—namely, to get ordained as soon as possible and get back to the mission field to fulfill the Great Commission. I felt like I was wasting my time as millions were lost and dying, going straight to a Christless eternity in a literal burning hell. It was my assigned job to warn them! I knew I was up to it; but like the military, the Church has rules. You don't just hop a flight and run headlong onto the mission field without any training or backing. I realized that, so I was hot to trot to get on with it all. I left the service in January of 1972.

I drove immediately to Santa Cruz, California, where the Assemblies of God had a regional seminary. Actually, it is more accurately called a "Bible School." The mission of that institution was to train ministers in Bible content and church doctrine, as well as church administration and homiletics (the art of preaching), and other things that any rural Pentecostal pastor might need to know. I loved the quaint little campus in a very nice part of California, but left in a rather distressed mood, imagining myself studying there with all those P.K.s and M.K.s and all those other "church kids" in general. I imagined sitting in classes filled with hundreds of Dave Loyals, lukewarm children of the clergy with little or no calling on their lives to serve Christ unwaveringly. Everything seemed so small, pat, and pointless. That was the summer of *Marjoe*, a shockumentary film about a young Southern evangelist that was sweeping the country. He was a religious huckster and a self-proclaimed fraud who exposed the soft underbelly of Southern fried Christian Fundamentalism. Of course, I didn't see the film (at the time), as it was obviously of the Devil and I had to keep right and pure. But although I was aware of it only tangentially in my personal life at the time, it was helping to shape the religiopolitical landscape I would travel in the years to come. Even so, my mind at the moment was on finishing my education and getting on with my ultimate goal—to get to the "mission field" to win souls for Christ, as quickly and expeditiously as possible.

I re-enrolled in both of my old schools, Lewis and Clark College and Portland State University, and I rented a small apartment that was located halfway between the two, intending to finish up a degree in Art at one school and Linguistics at the other. I burned the midnight oil. It was kind of a blur as I ran toward the finish line, knowing that I was facing years of Bible study/ religious education afterward. I tried to get pumped up about the idea, but I was quietly dreading it. While driving to or from one school or the other that summer of 1972, I was listening to the news on the car radio when I heard something incongruous about a former Miss America whom I had known of just vaguely . . . Anita Bryant. She was on some kind of a campaign down in Florida that had to do with gay rights or something. I barely noticed in the hubbub that was my life at that time, but indeed it was the first time that I had heard the words "Evangelical Christian" and "gay" in the same sentence. Little did I know that this was the beginning of a lifelong personal struggle.

At that very time a letter came in the mail from Howard Foltz, the head of Continental Teen Challenge, inviting me to return to Europe and join his team as a graphic artist, German-speaking cook and bottle-washer—kind of an all-purpose assistant, and doer of whatever needed doing. I was about as nonplussed as I was thrilled. He challenged me to put my Bible school plans on hold and, after graduation from PSU, come back over to Europe for a year or two to work with the Teen Challenge program. I could go back later to the U.S. and do my Bible school after a year or so of intense missionary work "in the trenches" of modern drug-ridden, sinful, secular Europe. Or I could do my Bible school courses via correspondence from Germany! What? How cool was that?! It had to be from God! Since I had done a lot of various secular correspondence courses and extension courses while in the military, I already knew how to do such a thing. But why hadn't anybody told me about this option before?

It was a beautiful October day when I landed back in Frankfurt. I was reconnected. It felt like home. Howard and Pat Foltz lived in a village outside Wiesbaden. It was a helluva drive to civilization from there, but the prices were so high that anything within an affordable range of a missionary budget could not be found close-in to Wiesbaden, let alone Frankfurt! When I arrived in Germany from Viet Nam in 1970 the U.S. dollar stood at four DM (Deutsch Marks) in exchange. Since my military salary was paid in dollars, I was used to exchanging currency. I had begun experiencing "Dollar Shock" from day one, as the American currency began its downward spiral back then and went into a full-fledged freefall. Everything was so astronomically expensive that we had to learn to live on a shoestring. We never looked at the price of anything in a store. The question was never *How much is this thing?* but rather *Do we actually need this thing?"* It has colored my attitude toward money to this day. Since we never had discretionary money of any kind, I got used to spending wisely. It has always stood me in good stead, as I am a successful budgeter and money manager, but never a penny-pinching miser like my dad. I related to the Apostle Paul's statement that he had learned how to *abound and abase*.

In the headquarters of the Teen Challenge office for all of Europe—which consisted of Howard's office, a secretary out front, and a drawing table for me in the basement of his house—I thrived right away. I was given the job of setting up a bona fide graphic arts facility that could help out various TC ministries growing rapidly throughout Europe. I was thrilled. Looking back, I see how happy I was about being so totally connected. I was definitely a square peg in a square hole. The secretary, Beth, was from Los Angeles. We hit it off right away, and became fast friends. I lived in the guest room and Beth had a nice little room in the basement next to the office. It sounds hokey—and it was—but it was clean, dry, and carpeted. I figured quite rightly that "you have to start somewhere," as I sent off for my first few correspondence courses in the *Berean School of the Bible*. Beth was a graduate of an institution in Minneapolis much like the place I had visited in Santa Cruz. I asked why she had gone so far away from home to do her Biblical training. "You would have to know the place I grew up in L.A. to understand," she replied. Little did I know that I would indeed get to know that place quite well as time went on.

Life in the wee little village of Breithardt im Taunus was laid-back and peaceful. I liked hanging out with Pat, Beth, and the two little Foltz boys, who were indeed untreated ADD mini monsters. Eventually they got help and grew out of it. During the time I was in town, though, they were the bane of my existence. But my travels soon began and I was "on the road" for Jesus most of the time from then on.

Howard was a gifted organizer. He had been sent out by the Church headquarters to "plant" Teen Challenge centers in every country within reason on the European continent (kind of on the Servicemen's Center model, but far more indigenous in nature). At the time the concept was to address the scourge of drug addiction which had been sweeping Western Europe all during the 1960s (like in the States). I had skipped the drugs during high school, college, and the military, so was rather unschooled in the subject. But I got a crash course right away.

I was thrown together with other American-grown missionaries in several of the countries where TC was evolving in Europe. My assignment was to help them develop any kind of concomitant literature that they might need, to aid in reaching the lost and the dying youth of Europe, for Christ. As I knew already, organizations of such type run on a sea of ink and paper; and that was just up my alley. I was befriended by Al Perna, an American-born, Italian-speaking missionary in Italy whom I had met back in Augsburg when we had worked together to start a Pentecostal "fellowship group" there, much like the 97th Hospital Chapel model in Frankfurt. We got along famously and I visited him now and then in his place in Vicenza. We traveled together now and then. He preached and I tagged along, connecting with church pastors and evangelists of every stripe in Germany, Netherlands, France, Sweden, and just about everywhere west of the Iron Curtain.

All this time I was dragging around my Berean Bible Correspondence School materials. Beth and Al were both the product of an Assemblies of God religious upbringing; so I was on a learning curve that lasted until one day when I actually finished my final test, and threw it into one of those bright yellow Bundespost mailboxes in Frankfurt—done with my Biblical training officially. I received back an official certificate indicating that I had finished a course equivalent to a four-year "real" Bible college. Piece of cake. As Beth had watched me dutifully reading the materials and sending off for the tests, the day they arrived in the mail, she kind of lamented that she had spent so much time covering the exact same material with the exact same textbooks back in snowbound Minnesota. I made it look easy. Actually, it was. The trick was, I learned, to just parrot back exactly what the text said—no thinking, arguing, or imagining. Just learn doctrine by rote. That worked well for me (for a while, that is). There were many great moments. I spent an entire winter in Great Britain, traveling with two characters that I couldn't have invented. Tyrone was a black guy from Evansville, Indiana who had played the part of Judas Iscariot in one of the many touring theater companies doing *Jesus Christ Superstar*, a wildly popular rock opera at the time. It was already in film form, starring Ted Neeley as Jesus and Carl Anderson as Judas. Everybody in Europe had seen the film, and just assumed that Ty was really the guy in the film. They were swooningly impressed, and it was not our intention to dissuade them. Well, after all, one black guy singing was the same as another, right? LOL. After all, the "Jesus movement" was sweeping over Europe in mighty ripples, and it was our job to capitalize on the success of the Andrew Lloyd Webber production to achieve a far higher purpose — to win the lost and dying souls of tired, old Europe to Christ (and to do so in as American as possible a fashion).

Rodney, our British go-to guy, and I likely invented the term bromance. We were tasked by Howard and the powers that be in the American Assemblies of God headquarters in Springfield, Missouri, to make a documentary film about what Continental Teen Challenge was doing over across the pond in the Old World where centuries of Church (read: Catholic) rule, then colonialism and world wars, had turned the populace toward skepticism, secularism, and drugs. I saw through a lot of the truth-fudging, but considered the greater, nobler goal; so I was totally on board with the whole thing.

Rodney had been a banker in a small town in Kent. He and I bonded right away and began marathon-talking before we even got his British Ford station wagon out of the driveway of the Teen Challenge Center in Tunbridge Wells. We were fast friends by the time we hit the M-1 Motorway and headed for all points north. Rod and I sat in the front, trading off driving, while Ty worked on his music in the back. We were on the missionary journey that was destined to take the whole winter and cover every corner of England, Wales, Scotland, and Ireland. Rod and I started our conversation immediately and didn't stop for four months until I finally got on a plane heading back to Frankfurt. We locked into serious conversation about everything from theology to the war in Viet Nam; the demise of the British Empire; pop culture, music, and films; and—above all—the differences between two peoples divided by a common language. Neither of us had ever crossed that divide before. I had come to understand the Germans quite well (in part due to those years spent in the military), but the British were a totally new challenge. And, to my surprise, the Americans were as much of an enigma to Rod as the Brits were to me. He knew nothing more about the "Yanks" than what he had seen on television, and I knew even less about the "Brits."

Both of us were like vacuums, sucking up information like crazy. Rod was very well-educated—a product of the British "public" school system, which translates to "private school" in the States. He had what could be called a classic European education. He had read all the literary classics; knew geography, politics, and economics; but, most of all, he loved history—as did I. Since we were in his territory, I learned all about Cromwell, the Round Heads, and the battle of Bannock Burn. Meanwhile, I dusted off my American history and told him all manner of facts and issues from the Lewis and Clark expedition to the Civil War, Valley Forge, and the battle of Brandywine. We took turns being the odd-man-out regarding sleeping arrangements. Usually flipping a coin, I more often than not lost the toss, but lucked out on the cultural experience. In Edinburgh I stayed with a very Scottish family who had never even known an American before that, save for a handshake here and there. They were very much Scottish nationalists—very proud "home rule for Scotland" types.

I spent a week and a half with them, intermittently going out during the day to drag through the slums of Edinburgh in search of the illusive *Nidery Terror*, and at night going to various church services where Tyrone gave his testimony and played his guitar and sang. I had never actually seen real slums in Germany, but Britain had them in every major town. Many of the northern mill towns that were once the powerhouses of the British industrial revolution were in ruins. The Nidery section of Edinburgh was the most notorious slum in Scotland. To quote Bette Davis: "What a dump!" We drove around deserted streets, wondering where everyone was. Finally we found a trio of dopers hanging out on a flight of cracked concrete steps in front of a dismal, rundown block of flats. The graffiti was everywhere, warning of the dreaded Nidery Terror, a street gang known for their violence and mayhem. We finally found three of them stoned out of their minds and looking very un-terrorist-like. We told them that we were making a documentary film and showed them the camera. Suddenly they got really interested. We asked where the rest of the Terror team was, and learned that they were normally sleeping during the day, especially if they had scored drugs the night before. We made an appointment for that night to do some on-camera interviews.

They showed up in droves to get face-time on film. We had told them to show up in their gang garb and to bring any weapons that might be normal or standard, for effect. They all dressed as frighteningly as possible, but there were no serious weapons. In a country where guns are not for sale to the public, only real hardcore "connected" criminals managed to obtain them. The kids that showed up for the photo shoot were anything but scary. They spent the evening posturing for the camera and for each other, talking big; but I saw through the act. The film was supposed to frighten the American audience into giving money to help reach these poor desperate youth find Christ, but we really never got much usable footage there or in any of the major cities of the British Isles. These young people were basically addicts. Their lives were not those of devoted terrorists. Their motivation was just to get more drugs. We got enough footage to splice it into more material that we later staged in Hollywood where we did the final editing and post-production. There were real terrorists in Britain, to be sure. However, they weren't a motley collection of dropouts and dopers. They were the IRA, and they were in Ireland, and they were scary. As we boarded the car ferry from Liverpool for the overnight crossing to Belfast, Rodney went on and on about how he got seasick the first time he crossed the Irish Sea in winter. I slept like a baby through the whole thing. But when we disembarked in Derry, I knew that I was back in a real war zone again.

They may call it the Emerald Isle (and it does have its moments of great beauty) but, on the dreary gray morning when we got off the boat in Belfast, it was anything but inviting. After running the anti-terrorist gauntlet rivaling Israel in the 80's or the United States today, we finally got back into the car and headed into town—a city under siege. It was in the midst of what the locals referred to as "the troubles." Whereas it seems that the basic human cause for conflict or war is competition over resources, it appears that religious wars come in a close second. I was amazed at the size of the churches in Belfast—they were huge. It seemed to me that the polarization between Protestants and Catholics literally drove the mushy middle to the extremes. Everybody had chosen sides A or B, and church attendance was a key element of one's identity. Tyrone played his guitar, singing tunes from *Superstar*. He even tried his hand at preaching a regular sermon, which lasted all of ten minutes. When he turned away from the pulpit to sit down, both Rod and the pastor glanced at each other with a look of alarm and panic. "Sing! Sing!" Rod said quickly to Ty, sotto voce. As he sang, they both frantically flipped through their Bibles looking for something to fill up the time. They came through! Afterward, Rod told us that folks there come for "the big preach." In places where there isn't much to do at night, or it is too dangerous to venture out, church is the entertainment; and the congregation expects its offering's worth. I found that to be the case in many places in the world. Years later, when I was living and preaching in the Philippines, entire villages would come to see a religious film or hear a sermon or gospel music. What else was there to do in remote villages in the "bundok" (the origin of our word Boondocks)!

Actually, partway through our trip, we were driving in Wales when I mentioned to Rod that I was studying for the ministry. He was impressed, as he had also done his theological studies by correspondence. Having a job at a local bank in Kent, along with a family and financial responsibilities, he couldn't take four years off to attend seminary. I, similarly, was working in Europe and didn't have the time or means for attending a live-in seminary. He volunteered me to practice preach at our next stop, Swansea; and I was a permanent fixture on the docket of our 3-man road show from then on.

One thing I really enjoyed about our extensive travels around Britain and Ireland was our near-daily visits to local high schools. The British have a class requirement called Religious Education (RE). This is an opportunity to expose students to various religions belief systems and theological doctrines of all stripes. It is an open forum style discussion and dialogue. The intent is not to indoctrinate the students with a particular religious viewpoint, but to give them the widest possible experience with as many religious disciplines as possible. We heard that many of the RE teachers frequently ran short of new material, so anything different was welcomed. Rod had learned to tip off local pastors who contacted their neighborhood schools, volunteering us to come to their classes to discuss drug addiction and Teen Challenge, etc. Having a celebrity singer from *Superstar* was a real draw. (duh)

We did our dog and pony show until April when Howard called from Frankfurt telling us that the churches in Scandinavia wanted Tyrone to tour, so we bade Rod a fond goodbye and hit the road for Stockholm. I saw him again at TC conferences in Switzerland where we dragged out all the old jokes that we had come to enjoy while on the road. I didn't realize until years later how much those months helped me; not just in the confidence I gained as a public speaker; but when I was finally assigned to ministry in British Hong Kong, I was already so familiar with the British side of the Colony's culture that I could concentrate all my efforts on learning the Chinese side!

Back on the continent, I was really enjoying life working for the Lord. It was great; and when I finally sent in my last exam for my ministerial license requirement, I was satisfied. I knew a lot about the Bible and doctrine. I had passed the "Bible content test" with flying colors. Together with my ponderous knowledge of scripture verses that I had been packing into my skull since Viet Nam, I was a little Bible machine of sorts. Yes, I had read the required books about church administration and a great eye-opening textbook entitled *Great Church Fights.* So I guess I was ready when they proved so unavoidable in the years ahead. . . . Sigh.

My graduation diploma arrived in the Bundespost, and I immediately applied to the Oregon District of the Assemblies of God for what is referred to as a *license* to preach. Like a novice in the Catholic Church, or an apprentice, I was allowed to perform all the ministerial duties, like baptisms, marriages and funerals. I kept my secret, since I felt it was always smart to have an ace up your sleeve. No need to mention that I was now officially entitled to put *Reverend* in front of my name. A two-year period of active ministry was required before one could undergo the actual spiritual ceremony of *ordination.* I was definitely in active ministry by then, and the other ministers were told of my new status. I was welcomed warmly into the ranks of the bona fide, recognized clergy. Then came the news—a harsh reality that I was marginally aware of up to that time, but had to confront if I expected to make a career out of missionary work. Most Protestant denominations do not send out unmarried males to the mission field. The reasoning is that a fellow burning with lust cannot concentrate on his God-given assignment to reach the lost for Christ. Unlike the Catholics, who send out only single male missionaries in the garb of priests, Protestants were totally gung-ho for real Christian marriage—one man and one woman *and children!*

I was totally conflicted about this whole dilemma. I wanted to serve God, preach the Gospel of peace, and bring the blessings of Christ to a lost and dying world. But I had to have a wife if I were to be allowed to fulfill my ministerial calling. I had always gotten along with women and enjoyed their company and conversation. But I just wasn't attracted to any of them sexually. What to do? I ruminated on the problem for some time, but recognized that sooner or later I was going to have to do something. But what? I thought about it for months, and finally came to a conclusion that I was never going to be fulfilled sexually in my Earthly life. Like a Catholic priest who would never know the touch of female flesh, I too was going to have to forgo any male sexual encounters—ever. It was a rather dismal proposition, but it was a sacrifice that I was willing to make for the Lord. So I went in search of a wife.

I didn't have to look far. Beth and I were best of friends. And I figured that if my sex life was never going to be anything, at least I should be married to someone who I enjoyed spending time with. Could I make that lifetime commitment? Well, unless I was willing, I had no future career with the Assemblies of God or any comparable denomination. So, one summer evening as we were out walking, I proposed marriage to Beth, my "bud." I know she was shocked, so I quickly added that I did not expect a quick, off-the-cuff response, but a prayerful one. A few weeks later we were engaged. As was our typical style, we did not announce it right away—but waited for the right moment to drop the bomb. It was classic.

But the announcement of our nuptials was not a total shock to the Teen Challenge staff and the trainees who were live-in students from all over Europe. A rash of marriages had been springing up all during that particular time. In fact, it was sort of a mania. There were a lot of weird theological traumas and dramas going on at the time, and avoiding being swept up in this or that "new truth" was difficult. The prosperity doctrine was creeping across Europe and had already more or less peaked in the States. "Name in and claim it" was the order of the day. In a nutshell, the concept was simple: God blesses his children with material things to prove his love. Poverty is for suckers and those lacking in faith. If one wants to drive a Cadillac (note the American bias), one need only to ask the heavenly Father to provide it.

"We're King's kids!" exclaimed a Swiss friend of mine who had fallen hook, line, and sinker for the new "truth" du jour. "We deserve the best!" he explained as he turned his beat-up, aging Peugeot into the hardware store in Friedberg, where we had come to get some shelf fasteners. "The Bible says that God will not deny any good thing to those who love him!"

Along with the claiming of riches to which all Christians are entitled, came the next logical step—claiming perfect health! That winter was particularly miserable and cold in Frankfurt, and germs were everywhere (I guess that is why they call it Germany). Anyway, catching a cold was considered a sure sign that one was not really up to snuff in his prayer life, since "God does not want us to be sick." Everyone got the flu at some point, and I was no exception. I wasn't buying the line that getting sick was equivalent to falling out of God's favor, so I just stayed home and got over it.

The "name it and claim it" doctrine was playing it's course out at the Teen Challenge Training Center where Howard had hired a wild-eyed, Southern-fried preacher from Georgia to teach Basic Christian truths and personal evangelism to would-be Teen Challenge workers from all over Europe. He had made a name for himself the previous year by carrying a wooden cross all over Germany, preaching in lousy German in parks and on street corners in places like Frankfurt, Munich, and Berlin.

Heavily invested in American religious trends and movements that come and go, he was convinced that one sure sign that one was out of touch with the true will of God regarding our health, was eyesight. "Why would God create you with bad eyesight?" he roared! "If you truly believe God made you whole and perfect, throw down those glasses and trust God for your healing! Do it right now!" They did. I still get a chuckle when I recall seeing all those glasses piled on the altar in the chapel at the Center. A Danish friend of ours in the program nearly killed herself and some innocent bystanders near the Frankfurt airport one night due to bad visibility. (I'll say!) : -)

What a spectacle! But the doctrine that took the cake that year was the "perfect marriage" concept. It goes something like this . . . God has a perfect mate for you; and every man should simply pray for divine direction, then simply ask whomever he felt "called to" for her hand, without hemming and hawing about it. The woman should pray that God will "send" her the right man and that when he asked, she will know it is God's plan. The number of weddings announced shortly thereafter was legendary. Being engaged already at the time, I was looking forward to building a new life and ministry with Beth, whom I loved and admired greatly. I prayed about it a lot . . . with a heavy dose of "God, please make my health perfect; I claim my right as a King's kid to what I truly deserve . . . *heterosexuality!*" (Still waiting!)

We had no plans for the wedding whatsoever, as everybody was getting married in elaborate, expensive ceremonies that we attended regularly. Since some of our friends were getting married in Europe—and others, the Americans, were going back to the States to much folderol—we decided to go back as well in December as our cheap airline tickets were nearing expiration. Our intention was to return to Europe in the spring and put together the big fat Christian wedding then.

My fiancé's family was still living in the little East Los Angeles enclave of El Sereno where she had grown up. They were still attending the same little

Assembly of God church that they had always known. And the pastor hadn't changed in over thirty years. It was quaint, traditional, and charming. One thing had changed, however—and that was the congregation. From a collection of nice, kind, pleasant, white Christians, it had become a collection of nice, kind, pleasant, brown Christians. In fact, the Taylors were the only remaining elderly white couple in the almost completely Hispanic congregation. Although they stood out a bit, no one seemed to notice. We all had a grand time.

Beth's parents were delighted about the upcoming nuptials, but were crushed that we were planning to do the big fat wedding in Europe. We both felt bad, but they understood that in many ways they were a little out of step with the times. We spent our time itinerating —a euphemism for fundraising. Meanwhile, letters and photos of massive weddings and receptions poured in from all over Europe and the States. Everyone was so happy happy happy. We were happy too. But were both starting to get a funny feeling. Since we had been living on a shoestring already and were used to frugal living, planning a big expensive wedding in Europe seemed like kind of bad stewardship of God's money. So, like all good Christians, we prayed about it and decided to throw together the most inexpensive, practical, spur-of-the-moment little wedding that the law would allow. Beth rented a wedding dress from a local shop and volunteered her best friend from High School to be the maid of honor. I recruited Jim, an old Army buddy from Viet Nam days who was attending a local seminary, to be best man. That Sunday morning the pastor announced: "God has spoken to Tom and Beth about their wedding, and has told them to get married right here in Calvary Chapel! Hallelujah!" It was like Jesus himself had made the announcement personally. Everybody went wild. "We are going to have the wedding next Sunday afternoon after the morning service; so you can all just bring a hot dish for the reception and you don't even have to go to lunch or change your clothes . . . come on out and we will have a wedding celebration and feast just like in Cana!" (Minus the wine, of course.)

The wedding went off without a hitch. What was there to rehearse? The regular Sunday service ended in the conventional way with the doxology, prayer or two, and the benediction, whereupon the organist pulled out all the stops and began pounding out the wedding march on the electric Wurlitzer . . . and we were off. A few minutes later we were married. Beth and I retired to somewhere behind the curtained baptismal tank, and changed into our traveling clothes, which we had organized in advance. The congregation made its way into the large room in the back of the church. They had opened the sliding plastic doors to reveal a sumptuous feast of enchiladas, frijoles, tacos, and fixin's of every kind; salsa of every kind, and manudo. It was better than Cana! Someone had even thought of a cake! We stayed and soshed a while, then hit the road for San Diego where I was preaching later that night. We couldn't have planned it better.

We heard later on that the whole affair was such a success that everybody waddled back into the sanctuary from the fiesta, and started singing choruses and carrying on praising God; and the pastor took to preaching. They just had a whole 'nother service right then and there!

ITINERANTS: HITTIN' THE ROAD FOR JESUS

Many fits, many starts, and many decisions

We arrived back in Europe directly from our honeymoon in tasteful La Jolla, California, just north of San Diego. After the skinny little Mexican wedding, we hit the road south, and found a funky sort of hum-junngin' little motel that was within our price range, and stayed a week. But we were ready to get back to the "field" . . . (the mission field that is). And our arrival was barely noticed, as we had not been away all that long. The only difference was that Teen Challenge had rented a ground floor flat in the building directly across the street in Nieder Woellstadt, a small village between Frankfurt and Friedberg Hessen. They figured that we, as a married couple, deserved our own place. We thought that was very cool. Of course, along with that came far more responsibility. We were going to be the *Hausmeisters*—the chaperones and go-to guys for everyone in the center— as we were an old married couple of at least three weeks by then!

Howard took us to a light lunch in a small local cafe to ask us to hold the fort while he and Pat went back to the States to itinerate. *Itinerate?* Well, like the itinerant pastors of the American West (the circuit riders), all missionaries were required to return to their home districts in the States every four years and itinerate—travel from church to church to tell the congregations of the wonderful things that God was doing through them back in Belgium, Bolivia, or Botswana. They would raise money in the process, and were not allowed to leave for the field until they had raised their budget, which was set by the missions department. It sounded dreadful. Little did we know that we would be on the itineration trail soon enough ourselves! In a flash, Beth and I were in charge of the Foltz's ministry, and we prayed to God that we were up to the task and the responsibility that we were entrusted with. It was actually fun, and we enjoyed every minute of our time as interim directors. But one day we got a letter from one of the honchos in the foreign missions department, and we were "allowed" to apply for an open position with the fledgling Teen Challenge Center in Saigon, Viet Nam. I was stoked. Beth was freaked. We were aware of the stipulation that all missionary candidates were required to go back to their home districts in the States (namely, Oregon in our case), and pastor a small church somewhere in the sticks as a trial period before any could be appointed to full-time overseas service. I saw it as a wasted two years of preaching to a tiny congregation of lukewarm half-wits with no vision. The very thought of it gave me the dry heaves.

Then the opening in Saigon fell into our laps as an alternative. Apparently we could be assigned a special designation—*approved* missionaries, as opposed to appointed—kind of like a non-tenured college professor. But the great thing to me was that they would count the two years in Viet Nam as equivalent to two years pastoring in the U.S. I was elated. When most people—including my non-Christian parents—heard that we were returning to the States, they were happy. When they learned that we were then going on to Viet Nam after that, they were unhappy. Imagine that.

Actually, we didn't know the whole story about the situation in Viet Nam. Apparently, a rather crazy evangelist with a radio and TV ministry had donated a ton of money toward the construction of a Teen Challenge Center in Saigon. My new boss-to-be had spoken to her in Southern California and convinced her that she should consider it a sign from God if the Government of South Viet Nam would give the church property to build such a center. The reason given for the need was that the American G.I.s had brought a drug culture to South Viet Nam during the war, and thousands of drug dependents had been left behind in their addiction. It was actually a fairly accurate story, and John Hurston, our future boss, was a master fund-raiser.

Little known to the potential donor and her congregations, he had already met with the president of the country, a veritable puppet government of the U.S. and American corporations. Apparently, Madam Nguyen van Thieu had been moved by Dr. Hurston's presentation of the need in the country, and had pledged a certain piece of property right on Tran Hung Dao, one of Saigon's busiest boulevards. Beth asked who the donor was, as she was from the L.A. area and might know of her. Her name was Katheryn Kuhlman, and her name was whispered in hushed, almost angelic tones. I blurted out that I had never heard of her, but Beth kicked me under the table and gave me one of those looks. You know—like, I'll explain it all later, you convert! Beth was always a great source of wisdom when it came to Church history, as she had grown up in the Church and delighted in blowing my mind with all the weirdness that she had witnessed growing up. Kind of like Jerry Hill and his snake-handling relatives back in Texas, she had concluded that the Assemblies of God was a church full of kooks as well, but she had stayed within. Her faith was real. And she could see through a lot of bullshit. I thought back on Dave Loyal quietly sitting in the back of the church while all us new converts were carrying on at the altar in services like idiots. He too had concluded that he just had to put up with a certain amount of strangeness if he was going to remain in the Church.

Well, we were all rejoicing about the gift of the facility and how we would really like to join the team there in Saigon and *push back the darkness*, preaching the Gospel of deliverance from drug addiction by calling upon the name of the Lord. Then we were given another bit of information that completed the jigsaw puzzle. The appointed missionary and his wife, whom we were going to replace, had run into some difficulties on the field. Well, the guy—who, like me, was a Viet Nam war vet—had fallen into sin (bed) with an attractive Vietnamese woman (read: prostitute) and had committed adultery. They had left on the next flight out, and the A/G was in dire need of a replacement with a Teen Challenge background. Although Howard was loath to lose us, he had recommended us highly.

Once we arrived at the church headquarters in Springfield, we took all the personality tests (like the famous MMPI) and interviews, probing into our backgrounds and experiences. I was totally in the dark as to why they kept talking to me about my marriage and how solid it needed to be if we were to go into that "stronghold of Satan" that was Saigon. In private meetings with our new boss, Wess Hurst, and their personnel director, a certain Delmer Guynes (who I ended up working for years later), I was flat out asked if I could withstand the temptation of those wily Vietnamese women of the night. I was dumbfounded in a slightly humorous way, but I just assured them *honestly* that I was sure I could handle any tricks the devil might put in my path. I could definitely deal with the "desires of the flesh" that those "Vietnamese whores" could inspire in any man. But I let it go at that, and in a day or so we were "approved" for missionary service and were on a flight to Portland to begin our new adventure—itineration. . . raising our budget.

The folks in Springfield—come to find out—really needed us to get to Saigon as soon as possible. Although the land for the project had been donated by the government—the cost of building borne primarily by the Katheryn Kuhlman Ministries Incorporated—the operating budget was the responsibility of John Hurston, a rather famous missionary within the framework of the Assemblies of God church structure. He had more or less engineered the massive growth of the first of many megachurches in South Korea. He was a fundraiser par-excellence, and was needed to itinerate permanently and constantly just to keep the whole thing afloat. Neither the church, nor the Division of Foreign Missions, nor the Katheryn Kuhlman people, nor any donors on either side, wanted to see the mission flop. Viet Nam was still mighty big on the minds of most Americans, and the Teen Challenge name and reputation was at stake. They needed us to get over there as soon as possible and give the whole operation some umpf.

The mucky-mucks back in Springfield had promised to make some calls "out" to the officials at the Oregon district office in Salem, indicating how desperately they needed us to do our itineration, raise a barebones budget, and get our butts over to Saigon as soon as humanly (or divinely) possible. They were right; they did call ahead, and we were greeted like heroes when we first hit the deck running in Oregon. We had no idea what we were doing, but whereas the average seasoned missionaries usually take a year or more to raise a sufficient budget to live four years abroad in the land of their calling, we were given the goal of two months! But we did it! Considering the fact that this was a two-year assignment in lieu of pastoring in the States, our budget was reasonable. The big churches all broke the rules for us in light of the tremendous need, and bumped us to the head of the line. They took a big risk on us, but we came through. We bought a 1965 Ford for $500 and hit the road.

The A/G had like a hundred and fifty churches in the Oregon district at the time. We preached in about a third of them, from Astoria to Brookings on the coast, throughout the Willamette Valley, and all points south to Medford and Grant's Pass . . . through Bend and the entire central section, and all the way as far as Ontario—clear over on the Idaho border (and even in a different time zone). The fact that I was a native instead of a transplant, went a long way. Beth, a Californian (usually a term of derision in the Pacific Northwest) was welcomed as well. She only complained about the rainy weather once; but I corrected her for that, and we did fine.

Our arrival in Saigon was warm. Well, it was actually hot; but I knew from the weather report and from experience what to expect in advance. LOL. The Hurstons were on their way out of the country for a speaking engagement in Singapore or some such place, and met us briefly before they flew off. John was a big-picture kind of guy; and at this moment in time, we were a very small but important element in the grand scheme of things. The Teen Challenge center was unlike anything we had seen in Europe. It was more or less a glorified church with a few rooms in the back to house in-treatment drug addicts. It was a pretty good deal for them, as they had a place to live and food to eat, and very little else to do but sweep out the sanctuary. In exchange, they had accepted Jesus and had become born-again. I baptized several of them right away. The operation came with a full tank of water in-waiting for a spur-of-the-moment baptism. It made sense, especially as in the spring of that year, the North Vietnamese and Viet Cong had decided to make a quick land grab in the north of the country. Later they confessed that the move had been designed to be small and even rather innocuous, as other parts of South Viet Nam had been controlled by the insurgents—the Viet cong communists—on and off for years.

But the whole house of cards began to fall. I wasn't alarmed at first; but when Hue fell, I was terrified. A week or so later, when Da Nang was overrun by NVA regulars, I knew it was all over. The refugee flood had begun, and the images were life-shattering. We all met in the chapel of the Teen Challenge Center, which was standing-room-only all the time. I don't really know if all those Vietnamese had come to seek salvation in Jesus, or if they were hoping that any link to the Americans might be a ticket out once the North Vietnamese tanks were on the perimeter of Saigon itself. That came soon enough. By then, the word had come down from Mecca— er, I mean Springfield—that all missionaries were to be evacuated as soon as possible.

We had been given a packet of evacuation information from the American Embassy as a "Just In Case," so we read it carefully. The Armed Forces radio station in Saigon was still broadcasting, but the secret "password" or indication that the embassy would be soon shut down was to be when they played Bing Crosby's *I'm Dreaming of a White Christmas* on the air. At that point everybody should have a plan, as the embassy could not be counted on to rescue any recalcitrant missionaries wanting to be heroes. Our church, and most others with American workers, had the good sense to get us out well in advance of that. Some Catholics (especially French and Italian clergy) stayed through the takeover. I wanted to go to Bangkok, but there was no choice. "Grab any flight that is leaving the country" were our instructions. We ended up in Manila in the middle of the night with the shirts on our backs. Fortunately, we had some newfound friends we had met in Viet Nam who were there to greet us; and we were just happy to be anywhere where the rockets would not be falling on our heads.

* * * **

I opened one eye. Where was I? I quickly glanced around the small room. Right next to me was a second twin bed. Beth was sleeping profoundly. We had been evacuated and were sleeping off the drama of the previous day. I was just enjoying the silence. Everything seemed so peaceful. The war was over—at least for us and for now. I went outside into a postage-stamp-sized, enclosed, little patio surrounded by fan palms and bougainvillea. I sat in one of the rattan chairs under the friendly green-and-white deck umbrella, as it was already hot so early on that first morning in Manila. The whole household was sleeping. Meanwhile, I prayed. I still relished my morning quiet time, and this peaceful atmosphere was a real treat. Of course, I was mindful of all our Vietnamese friends that we had left behind to their collective fate in Saigon. I prayed for them too. I felt good. I looked at my watch and saw that I had lost track of a few days amidst the melee. And as I was decompressing, I tried to reorient myself to time and place. It read: Wed 18. Hmmm. The eighteenth of April. What was it about that date that struck a chord? It was indeed 1975, and it hit me . . . Oh, how weird . . . it is the 18th of April in '75. I recalled the famous Longfellow poem that I had partially memorized back in fifth grade: It was the eighteenth of April in '75, and hardly a man is now alive who remembers that famous day and year, and the midnight ride of Paul Revere. Two hundred years to the day, after the famous warning ride, I was still mindful of it as I sat quietly in the humid Philippine dawn, reflecting. Now what? That day, we managed to get a telegram off to our boss, Wes, back in Springfield (and by extension, the Hurstons), noting that we had managed to evacuate from Saigon and that we were safe in Manila, staying with the Ohlerkings in their home in Makati.

On the phone a few days later, Springfield actually gave us a choice: Would we rather return to the U.S. and pastor a church somewhere, or remain in the Philippines and pioneer a Teen Challenge Ministry there? That was like asking me whether I would rather have a bowl of boiled lima beans or a bowl of rocky road ice cream. They were all quite pleased that we were so resilient and willing to stay "out in the field" instead of taking an easy job like pastoring a rural church. I would have rather been dragged over broken glass than even imagine pastoring a rural church anywhere— especially in the South. But even the Pacific Northwest has its share of hicks and hillbillies. We had gotten a taste of that during our whirlwind itineration experience, which was still vivid in our minds. It was kind of ironic that the need for a Teen Challenge outreach in the Far East was, and had been, already on the mind of Springfield for some time. A quick note here: we all (and often) referred to our headquarters and its officials collectively as "Springfield," as if it was a personage. I didn't bat an eyelash when I heard others preface a sentence with: "Springfield says . . ." or "Springfield is going to institute a new policy."

A seasoned missionary from Japan had been assigned to head up the organization and operation of Teen Challenge Centers in various countries in the Far East, putting the headquarters in Manila. It was supposed to kind of mirror the European model that we had just left less than a year earlier. We were just perfect for the job, and all of Springfield was rejoicing in the Lord that we were ready to show 'em how it's done. Our boss, a certain Paul Klahr, and his sweet wife Lily were a delight. I had met Paul back in Germany briefly when he was visiting the various European TC programs in Germany, France, Switzerland, and Great Britain. He knew of Beth and me from then, and was overtly thrilled that we had been assigned to work with him, as he had no experience with the program whatsoever. That was perfect for me, as he basically gave me carte blanche to invent whatever kind of program that I felt was doable. Being the creative guy that I am, I rose to the challenge :-)

Fortunately, I did not just run headlong into the project in a willy-nilly fashion as many Protestant missionaries assigned to the Philippines tend to do. Both the Klahrs and we had served on other mission fields where knowledge of the native language was necessary. "All the Filipinos can speak English" was the mantra of so many clergy that we met right away and as time went along. It was definitely true that while the Pilipino clergy were mostly trained in Bible Colleges in the States and spoke great English, the average pew-sitter did not. We enrolled in Tagalog study immediately. By the end of sixth months of daily mind-bending work, I preached my first sermon *in Pilipino*. I hasten to add here that it was a rather Methodist-like, canned presentation. Most Pentecostal preaching is high, fast, loud, and extemporaneous. I got there, and extemporaneous exposition was always my best suit; but I carefully wrote out my sermons thereafter for quite a while before really launching out into the deep at one service in Pangasinan when the power went out during my homily, and I had to forget my notes and wing it. It went fine and I lost my linguistic stage fright from then on.

The language barrier had not offered an insurmountable challenge, but other factors did. It had never crossed my mind—given my call to China and the classical cultures of Asia and all—that I would ever be required to do missionary work in a *Catholic* country! That was for those called to Latin America, I had assumed—never me! But here we were in the Philippines, a nation of 7,000 islands with a history of Spanish colonialism. Pilipino is indeed saturated with zillions of Spanish words, but other than the religion, Spain had given the islands very little in their over 375 years of domination. The Jesuits and other Roman Catholic (RC) orders had done a magnificent job of transforming a motley collection of pagan island tribes into a motley collection of "Christian" island tribes, to be sure. And layered on top of that was a veneer of Protestant sects too numerous to count. And other than the wild and woolly provinces in far southwestern Mindanao, where Muslim separatists were constantly stirring up trouble, the country was RC all the way . . . lock, stock, and barrel.

I never had any doubt that the entire Catholic population of the country was headed for a literal burning Protestant hell. I had learned *that* clear back from Ernie in Viet Nam during the Army. And, of course, all my religious training in the interim reinforced that absolute certainty. Catholics *are not* Christians, and they need to be saved—converted to Protestantism in order to enter the Kingdom of Heaven. That was never in question. I knew full well that my mission assignment in the Philippines was simple:

Convert Catholics. Save them from the fires of Hell to which every one of them was doomed—or damned . . . take your pick.

But years later, during the antigay culture wars that were to come, when the Assemblies of God, Baptists, and other Evangelical denominations teamed up with the RC to "fight the fags," I marveled at how hypocritical both were. They hated each other's guts, but hated the queers more. I did not really know why back then, but over the years I learned a lot about Christian hypocrisy—no matter where the Church headquarters was located . . . Springfield, Dallas, or Rome. I hasten to throw Salt Lake City into that toxic stew as well, but that is coming up :-) During our first months in the islands, we were kind of hermits. We studied Tagalog from nine to noon with our private tutor, Isabel, who was famous as one who knew how to teach missionaries how to talk the talk. She was good at what she did, but I really wish that we could have had a textbook. Nevertheless, her lesson plan was complete, and she could guarantee success if we just stuck with her program. We did.

I was simultaneously taking nightly tutorials in Mandarin from Mr. Wang, a native of Beijing who had fled the mainland in 1949. He had grown up in Manila as a Hua-chiao (an Overseas Chinese), and spoke both Pilipino and the local Chinese dialect, Fukienese. But he had never forgotten a single word or character of Mandarin, and he never let me slide a bit. He was a perfectionist, and I will always give him a lot of credit for helping me pound those thousands of ideographs into my overtaxed brain during those days in our quiet little home in Quezon City, near the UP (University of the Philippines). It was a nice, calm life. After our obligatory morning classes with Isabel, Beth and I retreated, notebooks in hand, to a small local swim club that we had joined, and did our homework together while working on our tans.

We had not yet been thrown into the melee of the missionary scene yet. Language school was kind of a reprieve between evacuating from Saigon and jumping into the new life as real professional missionaries. But I was then, as now, a news junkie; and was as aware as anyone could be in our position during those years of martial law under the much-hated Marcos regime. The Catholic Church opposed Ferdinand and Imelda. (Yes, the bitch with all those shoes :-) But the Protestants loved them both, as they do all Right-wing dictators. Like Madam Thieu, who had donated property to Teen Challenge in Viet Nam, the Marcoses constantly leveraged the Protestant missionaries against the Catholic hierarchy in the county—his only real opposition to undisputed power. Over and over again, we saw how Right-wing dictators like Marcos, Thieu, the Shah, and Rios-Montt could bait the Protestants with freebies and concessions as a dig to the Catholic Church, an institution far bigger than any of them and certainly more longstanding. Dictators come and go, but the Church goes on long after they have looted their countries and have fled or have been overthrown.

Catholicism aside, one thing really rocked the whole Evangelical Protestant missionary world in that year of 1975 . . . a simple off-the-cuff statement offered by the then-President of the United States, Gerald Ford, in reply to a question about how the CIA had blundered in misreading the situation in Viet Nam in April of that year, and had suffered a great discrediting in the process. Ford tried to downplay the need for the CIA in any case by quipping: "We don't even need the CIA; we have missionaries!" Thud. That remark hit the deck like a ton of bricks. What? With that single remark he put the lives of Western clergymen and women in danger everywhere. There has always been the suspicion and even claim that the American missionaries that are sent out by the thousands are really just spies in disguise. Of course, it makes sense, and I was personally approached by the State Department right away—during language study. Of course, that did not surprise me one bit. I was well within the radar zone of the U.S. intelligence community as far back as Germany when I was called out of the G/A department once or twice to meet with the spooks upstairs in the NSA, testing out my possible interest in doing patriotic duty as a future agent of some description. My arts and languages skills did not go unnoticed.

So when the U.S. president casually hinted that at least some of the overseas missionaries might be actually spying for the U.S. government, a whirlwind of speculation ensued. It wasn't a real big deal in the Philippines, as Marcos was so deeply entrenched at the time. But of me they knew a lot. I had left the U.S. military only three years earlier, which included a five-year travel restriction due to my top-secret crypto security clearance and access to all that classified stuff that I had been handling during my time in both Viet Nam and Europe. Of course, I had never breached any travel rules, and God knows I knew how to keep my mouth shut. I was no threat—just a possible asset at the time.

It was no trick for them to keep up with me. They even knew of my continued Chinese study, and asked why I was doing that. Of course, I was such a la-la Christian at the time, I took the interview as an opportunity to witness to the polite embassy people who were hosting me for lunch at the downtown Manila Hilton Hotel. Neither of us had much to discuss at the time, but they were very supportive and encouraging about my interest in China. Hmm. Indeed.

LITTLE BROWN BROTHERS

A mole in their midst

Language school was over, and the fun was just starting. I didn't choose to come to the Republic of the Philippines. I landed on the beach like Jonah being burped up by the whale. I had been in the country before a few times, and never saw much more than the pool at the downtown Hilton. But now we were living in the culture, and it was definitely a shock.

Oh, the Pilipino culture wasn't all that remarkable. I had had my own third-world experiences by then, and compared to my ghastly time in Mexico as a foreign exchange student, and my fun war frolics in Viet Nam, Manila was not much of a challenge. And once we had graduated from language school, we were clear in our task—our mission to establish Teen Challenge Centers throughout the Philippines and convert Catholic youth. No sweat. But, although I had had a taste of Christian infighting back in Germany, and the TC Center situation in Saigon, nothing really had prepared me for one of the biggest issues that missionaries and church organizations deal with everywhere and constantly—namely property.

Yup, property. The vision that most pew-sitters back in Itinerationville have of the mission field is of noble missionaries toiling dawn to dusk for Jesus, building churches full of happy black and brown people, smiling and singing local versions of the very songs in their own hymnals. They envision their lovely facility transported to Nigeria, Nicaragua, or Namibia. But the key element of this vision is the church building itself. Of course, those dear dark brothers and sisters in Christ out there in Togoland or Tobago don't really need a church quite as nice as ours; they can skip the shag carpet and padded pews. A simple structure should do.

Well, that vision is not too far off really. And most Third World converts actually love the buildings that are built for them with mission offerings. But the rub is often closer to the ground—that is, the land on which the church physically sits. Remember back when I mentioned that fun book I read when I was doing my correspondence courses, entitled *Great Church Fights*? Well, I should have read it twice. It was oh-so accurate.

The truth is that whenever you have a bricks-and-mortar church building, you have land disputes. In the Philippines back in the day (of Ferdinand and

Imelda, that is), foreign persons and corporations were not allowed to own land in the country. This was common throughout the Third World in places like Thailand, Mexico, and Brazil, where—if given half the chance—multinational companies and multinational churches would simply buy up all the good land for factories and retail outlets, churches and seminaries, conference centers, and missionary housing. Of course, the Catholics (smart guys that they are) knew that centuries ago, and snapped up some of the best downtown real estate in places like Manila, Malta, and Mexico City. Of course, they frequently had their property ceased by revolutionary governments and then turned into girdle factories or other useful establishments only to be returned to the Church a generation later under a new administration.

Well, most Protestant denominations were lousy at this game. In fact, many lost their shirts in bad land deals with the natives. If it is true that the Dutch bought Manhattan for twenty-four dollars' worth of junk jewelry, the natives have certainly wised up since then. The Baptists, the likes of the Christian and Missionary Alliance (the CMA), and the A/G all got swindled constantly around the Globe. When I arrived in Manila, I heard of the endless ongoing legal court cases for the possession of Bethel Temple, a large A/G church building in downtown Manila right on Taft Avenue. It was a monstrosity, but everybody wanted it! God knows why. To quote Bette Davis again, "What a dump!" We referred to it as "Battle Temple" throughout my stint in the RP, and the legal war was still raging when I left two years later. I hasten to mention that I had actually been through another similar scrimmage back in Germany, in a place called Bensheim where a couple of A/G missionaries went "rogue" and hijacked a Teen Challenge center (which had once been a real girdle factory during the Nazi-Zeit). I kid you not. I was still doing my thing in correspondence school in Frankfurt during that time, so was spared the slings and arrows tossed back and forth among all those "good Christians." I stayed clear of the Bethel Temple saga as well, knowing that I was just putting my time in and didn't want to get my hands dirty.

Doing missionary work on my own was actually rather fun and challenging, as I had no interest whatsoever in building some big, fancy, highfalootin' Teen Challenge Center with all sorts of bells and whistles. I saw my talents in art as sufficient, since ink and paper were far more effective than bricks and mortar IMHO. Well, Teen Challenge is an Evangelistic youth outreach, and a key element from the beginning has been drug rehabilitation and "deliverance" through prayer and salvation through Christ. I got that, so I listened carefully when I heard a public service announcement on one of the radio stations in Manila, regarding the horrors of drugs, and aimed at young people. It was vivid and gruesome—designed by the government to scare the shit out of everybody in the country. Like a Pilipino version of *Reefer Madness*, it really was a scream! I decided that this was an ideal entre for Teen Challenge and that it was the newest thing: "positive alternatives." Way cooler than freaking everybody out with messages of death and ruin brought about by drug use (kind of like those kids back in Nidery), positive alternatives were so much more, well, *positive!*

I contacted the Government's department dealing with such matters, including the airing of those wild radio and TV spots, and made an appointment with the DDB (the Dangerous Drugs Board). Cool name, huh? Sounded like a totally contrived bureaucratic tangle of FUBAR proportions, and it was! Like, Duh. I could have predicted it. But there was a silver lining. The woman who ran the place was totally wonderful, and she fell in love with me immediately. I don't mean that kind of "in love" . . . come on. She was what a true polite, well-educated Pilipina should be like. Her name was Aruora Cudal and she was charming, and delightful, and frustrated. She knew that the government was failing grossly to curb drug use in the country, as it was exploding and expanding all over the place—and not just in Manila and other of the large cities. I had met dopers in small towns as far away as Gen. Santos, Mindanao, and way in the extreme south of the country. After she learned that I was a missionary, she mentioned that she had been raised a Methodist, and had gone to mission school, and had a real heart for guys like me! Yea. I had dummied up some sample ideas for an antidrug campaign that offered "Positive Alternatives," mostly in the person of Jesus Christ, as the best alternative of all. She loved it. I was practically hired on the spot. But, as I was still running on high-octane for Jesus at the time, I more or less made common cause with her; and we really did get a lot of Gospel literature out into the hands of kids throughout the country, from the biggest cities to the little barrios and barangays in the sticks. It was fun, and I enjoyed it. I realized something about myself during that time. I love to start things—get things off the ground and explore new and creative ideas. But once they are up and running, working well and self-maintaining, I get itchy feet, wanting to launch out into something else—something new, different, and challenging. But, like Howard, I had a certain ability to recognize the talents in others that I did not have myself.

Way back at Calvary Chapel, right before the skinny wedding fiesta in Los Angeles, I had met Byron, the son of the pastor. I mentioned that Brother Berwick had pastored that quaint little church for years. Well, his kids—all four of them—had grown up with Beth, and we were all more or less contemporaries. Byron, the youngest Berwick, had been the black sheep of the family and kind of a disappointment. He had pulled his life together by the time I met him, but he was at loose ends trying to form a Christian rock band.

OMG, every church I ever preached at in the United States has one—an aspiring musician with rock star envy who wrote his own songs. He appeared to me to be a wannabe, but with obvious talent I set him up with the CTC traveling band in Germany and he really blossomed there. When I needed a guy with musical talent and Teen Challenge experience, I called on him. He arrived in Manila a few months later and began taking over the Teen Challenge operation. I was so glad to give it to him, as he turned out to have the magical gift of administration, in addition to guitar playing. He never learned to speak Tagalog, but memorized lots of Christian hymns and tunes by heart, and his following among young Pilipino kids really melted my heart. I was so proud of him, and also realized that my time in the country was shortening. I had already made it clear to Springfield that my call was to China and that I needed to get back to language study and preparation for when China was going to open up again to the Gospel.

* * * * *

I had always been careful to avoid blurting out stuff like: "I'm called to Mainland China—not Taiwan—and I expect to be there very soon" . . . in general audiences, that is. But the FMD in the Hqs. in Springfield believed me right from the start. When Chairman Mao died in 1976, I predicted that we would all be doing missions work in the People's Republic within five years. A big prediction, but—hey, guess what—I was right (again). I am also a prophet, or didn't I mention that? LOL. The Chinese church in Manila was often referred to as the First A/C. It was the only church within the A/G chain of congregations that was air-conditioned :-) I took a bit of flak from the *tunay na mga misyonero sa Pilipinas* (real Philippine missionaries); but they all knew that I was building bridges to future work among the teeming millions of Chinese, so they just dug a little about spending so much time at the (much cooler) Chinese church. Actually, the Philippine-Chinese had already been building bridges of their own to their relatives and friends in Mainland China. I was jealous that they could actually begin traveling there right after Mao's death, but assured them that I would be right on their tails as soon as they let gwailos (white Westerners) back into the country. Of course, we all knew that openly living there and preaching the Gospel freely was years away, but there were plenty of things we could do in the meantime . . . like smuggling. Of course, the local Fukienese-speaking hua-chiao were very discrete in their efforts to smuggle a few Bibles and other Christian teaching books, etc., in. But once some missionaries, and especially visiting pastors and evangelists, from the States, Australia, and

Europe caught even the faintest whiff of such an endeavor, they had to blab. It is the nature of some to talk too much. With my background in military intelligence, I knew full well how to keep my mouth shut. But evangelists make their living and raise tons of money by doing the opposite. They just can't ever shut up—even if it ruins quiet work being done successfully without fanfare. What, no fanfare? How is that possible? Strike up the choir, tap tap tap on the mike . . . Ladies and gentlemen, welcome to Christian media! Da dut da duh dut duh!

It's time to play the music, it's time to light the lights, it's time to meet the Fundies on your TV set tonight . . . It's time to put on makeup, it's time to dress up, right. It's time to raise the curtain on the most sensational, inspirational, celebrational . . . this is the Christian dog and pony show! Oh well, that didn't quite rhyme, but you get the picture. The year was 1976. I had been out of the United States since 1968 (except for the brief stop in to get married and then itineration), but was really unaware of what was going on in the world of "Christian Media" during that intervening time period. A lot, as I found out!

I was preaching in an Assemblies of God church in Kabanatuan, and staying in a very authentic local motel (I guess you could call it that). It was rather primitive, but in the lobby they had a television! It was kind of ground zero for the neighborhood, as I noticed the same townspeople watching it when I arrived; and most were still there when I checked out. I was told that they charged admission to watch the thing, and that it was in living color! (Sort of :-) But I was stopped dead in my tracks when I took a look at what they were watching! It was an Oral Roberts Crusade in India! OMG. You've got to be kidding! At that very moment, I felt a tad bit out of touch. Once the yokels get hooked on religious broadcasting, why would they need to go to church? Heck, why would we need missionaries? I considered a vacation. But I watched for a few minutes in utter amazement. I was flat-out impressed. Like, how did the ORU crowd pull off a coup like that? Within a matter of a few weeks or months, I witnessed all manner of Christian programming, from Jimmy Swaggart and Jim and Tammy Faye Bakker to Pat Robertson's 700 Club, and even local pastor/evangelists from places like Buffalo, New York piling into the fray. Praise the Lord! The electronic Jesus movement had just hit the Philippines.

I was used to the big crusades sweeping onto the shores of the RP, and crowds of up to a million jamming into Rizal Park or some other stadium-style venue to hear the pope or Billy Graham; but now even totally unknowns could buy some TV slots at odd times and odd locations throughout the country—preaching in English! And claim to be reaching millions of souls for Christ! The missionaries could just retire. I was definitely ready to do so—from the madness that was becoming the Christian TV extravaganza of the Philippines. Our flight left Manila two years to the day from that dark and scary night of our evacuation from Saigon. But, to tell you the truth, this evacuation was just as welcome to me as back then when the rockets and mortars were falling on Saigon. Manila, like other places around the world where television was relatively new and airtime was cheap, had joined the globalization of the great commission. Jesus had gone viral! Hallelujah!

We were back at the itineration game again. But this time with feeling. We had been reassigned to Hong Kong, a city that I had visited several times since my first visit on R and R from Viet Nam, back in 1969. It was like Frankfurt—love at first sight. But I genuinely intended to live there for the rest of my life—to really put down roots. Itineration was a snap. I had figured out that the average church pew-sitter had no idea where Hong Kong even was (especially when a well-meaning woman in Medford asked me if I was going to have to learn Japanese when I got there). LOL. I emphasized China instead, and that got their attention. I didn't even mention the Philippines in my presentation, as most people thought you could drive there (but that it must be a long drive). But everybody knew China, and they all referred to it as RED China. They had remembered my Viet Nam stories from the past, and together with my grand march to conquer Red China for Christ (and push out all those Commie bastards in the process), I was their guy. Beth and I raised a ton of money. Vincent, our son, was born in March, and we were not scheduled to hit the deck in HK until July or August, so I itinerated on my own for a few months. It was okay, but I missed Beth. It just wasn't the same without my favorite critic and fellow itinerant to share the foibles of deputation with.

But I made it. This was 1978, and I had access to a far wider variety of news sources than I ever had in Manila. I began reading of a new phenomenon that caught my attention. The news was talking about this thing called the "Gay Agenda." I was interested, and read up on the various happenings around the country, especially in New York, L.A., and S.F. It all still seemed too far away and remote, but I did some research in the library of PSU, where I was taking some classes in the history of China and more Mandarin study even though I would be immersed in Cantonese soon.

But during those few months with a lot of alone-time, I had a gentle introduction to the gay world. I could certainly not be accused of living a "gay lifestyle" but I was then, as we say now, gay curious. My research was not confined to libraries, but I was pleasantly shocked at the number of books and articles I found on the subject. One thing lead to another, and I walked into a gay bar in Portland for the first time. Though I was scared shitless, I figured that I would never get to know that side of my inborn nature unless I checked it out. So I did.

It was a "marvelous work and a wonder" :-) I don't know what it was, but within no time, I was right at home, meeting new friends, and getting laid. Perhaps that sounds crass, but as I learned rather quickly, sex is indeed the touchstone issue that brings men together from the most disparate backgrounds possible. Within a few weeks or so I had gained enough experience and confidence to finally admit to myself that I was gay—not bisexual or even questioning. I now, for the first time in my life, had a point of *comparison*. And, well, there was none. I finally knew what all the fuss was about. For me, and IMHO, gay sex is flat-out better. I will emphasize "for me" one last time to make my point. It had always been a choice before (not to even try it). And once I tried it, I decided to try it again :-) It *was* a choice. Unlike what I was hearing on Christian radio and from televangelists populating the air waves back then—that all men are straight by birth, but some chose to "engage" in immoral, unnatural acts, and get *sucked* into the dreaded "homosexual lifestyle."

The choice is really, I found out, to either actualize one's biological nature or to fight it. I had fought it all my life thus far, but now had chosen to follow my inborn nature—my DNA. I was happy and relieved, but knew full well that I was not going to pursue a gay life, as I was still a Bible-believing, born-again, Protestant, Fundamentalist clergyman, and missionary. The struggle of whether by nature I was a homosexual was over, but the struggle of faith had just begun. It was going to be an interesting and gut-wrenching time as I faced the years ahead in the ministry, knowing that I was going to have to subordinate all my natural feelings and sexual interests and keep playing the game, pretending to be straight. Heck, I figured, I got through grade and high school, college, the army, and this far in the ministry by faking it. I was an expert, as so many guys like me are. I would just keep pretending. But, as I sort of suspected in the back of my mind, it wasn't going to be easy. It wasn't. I began a new and double life, like a "mole," a spy sent in to infiltrate enemy territory. But I didn't consider the church, my fellow ministers, or the doting congregations to be the enemy ... at least not yet.

We arrived in Hong Kong and settled in. I had made a pact with myself on the long flight across the Pacific to put my time of experimentation and discovery behind me and to run full tilt into my calling: winning millions of lost Chinese souls for Jesus! I was stoked and entered language study with firm resolve. I skated through the experience with little effort other than trying to keep my eyes to myself. One interesting thing did happen in language school, however, that hinted to me that I was beginning to develop a new sense of gaydar. A word not yet in common parlance at the time, it is like radar, detecting signals in the atmosphere—vibes of gay persons.

My first real bell went off in my head during the second semester when two of the new students in first semester came to my attention. They were Italian priests and very good-looking ones at that. Language school is kind of a religious neutral zone, as we were all in the same boat, struggling together to learn Chinese. As if we had a self-imposed truce, our doctrinal differences never came up. I liked all the students of every stripe—even the non-clerical types who were working for large multinational corporations, travel agencies, or the like. We thrived on a certain kind of mutual camaraderie.

Paolo and Francesco had been put together as a two-man team back in seminary in Rome. They were committed to being China missionaries from the get-go. They spent two years learning English in London so that they could come to HK to learn Cantonese—and likely Mandarin should the opportunity develop. It did. I was not only attracted to the two intellectually. I had read Dante, and knew the story of Paolo and Francesca, a straight couple in hell for being too sexually hot for the Church of the Fourteenth Century . . . I so wanted to ask them if the Church had put them together on a whim, as certainly all good Catholic seminarians would be familiar with the *Divine Comedy*. Of course, no Protestant could possibly get the joke. But it was just as well . . . I couldn't explain it to them anyway. But the three of us came to be friends—hanging out together now and then in the one and only (somewhat gay) bar in Hong Kong, or together at the only gay beach.

My life as a mole had its moments. I began picking up on more and more obvious racism and certain homophobia from my fellow missionaries and other sundry church people in the Colony. Maybe I was just more attuned to such things after my brief dip in the pool of the gay world, or maybe I was just becoming more in-tune with politics in general at the time. It was in 1980 that Ronald Reagan was elected president. I had voted for Jimmy Carter. Of course, I couldn't vote four years earlier in Manila, as getting an absentee ballot was like pulling teeth. But I did vote in 1980 and was distressed to see that doofus Reagan win so handily. We missionaries all met with the Wall Street types and various businessmen and women at the American Club where election information was coming in as close to live as was possible at the time. I presume someone in the States was calling in the election results to some member of the club. Anyway, I had a strange sense of foreboding as all the others in the place went wild! Hallelujah, the Republicans are in the White House! Hmmm. Why was I not cheering?

Actually, I had loved Carter from before the 1976 election that he won. I was shocked at the response of the other missionaries at the time. "But he is born again Christian . . ." I whined. "A Baptist!" But hey, Tom, get with the program. He is a damndemocrat! Ah, shades of my past. My dad loved Ronnie, a true conservative. Most of the other missionaries in both Manila and then Hong Kong loved Reagan and were true born-again Republicans—party members all. Well, almost. I did have a few cohorts who had not fallen into the political net of political-cum-religious conservatism . . . yet.

But the bubbling, gurgling toxic stew of the rising "Religious Right" in America was seeping into all manner of ecclesiastical conversation, growing stronger all the time. I noticed, but tried to ignore it as best as I could, since I had China on my mind, and lots of great opportunities for evangelism of various kinds began showing themselves on the horizon. I was really jazzed. I loved Hong Kong and my cool flat up in Jardine's Lookout with the million dollar view of Victoria Peak and the stunning harbor below. I loved my work as it developed, drawing from my experiences in Europe, Viet Nam, and the Philippines. I began with a built-in set of missionary friends and contacts, but they were all rather insular and incestuous. Everybody in the church world knew everybody else. All our "fellowship" was with like-minded people, and there was very little cross-pollination with the world at large.

I was twenty-seven years old when I first began what I had planned to be my life's work, my occupation, my calling. I was in the right place at the right time. I had been in Cantonese language study less than six months when the news broke that foreigners were being allowed into China (as tourists). I figured that it wouldn't hurt to get the "lay of the land," so signed up on a tour to Guangzhou (Canton) right away. Well, as I so expected, it was a dump. There was one hotel that was able to house foreign "guests," the *Dong Fang* (the Orient). It looked like it had been transported from Irkutsk or somewhere else in Siberia—very Russian—very much the kind of place you would want to take people who you wish to impress with your country's incredible progress under a Communist dictatorship. It was just as I had imagined it. The reactions of the other foreigners was predictable. Yuck.

But I could overlook the crud—the lack of modern infrastructure like traffic lights and electric light bulbs over 40 watts—as I could see the sea of Chinese faces bicycling everywhere to and fro on the crowded streets, and felt a true desire to reach them with the salvation in Christ. I can't say that I was overwhelmed with what I saw, but I was definitely challenged. I prayed on the few private walks in the city I was allowed when we were not off visiting factories and mills that were supposed to impress us. They didn't. But I got a lot of ideas on that trip and others that followed as restrictions on travel eased more and more and we sneaky missionaries were allowed to enter the PRC (People's Republic of China) on our own.

I need to interject here that clergy were not given even tourist travel permits into China. We all had to lie on our visa applications in order to gain even limited access into the country at the time. I had run into this problem before, so had thought through my response to the question: *What is your occupation?* on the application's questionnaire. I had been refused entry into Burma (Myanmar) a few years earlier when the well-meaning Filipino travel agent had simply typed "missionary" into the box requiring occupation. I resubmitted the application as an "illustrator" because, although they likely had no idea what that was, I had learned that most Asian countries have long and dark memories of missionaries. And I don't blame them. Whereas all the Hong Kong missionaries and American pastors and evangelists who were also flooding into China to do God's work, were calling themselves "teachers," at least I was honest. I was a bona fide graphic artist, whereas all those liars could not even tell where they were teaching or what. A weekly Bible study class is hardly professional teaching. But, I had learned a long time back that lying for Christ is okay :-)

Actually, I had no real qualms about lying, as I had been lying to myself and others all my life about my sexuality. I was not righteously indignant about all those clergymen and women calling themselves teachers any more than I could fault myself for identifying as straight. It was a game and we all had to fake it here and there, now and then, in order to participate. Of course, the lying intensified as we began coordinating the new thing, the new missions endeavor—Bible smuggling. Now, that required more than just lying. We had to conspire to openly contravene the laws of a sovereign nation—namely China—and secretly arrange to surreptitiously import thousands of illegal religious books and other materials in direct defiance of the law. Breaking the law for Christ is alright too. After all, we chanted: "God's laws are above man's laws." I was still okay with that, as I was all wrapped up in the smugglers pipeline.

Back in the States and in the Evangelical churches in Europe and Australia, tongues of fire were wagging! Everybody had read the famous book entitled *God's Smuggler*; and, believe me, everybody and his dog wanted to be a mini Brother Andrew, the hero of the book. By now I was familiar with religious fads that constantly sweep though the Evangelical community worldwide. Usually it is in the form of a "new truth" or a doctrine that everybody loves and gets behind—at first. Then it morphs into something weird and then just plain ugly. The prosperity doctrine was largely discredited by now and the emerging power of Christian media was gaining speed everywhere, so it was no surprise that once the word got out that missionaries in Hong Kong were able to assist in smuggling Bibles into mainland China . . . well, everybody was ready to line up, buy a ticket for a China tour, and carry some contraband religious-anything into the PRC. They too could be a smuggler for Christ and see the Great Wall of China to boot! What a deal!

The problem with Evangelical Christians (as I have already noted) is that they are self-centered and love to talk and gossip. It would never occur to them that a smuggling operation should be kind of on the QT—like hush-hush. Oh no, they had to broadcast it on the 700 Club, PTL, and from every pulpit in Jesusland, USA . . . "Well, our church just smuggled a hundred Bibles into China! . . . Well, ours just smuggled a thousand! . . . Oh, have you heard, Pastor Joe Blort's megachurch has just funded a massive project to smuggle ten thousand . . . or more! "

Well, I wasn't the only missionary in HK to roll my eyes when hearing of such bullshit. Telecommunications were developing so rapidly at this time that one could actually pick up a telephone in Indianapolis, Indiana and dial Hong Kong directly! Rapid and direct communications between the mission field and donors was shrinking the distance between the two rapidly. Even in the brief course of a year or so, overseas phone operators became a thing of the past, and you could talk to a missionary right in the field by picking up the receiver! It was scary and a definite sign of things to come. Who needs missionaries anyway? Heck, anybody can just hop a plane to anywhere and be a weekend warrior for Christ. Cool, huh? I had my doubts.

GOD'S SMUGGLERS

God's laws are above man's laws, so breaking China's laws is okay :-)

I was still on-board with all this maelstrom of disjointed religious fervor and mayhem. Everybody had missionary envy, and was sure that God had called him or her to China—if for no longer than a week or two-package tour would allow. Gospel smuggling was oh so exciting—and dangerous! LOL. The only danger that most of the missionary wannabes faced was lifting their overweight luggage, filled with illegal religious literature, onto the carts at the Hong Kong airport. It was so funny to note how much lighter their packs became on their return trips. Not that the Chinese didn't notice. *Come on.* A communist police state like the PRC was totally aware of the whole operation, but turned a blind eye as long as the tourism industry continued to grow. Hell, whole Christian tour groups were being formed by travel agents in America and elsewhere, touting the whole smuggling agenda right in their brochures! It could not really be called stupid. It was way beyond that.

My impression of the church world was rapidly descending into a kind of pity. God, these people are dumb, I thought. Like, once they get all these materials into China, who are they going to give them to? Where are they going to get a suitcase full of Chinese language literature in the first place, and who was going to have to arrange a drop-off contact once they lugged their load of spiritual propaganda into the country? Well, remember the bottleneck I mentioned back in the graphic arts department? I found myself at the neck of the bottle once again, but this time for Christ! I was happy and willing to make connections for the would-be smugglers, but that would involve drawing attention to myself with the Gung An Bao. Like duh. Not very nice folks, those.

Well, I didn't think the whole fiasco would last long. It didn't. Actually, the Communist government up in Beijing was aware of all the skullduggery going on down in Hong Kong with foreign tourists bringing tons of religious literature into the country. They let it slide as the tourist dollars rolled in. But finally it became a matter of face. The government couldn't be seen as just allowing all this contraband to filter into the country. They were especially weirded out by all these gweilos bringing in Bibles, because they were printing them in China already! And that was true.

Anybody in China by 1980 or so could simply buy a Bible, a Koran, and most other well-known books at a government-run bookstore! Hey, the days of the Cultural Revolution were over, and China was on a path to modernization. The Chinese under the Communist Party had long ago caught onto the value of the printed page. For years I subscribed to the China Pictorial (Jen Min Hua Bao) in both English and Chinese in Manila and Hong Kong. It always had a most peculiar smell—weird ink or paper or something. And, let me tell you—the Bible, like the Koran, is not really self-propagating. You don't just pick up the Bible, open it at random, get hooked on the great rhetoric or the catchy storyline, and then get saved! Somebody has to explain it all to you. The publication and sale of Bibles was not much of a threat to the government as they controlled everything in the country, including religion! It comes as a shock to most uninitiated folk that the constitution of the PRC does allow for freedom of religion.

Well, like most things in dictatorial regimes, their choice to use the word "freedom" comes with a caveat. One is free to choose to be a Christian, a Muslim, or even a Jew (I guess) . . . but not so much a native indigenous concoction like the Fa-lun-Gong. Of course, the whole thing is totally whack, because if you want to attend a Christian church service, you have to attend one of the state-sponsored churches! Some freedom, huh? But in a political system that insists on controlling everything and everybody, it makes sense. If the masses want religion, well, package it up for them and dish it out with a heavy dose of Marxist rhetoric. Both Catholic and Protestant churches limped along for years in the PRC, but they were totally moribund, as all sermons and any presentations whatsoever had to be approved in advance by censors and then read verbatim as approved. Not much room for speaking in tongues, or for words of wisdom or personal prophesies, huh?

The "State" Church is called, ironically, the "Three-Self" Patriotic Movement (TSPM). The three selves included self-governing, self-financing, and self-propagating. Like total LOL, since they were not allowed to propagate, but were free to promote atheism. Like, how stupid and heavy-handed is that? The total warp and woof of the Christian message: The Great Commission is to propagate, evangelize, and preach the Gospel far and wide. Christianity is a missionary religion, but in China it was, by law, not allowed to do the very thing that Jesus commanded his followers to do with their lives: propagate! So we all considered the "Three Self Church" to be a total joke, and paid it no mind. Ours was the real church—the real message. And besides—church attendance, though legal, was strictly monitored by the party. The apparatchiks were at every service with note pads—taking names.

Of course, the big thing then, as now, was what is often referred to as the "underground church." Also known as the "house churches," these were secret meetings in the homes of believers. Although quite risky, they had flourished even during the darkest moments of the Cultural Revolution. Even so, the law against more than four or six people getting together *anywhere* was strictly enforced; but this kind of "on the sly" church attendance was a very viable alternative to the state churches. I participated in many such "services," which were more akin to in-home Bible studies really. Of course, I was always whisked in and out of such events in the dark of night . . . and usually with a purpose. Like, one time in the outlying areas of Guang Zhou, I went specifically to perform a baptism. The idea of doing a baptism of any kind was against all the rules. But I did it anyway. Fuck the Communists. It wasn't like I was being more rebellious or contrary than usual, because, in fact, I considered it an obligation. Some missionaries from HK were quietly slipping into China to do such services, but it was super hush-hush, and for the most part we never talked about it—especially to the loudmouthed evangelists and pastors who would surely blow our cover if we mentioned it to them.

I distinctly remember picking my way down dingy, narrow alleys devoid of any street lighting whatsoever, with several Hong Kong friends and a flashlight, dodging mud puddles in the dark. The local believers had heard through the grapevine that a real white missionary—a mok-sih from Hong Kong—was in town; so I was called upon and went willingly. My mission was to baptize an elderly couple who had converted right after the Second World War. The house was typical. It was near the end of a muddy lane. It was of dull, colorless bricks partially covered over with equally gray, dingy, cracking plaster. Inside the place was the humble dwelling of Mr. and Mrs. Leung, a very elderly crippled couple seated in the midst of a collection of believers from around the area. The single room was lit by a naked 40-watt bulb hanging by frayed wires from the center of the ceiling.

In the dim room we had an ad hoc service without the trappings of formality of any kind. The Leungs talked of their lives. It was pretty grim, and though I had made several trips into China already at the time and had heard many such tales, I felt really crushed and sad that these two little old people had once been young, strong, and hopeful. But their lives, as millions like them, had been destroyed by war, invasion, and revolution. They had spent their adult years faking their way under Communism, pretending to be "true believers," but knowing full-well that it was all a big lie. Like all others, they had learned to just keep their heads down and not to draw attention to themselves.

Of course, we all knew that this meeting was definitely in the category of drawing attention, but they had taken my presence as a sign from God that they should be baptized—even at this late date. So they were. They felt that it was a divine risk, saying honestly, "At this point, what can they really do to us that we haven't already been through before?" Good point. And I knew they were right.

I had struggled with the notion of doing a baptism without standing water, totally against my doctrinal training and all. I figured I would just do it and let God sort it out in Heaven when these two would stand in judgment. *Come on.* There is no such thing as a bathtub in those parts of China, let alone a pool, a stream, or a river. An open sewer? Oh sure. And besides, did I mention these people were crippled and could not even walk? I did the traditional baptism prayer in Chinese and carefully poured a small bit of water on each of their heads in turn. And that was that. We very quietly sang the doxology. It was very touching. It was followed by an unscripted silence. In any Pentecostal church I would expect someone to shout forth with a message in tongues. Like that would be a wise thing to do at that moment. LOL. But instead, Mrs. Leung quietly pointed to a picture of Jesus hanging on the wall. It was one of those Catholic prints with a beautiful glowing Caucasian Jesus, complete with a halo and flaming heart. I had seen it upon entering, and had just tried to ignore it. But then everybody was looking at it as she reverently said, while pointing at me, "Wah, ho-chi Yeh-So gam! "Just like Jesus! It was the beard. Does it every time :-)

Months later I was talking to an American pastor from California about my dilemma—performing a baptism in a most Lutheran way, by "sprinkling!" I didn't mention the part about the flaming heart, of course. Why make it more weird than necessary? "Well," he said rather wistfully, "I see the problem. But I can't help but think that if it had been me, I would have tried harder to find a river or something." I never mentioned that baptism again, figuring that word might get around in churches in the States that Tom was over there dripping water instead of doing real baptisms!

The next time I was in the city, I walked across the only bridge over the muddy fetid river flowing through town. I stopped near one end and looked over the railing. The river was low, exposing wide mud flats on both banks. There, sticking out of the grayish, filthy, oily mud, and covered in raw sewage, was all manner of disgusting refuse from upstream. The broken bottles made the biggest impression of all on me. I tried to imagine if it would have been possible for us to carry those two old folks through the muck and mire and broken glass to immerse them in those putrid waters—would that have been a real baptism? Or did their home baptism really count at all? Well, I figured that it would be up to God now. But it bothered me.

Meanwhile, the smuggling continued. But, as I had predicted, sooner or later some hotdog evangelist or pastor or missionary-wannabe was sure to bring the whole thing to a screeching halt. And they did. As the story unfolded—and I had no part in this galactic stupidity—a certain visiting Christian from the United States was talking to a "pastor or church person of some kind" somewhere in Fukien Province in coastal China, across from Taiwan. The Chinese fellow was bemoaning the lack of Bibles in their rather backward and off-the-beaten-track township. Whereupon the American churchman asked how many Bibles could be distributed if they could be supplied from sources in the West. Well, I couldn't believe my ears when the tale reached me that the guy had said local believers could easily use a *million* copies. What? Oh, it gets better. The next thing we all heard was that a massive fundraising campaign was being waged throughout the U.S. and Canada by various sponsoring churches, parachurch organizations, and Christian broadcasters, to print a million Chinese Bibles and buy a barge of some kind to deliver them in the dark of night, floating them ashore on an isolated beach area somewhere between Fu Zhou and Xia Men (about a hundred miles between the two). I mean, it was so preposterous that I never ever thought such a colossal boondoggle could ever get off the ground. And like, why not just broadcast it all over—as if the Gung An Bao wouldn't ever hear of it? By that time, I was having serious doubts about the sanity of a lot of the Christian leaders everywhere. I had already concluded long before that the average pew-sitter was brain-dead anyway. They will buy anything. I was tempted to just start my own missionary program and raise funds for some totally fictitious scheme myself. Nothing could be more asinine than the million Bibles for China campaign.

I couldn't help myself. I grabbed a handy copy of a small-format Chinese Bible from my desk and measured it. Even though I was a math dunce in school, I still remembered how to figure volume of an object by calculating its length x width x height. So I multiplied 4" x 5" x a half inch, and then multiplied that by a million. By the way, that was just the New Testament and not the whole Bible, which would be way bigger. Well, I came up with ten cubic inches per unit. Converting that unimaginable number to cubic feet yields roughly 5,787 cubic feet of total volume. I happened to have a friend in the shipping biz, so I gave him a call and asked what the volume of the largest ocean shipping container would be. He knew off the top of his head: 2,500 cubic feet. So, 2.5 such containers would accommodate a million Bibles. Of course, he had to explain that that was not perfectly accurate unless you were shipping water or any liquid that would fill all the nooks and crannies. I always admire guys like that, don't you? Anyway, he said that likely three containers would accommodate a million Bibles. Think about it. Oh, did I mention that the people who were coming to pick up these treasures on the shore would be coming on bicycles? LOL. Bicycles.

But just to make me feel better, he pointed out that you could likely get the whole shipment in only two or so standard rail cars! Wow, I was feeling so much better. Well, did this project succeed? We heard—but only a rumor—that a barge of some description did appear off the coast of Fukien on a dark, moonless night, and some plastic-wrapped packages of Bibles did actually float ashore. But the dear Christian brethren were not there to pick them up. The Gung An Bao had simply informed the local authorities, and some military personnel were quietly dispatched to collect the contraband. End of story. I never did hear what kind of a fish-tale of an excuse was told to all those American saps who gave money to such a cockamamie scheme without even thinking of doing the math. Oh well, as they say in the church biz . . . "Praise the Lord anyway!"

I was so glad to be living outside of the United States during this time. The Republicans and the Reagan regime were in power in Washington, and the American churches were in love. Ronnie could actually walk on water—or so I heard-tell from his acolytes in church pews nationwide. LOL. It was during that time that many whole denominations were getting sucked into "get-rich-quick" schemes designed by Wall Street. The Oregon District, like most others in the General Council began investing Church funds in various money market kinds of programs designed to multiply church funds fast and furiously for the glory of the Lord. And we missionaries, like all the pastors in the district, were invited to participate by putting our retirement funds into this "sure thing." Most of the other missionaries in HK and around the Far East (and beyond, as far as I could tell) bought into the scheme. Beth and I did not. In fact, having lived as poor church mice in Europe, we had lost faith in the U.S. dollar years earlier and had secretly opened a savings account in Denmark where we were stashing every spare dollar (converting them into Danish Kroner). The interest rate was fantastic, but we just kept our business to ourselves, as we did another venture that paid off even better.

John Damson, a friend of ours who was working for an American retail conglomerate as a buyer, had decided to go into business for himself. After all, he already had tons of contacts provided to him on a silver platter by Macy's, Sears, Kmart, and the like. He was a wheeler dealer, but we trusted him. After all, he was a Christian. And besides, his dad was a big-time pastor of some A/G church in Missouri or some place. The U.S. dollar was strengthening against the Hong Kong dollar, so we put in 20,000 U.S. dollars from Denmark and threw in with him, thus owning twenty-five percent of the stock in his new company called *Startram HK Ltd.*; a retail venture at both ends of the Star Ferry line between Hong Kong Island and mainland Kowloon. It was your basic tourist trap, but as they say in business, the key elements are three: location, location, location. They are right. We made a killing from the get-go. It turned into four, then eight, glorified T-shirt shops. And I designed all the shirts. It was great, especially since all our clergy friends had lost their collective shirts in the failed aforementioned scheme back in the States. We just kept our mouths shut and made a bundle when we sold our shares some years later.

Now, we had heard of missionaries leaving the ministry to go into business before. Of course, I had read James Mitchner's famous book entitled *Hawaii*, which was about how the clergy cleaned up financially by representing large pineapple and sugar interests. And although we had heard that our denomination frowned on any of its missionaries actually doing likewise, I never saw it in print in our bylaws or anywhere else that we were forbidden to invest in such things on our own time! Like back in Manila when I worked as an inker for an American comic book publisher for extra money, I had done it at night on my own time. Or like back in Frankfurt when I worked part-time moonlighting for an American advertising agency as an illustrator, I likewise did it during off-duty hours instead of sitting around the NCO club drinking beer with the guys. Of course, in Manila, since we didn't even have a TV, I read a lot, painted a lot; and later in HK, I created a lot of T-shirt and mug designs :-) It is always neat to have a renewable resource—making something out of nothing. Works for me!

* * * * *

But another weird and interesting thing began happening around the time when the China smuggling was going out of fashion. I began meeting a lot of gay people here and there. I was not cruising bars or beaches and such, but I did manage to make a lot of new friends when I got the wild idea to join a gym. Don't laugh. Me, the ultimate non-sports-enthusiast, joining a gym. Well, I knew it was a great place to meet "guys," and that was true. In fact, the caliber of the other members was incredible. My new collection of quietly gay friends grew gradually. Of course, the British laws against homosexual activity were strict, and we all were closeted. Some were more than others, but we all understood our mutual secret and were totally discrete. There was one gay bar in Central (the financial district) at the time, but everyone was careful and mindful that any of us could lose our jobs or even be asked to leave the Colony if we were too "out there" in our behavior. Like most, I was careful and never dropped a hair pin (a very British expression meaning to slip and give away one's sexual orientation in public). I know full-well that I was totally in the clear. I was living two *separate* lives . . . until they began to merge from time to time.

One afternoon I was invited by a very nice American fellow to visit his flat for drinks. The sex was nice, so we got together again. One day we were having lunch with a mutual friend, a banker named Maurice, in the French Club in downtown Central. We all knew a lot of the same people, as the pool of possible sex partners was not all that big. He mentioned that he had a friend who worked in the American consulate who would like to meet me. I thought he meant for a sexual encounter, so told him to get in touch. He did. Well, it actually was for a sexual encounter; but there was more. I was not really shocked or surprised as I flashed back to my army time, the NSA, and my friendly interview with the CIA in Manila; so when he began appealing to my patriotism, I knew what he was getting around to. But this time I was more receptive. After all, he pointed out, lots of church workers of various types help their countries out by just paying attention to certain things during their travels and reporting back now and then with anything useful. Having the language was a big help as well. Of course, it was not possible to infiltrate a place like China and blend in (although I could pass as Chinese on the phone!) . . . There were still plenty of things that a savvy China hand like myself could glean from any trip into the Mainland. And since I was venturing way into the depths of places like Xinjiang and Tibet by then, I had a lot to offer my country. Of course, they already had my dossier in hand at the U.S. Consulate in HK, going all the way back to the military—ASA, M.I., and NSA all included—when I was first escorted past the marine guards and into the consulate one rainy March afternoon.

There I met a most attractive GS-18 named Charles. We became fast friends, and I visited him frequently at his office at the U.S. Navy headquarters in Hawaii. He had big time mojo at the place as he was the highest ranking civilian working for the Department of Defense in the Pacific at the time. Of course, he was in the closet big time, but his travels around Asia afforded him plenty of opportunities to mix business and pleasure. He even managed to route himself through various places where I was preaching or helping Teen Challenge with artistic assistance in places like Manila, Bangkok, or

Singapore. He also helped me to route myself through Honolulu on occasion. Once I was even going to a big-time conference in Brussels and took an extra week going through Hawaii on the way. Talk about massive jetlag!

We remain friends unto this day :-) I also met another lifelong friend on that trip in Brussels . . . but I digress. My ever-expanding circle of non-church friends finally came to the attention of my wife, Beth. "Where do you meet all these interesting people?" she queried one day. "Well, you know me . . ." I replied, "Mr. Friendly." She didn't buy that for a minute. "Mr. Friendly?" she retorted with a tone of total disbelief. "You are so not Mr. Friendly. Mr. Snobby maybe, but you don't ever seem to hang out with your Christian friends much anymore!" Oh, it was starting to show. She was right. I was finding the missionaries and various church people rather boring and shallow. I was having far more fun with my private friends here and there. Mostly here. Hong Kong was my favorite place, and although I was away from it more and more, I still loved everything about it. I was genuinely happy. I was still quite fulfilled as a worker for Jesus in his vineyard, but my journey of self-discovery was clearly more fulfilling. Then something amazing happened.

The phone rang in the middle of the night. I took it in the office, as Beth was asleep. I was used to nocturnal calls from the U.S., since now that we had direct dial most anybody could simply pick up the phone and call the mission field for a report of the amazing things that God was doing in China. But this was different. The woman on the other end of the line politely asked me to hold for Mr. So-and-So, of whom I had never heard. He was the head of marketing or something for a large agricultural machine manufacturer in the Midwest. Having grown up on a farm (even though I hated every minute of it), I knew of his outfit for sure.

He was going to be coming to China with a big-time trade mission from Illinois, Ohio, and some other of those flyover states; and wanted to touch base with me. What? Why me? Well, he was a member of some megachurch in Chicago or someplace, and had heard me preach in California, and he was totally committed to helping spread the Gospel in China any way he could. We met a few weeks later at the newly opened Shangri La Hotel on Salsbury Road in Kowloon. He was truly jazzed about my missionary work in China, but he was really more interested in asking me if I might be interested in a part-time job as a foreign associate sales person for his company back in the States. The likes of John Deere, Caterpillar, and GMC were all keen to sell equipment to China, as the whole country was barreling full-tilt into a massive modernization kick. I was totally aware of this. And like the U.S. government, he had sussed out just how valuable a full-time resident China expert could be. He was right; and after he made a rather large donation to my work budget, I felt kind of obligated to see what I could do for him. He flew me to Beijing with him the following week after he had made no headway whatsoever during his first foray into the jungle of working with the inscrutable Chinese. I guess I kind of shocked him when I suggested that he bribe the officials who held the purse strings, for the purchase of a whole lot of foreign machinery. He confessed that he knew nothing about that, but was not the least bit opposed if it made sales. I had mentioned that missionaries, including myself, routinely pay handshake money to corrupt officials all over the world for various favors. Of course, it is for the glory of God, so it is alright. It is only a tiny step away from lying on your visa application to buy a television as a gift for an official's ailing mother. After all, it is not for the corrupt party hack himself at all. It is for his elderly mom who really needs it. Of course, any missionary worth his salt would offer to pray for the mother as well. Praise God. The Lord provides.

We talked about commissions, and I was offered a cool deal: a certain cut of his commission for each unit sold. Well, I figured, nothing ventured, nothing gained. And besides, I could use the money for religious endeavors—so why not? I didn't even have to go into China again to finish the deal. I simply walked into the PRC's trade mission in HK and sold a *huge* number of tractors (and other agricultural implements) on the spot. Of course, I had to cut various Chinese middle men into the mix, but I still made over a million dollars in a single transaction. I was happy. My guy in Illinois was ecstatic, and my phone rang off the hook from then on. I sold encyclopedias and all sorts of educational materials, phone-switching equipment that I didn't even understand . . . and used Cadillacs. That was my favorite of all time.

After the tractor deal, I was invited to trade shows in Beijing, Shanghai, Wu Han, Zhung Qing, and Guang Zhou. I was frequently met at the airport by a driver in a wa-wa la-la Chinese Communist limousine . . . the famous *Red Flag* top-of-the-line luxury car and dream boat of every party member. Those hideous, uncomfortable land yachts (with hand-embroidered curtains and seat covers) were kind of like 1950s vintage hearses. Really!

Up to this time, the only way for China to do business with the outside world was to have the sales persons come to them as I had been doing. But once American, Japanese, and German companies began inviting and hosting delegations of PRC buyers to visit their facilities, the game was over for us. Everybody who was anybody in the Party simply had to go on a buying junket abroad. It is there that they actually rode in real luxury limos for the first time. OMG, those stretch Caddies and Lincolns were like a cloud compared to those laughable Red Flags. Soon in China a Red Flag was sort of like a bathtub—nobody wanted to be seen in one. I had met a rather wealthy church member in New Jersey who was visiting HK and China sometime around then. He owned a dealership in suburban Newark. So I asked him if he could get his hands on some used Cadillacs for cheap. Once I explained that in China, even an old 1967 vintage El Dorado was a status symbol. I arranged a fair number of deals that followed. I discovered that free TV sets were no longer the bribe de jour. Cadillacs were the order of the day. But most of this was sort of done out of my hip pocket by this time. I had another brainstorm that really brought the house down. It came to me in a flash during a missionary conference that was held in Hong Kong. I was even on a panel discussion, but didn't even bother to open my mouth. Nobody noticed. Everybody else was too busy talking and listening to their own heads rattle.

MAILBAGS!

How I became an Evangelical celebrity overnight

Conferences conferences conferences! One of the salient features of my missionary career was the attending of multitudinous conferences. By and large, these are colossal wastes of time and money. Of course, they were seen by most as an opportunity to travel or take vacations on the church organization's dime. My wife and I had learned way back in Europe to travel to conferences, and charge the whole thing to the church, and then tack on a side trip as long as we were there anyway. We would pay for our own self-planned excursions, but the airfare to get there and back was covered by conference expenses. I used that deal to visit a lot of places that would have otherwise been prohibitive on our meager budget. But hosting the super China conference in Hong Kong was a no-brainer. Of course, it had to be in town where all the smuggling action was (or used to be).

But the big to-do was not just about smuggling, as everybody knew that the PRC was onto us, thanks to the total FUBAR million Bible fiasco. It was more of a *brainstorming* session. LOL. The idea was to "strategize." How can we take advantage of this divinely given opportunity to reach China for God? Everybody and his cat showed up, as the dogs in tow were already there. Everybody wanted to get into the act. During the meeting, I quietly whispered to Beth that a year ago half the people in attendance thought that China was something you eat off of; now, suddenly everybody has a call to China. It was definitely the biggest thing going at the time—and destined to get bigger. And it did.

The overriding question posed by our top dog at the DFM was: "How can we get in touch with the average man in the street? How can we contact him with the message of the Gospel?" Of course, everybody already knew that several church-related organizations were broadcasting religious fare into the Mainland, and had been doing so for years. But, kind of like being forbidden to listen to the BBC during the Second World War in Nazi Germany, listening to any foreign broadcasts was strictly forbidden under pain of . . . well, whatever.

Nobody really had radios anyway, and the ones available at the big state-run department stores (called *China Products)* were tuned to receive only state-run broadcasts. So it had been an exercise in faith to broadcast from Taiwan or Hong Kong. Local stations with a short broadcast radius could barely reach much over the border anyway, and the shortwave station in Manila had never received a single reply in all those years. Like duh! How many people in Mainland China actually had shortwave radios anyway? Come on. During the Cultural Revolution all media and books had been turned in and burned or trashed to prevent any contact with the outside world. Radio was mentioned, but in a rather pitiful tone. Like, isn't there some other way to get something into the hands of the teeming millions? I always quipped that it takes millions to actually "teem." You never hear of the teeming thousands. But, for sure, China had millions; and our job was to reach them with the Gospel; and all the king's horses and all the king's men were arrayed in Hong Kong that week to discuss strategy, but nobody had any real idea of how to do it. . . But I did :-)

Of course, I had no intention of blurting out my cool idea right there, as everybody in attendance would immediately claim it as his or hers. I just kept mum. After all the delegates had jawboned their way through the three-day conference and had left, I talked to my immediate boss, a certain Delmer Guynes, who was actually quite visionary in his own way. He was always willing to hear me out. I was aware that China was accepting advertising in their media outlets for foreign products. During the many trips I had taken to the Mainland already, I had noticed billboards for Coca-Cola, Marlboro, Seiko, and Toyota. Likewise, state-owned radio and television stations were airing ads as well for products that in many cases were not even for sale in the country! (Yet) The big corporations had been eying the huge potential China market for years, salivating at the prospect of selling anything and everything to that mammoth customer base. Most were taking advantage of a kind of pre-advertising concept to prepare the market so that when their products actually were made available in the country, their brand names would be recognized. It was brilliant, of course; and I saw right away how we could take advantage of the opportunity. So I ran it by Dr. Guynes, who caught my drift quickly without elaboration.

My idea was simple. (Maybe working at night for an advertising agency back in Frankfurt had turned me on to these kinds of possibilities. I suggested that we contact a similar agency in Hong Kong and try to buy some airtime on Chinese TV stations. I had a gay friend who was a wheel at one of the big HK ad agencies with clients all over Asia.

But what would we sell? Well, we really couldn't sell anything—at least not then. But we could give something away. I simply asked myself what we *had* that they wanted. Amazing. The answer was simple: English. China was on a kick to teach foreign languages to every student throughout the country to prepare them for higher education abroad. They were teaching French, German, Spanish, Italian, and Japanese; but by far, over 80% of all Chinese high school and college students in the PRC were learning English.

It is important to note here that during the much-touted Cultural Revolution of the years between 1965 and '75, all foreign language study had been suspended. But not only that—wild, raging students (called Red Guards) had ransacked all the universities in the country, burning entire libraries in their wake. They had done a remarkably thorough job, as there were very few books of any kind floating around in the country at all when I first arrived in 1978. Now they were years behind in areas like medicine, engineering, agriculture, astronomy, and all professions requiring an advanced education. So, what were they going to do? They had concluded that it would be totally impossible to buy up and translate textbooks from around the world into Chinese— let alone trade and professional journals that were coming out and changing constantly as the world of science, the arts, and politics developed worldwide.

The only solution was to teach everybody English so that they could access educational materials and read these materials for themselves. Of course, the country was totally gaga for English. This was not an isolated case of such phenomena. In countries of the former British Empire, like India, English had been a mandatory part of all college-bound students' curricula for years. And in places like the Philippines, anybody seeking to study science of any kind, including medicine, had to do their studies in English, as it—being the premier "research language" of the planet—was what all the textbooks and journals were published in. Like, there simply are no medical textbooks in Tagalog, Cebuano, Ilocano, Hindi, Marati, or Urdu. English (and to some degree, other languages) is the mode of instruction everywhere, and China had a lot of catching up to do.

I suggested that we simply buy airtime on Chinese TV and radio stations, and advertise a free English course (that could be heavily weighted with subliminal religious messages); or just send them a little something as a "loss leader." This marketing ploy is as old as the hills, and most all of us at one time or another have fallen for it. The merchant offers a freebie or a super discount to get the customer to come into his store; then he sells them something else. It is also referred to pejoratively as "bait and switch."

Of course, I was not recommending something as obvious as that, since the Gung An Bao would certainly catch onto such an obvious ruse right away. But we could in fact send them something and call it good. Of course, then we would have their address, huh? I didn't need to finish my thought. Brother Guynes' eyes lit up and a smile crossed his lips. He got it. Once we captured the addresses of people who replied to the ads, we could then (at a later date) just send them Gospel materials. It wasn't really bait and switch, as we were baiting and sending them exactly what they had asked for. So technically we were not switching, but just sending unsolicited materials in addition. Come on, we have all received junk mail. It is annoying to us, but nobody in China had ever received anything of the kind at all—ever before. They were like sitting ducks. Ducks who needed to hear about Jesus. What a concept!

Guynes swore me to secrecy about the whole thing, as he knew full-well that it was a religious football; and said that he would have to talk to the right people to get the money for the project, which he felt would be wildly well-received in the American churches. "It will be oversubscribed," he stated enthusiastically. He was so right. Once the scheme was proposed to the powers-that-be in Springfield, people were lining up nationwide to throw money at it. Meanwhile, he told me to contact my friend, of whom I had already told him, to find out how to go about implementing the whole thing from Hong Kong. I did so. And we were off to the races.

Once the money was designated, the agency bought the airtime for us. We quickly produced a sixty-second spot in their studio, and they did the rest. We didn't even need to take the video tape into China. They did all the work. Once the spots began running, we sat still and waited. A week went by. I walked down to the General Post Office (the GPO) on a bright Monday morning. It is located right next to the Star and Macau ferry piers. I opened up box 6840 in the usual way—and I got a big surprise.

The box was stuffed with mail. The letters had been jammed and squished in from the back. It looked like a jello mold! I peeled them out and counted 808 letters back at the office. I was wowed. I went to lunch and then went back to the GPO a few hours later that afternoon, and the box was full again! I bought a gym bag. For three or four days this kept up. Twice a day I made the trip to the GPO. Then one morning there was nothing in the box but a card that read: "There are too many. Go down to the window." There I retrieved two plastic tubs twice the size of recycle bins, full of mail from the Mainland. The gym bag simply would no longer do. I began coming with two of my Chinese staff and three gym bags. That lasted about a week as they dutifully helped me empty the plastic bins full of mail into the bags that we would lug back to the office, to open, read, sort, and organize for reply. But we were getting way behind.

A week later I came to the window as usual with my two helpers. I overheard the attendant inform the manager that the "weird foreigner who gets all the mail from China" is here. The manager asked us to follow him inside where the mail was sorted. One-hundred-pound canvas mailbags were waiting. We retired to my place and got my van.

For two or more weeks we spent most of our time shuttling back and forth to the GPO, picking up bags of mail, delivering them to the office, and going back again. The staff had long abandoned any notion of even trying to open them, so we began just tagging the bags with dates and piling them. At first we tried to pile them in neat, organized, chronological stacks, but that gave way to utter chaos in rather short order. We couldn't even start to open a bag when another would arrive. We just started stacking the bags. In no time they were up to the ceiling. The mail was rapidly taking over the entire place. And they just kept coming. I sort of flashed on mental images of the sorcerer's apprentice by Goethe, and the cartoon version featuring Mickey Mouse as Guido starting a magic spell not knowing how to stop it! Well, there was no stopping it now. I had had a really cool idea, but I wasn't sure where it was going, and how to even begin to deal with the deluge. Then one day I got a call from the postmaster asking for his bags back. The Chinese have an expression that goes like this: "If you pull the tiger's whiskers, you had better be ready for the response!" Like, no kidding!

Well, our success did not go unnoticed :-) The massive pile of mail from China drew attention from around the world, as every televangelist, preacher, pastor, and Christian tour group showed up to take pictures of themselves standing in front of the "massive response to the Gospel from China." Actually, I had always made it clear that these were really responses to ads for English lessons; but when these guys got back to the States they could spin it any way they wanted to raise more money. And I am sure they did. As in politics, Fundamentalist church and parachurch agencies are all dependent on the ability to raise funds to keep afloat. This was seen as the biggest fundraising tool that anybody could remember, and everybody wanted to be my friend—to take credit for standing by me when I dreamed of reaching into China with the Gospel. The bait-and-switch idea was really their idea. Yeah right. But I played along. I didn't care. After all, I had the evidence. The mailbags were stacked to the ceiling in my place in Hong Kong—so there. Haha.

The outcome for me was personally unexpected. I was catapulted to celebrity status overnight. Then I was compelled—first by my own denomination, then by other groups—to hit the circuit and tell the amazing story of the massive response to the Gospel that was taking place in China. I would get invitations—actually pleas—to come for even one service or one convention. They would offer a plane ticket for a flight from Hong Kong to, say, Chicago, St. Louis, or Miami, along with a guaranteed honorarium of $10,000, if I would come to one of the growing megachurches and preach (telling the mailbag story, of course). Naturally, if they could raise $300,000 in cash and pledges, it was a good investment. This tactic is still common fare to this day. Big churches can afford the top tier speakers. I was definitely top tier at that point. Well, pretty much everybody in Fundamentalism knew my name by then. I was getting around the world, preaching, and raising tons of money. Of course, I was not a recipient of any of it, as everything went to Springfield in the end, and they divvied it up at their discretion. But I didn't care about that either, as there was more money coming into my designated account than I could possibly spend anyway. Funds from Churches in Europe and Australia operated in much the same way; I was required to remit all of my "earnings" to Springfield for accounting purposes. That was fine with me, as not only did I hate paperwork like that, but I had my hands full hiring additional staff to deal with the cascade of mail that just kept coming.

Ironically, a new Chinese language computer system had just come on the market from Japan where they had developed programs to work in the Chinese characters, which they call Konji. They were selling like crazy in Taiwan already, as well as in Korea, Singapore, and of course elsewhere throughout HK and other Asian markets. They were expensive, but we didn't have to ask twice for the funds to go computer. We did have to send our staff for special training to use the new program. But they picked it up right away, and we were state of the art!

Of course, this did not go unnoticed by the PRC. I am sure they could have stopped the little English books from entering the country, but they knew full-well that we had all those addresses, so that would have been rather pointless. And besides, the responders had seen the advertisements on their own local state-owned television stations. I could imagine a committee of the Gung An Bao up in Beijing trying to figure out how to deal with this without losing face. After all, they sold us the airtime and we paid for it fair and square. Smile. And the mail just kept coming!

In fact, one day the postmaster mentioned to me in passing that I received more mail than anyone in Hong Kong, including the large corporations, the banks, and even the IRS! They call it the Inland Revenue Service, but their function is the same as in the U.S. And other countries. Now, that's a lot of mail. The whole Evangelical world was abuzz. I continued to travel and raise funds, but was growing weary of airports, different hotels every night, and the same breathless questions from well-meaning, but poorly-informed congregations all over the place. It was definitely getting old. But I had bought a copy of *Spartacus*, a guide to gay bars, spas, beaches, hotels, and restaurants all over the world; so I never was at a loss for new friends. And along with much broader exposure to the gay world came more information. I was gradually becoming aware of the actual gay movement—also known as: "The Gay Agenda." LOL.

I had caught a whiff of this growing phenomenon way back in Germany while working for Teen Challenge. The guy who started the whole TC organization and operation, David Wilderson—who wrote the famous title *The Cross and the Switchblade*—had gotten tired of running the program and finally given it up to his brother Don, who was—as I mentioned before—a much more collected personality and a very good administrator. Brother Dave, as we called him, was always the visionary—the dreamer. He was easily moved by events and was either ecstatic when things were happening that he liked, or horrified and totally pissed-off (righteously) when he saw things that made him frown.

Well, the gay agenda was happening in New York, and Brother Dave was beyond pissed. He was royally pissed. He was so uptight and indignant about what he was seeing on the streets of the Big Apple that he got a divine call to do something about it! He decided to go into the movie business. He had had just about enough of all those terrible fags running around the city and polluting everything with their mere touch; and all those drag queens marching in those early "gay pride parades" just made him want to shit a holy brick. He needed to begin making apocalyptic "documentary" films about the queer invasion of U.S. society, but he simply could not stay in the cesspool that was Manhattan. He needed to find a more accommodating and user-friendly location to work for God, so he got called to one of the holiest places on Earth—Dallas, Texas. (Actually, it was Ft. Worth as that is even holier, if that is possible.)

I had seen his films about drug addiction and gangs and genuinely evil things that needed addressing from a spiritual point of view. I agreed. I too felt for those dopers and lost youth in places like Nidery, but I couldn't get all stewed up about a bunch of drag queens trooping down Broadway once a year. I wondered why Brother Dave was so incensed about that as New Orleans had been hosting the Mardi Gras for years, and I never heard boo about that from any quarter—even in the Bible Belt. But the faggots really had everybody spinning in their pews! Dave's film, entitled *Return to Sodom*, was billed as his magnum opus —at least when it first came out. Even then, I rather enjoyed it. I thought it was kind of funny, if not downright entertaining :-)

But nobody was laughing. In fact, everybody was not just horrified— they were flamboozled, flustrated, and totally twitterpated! The whole Christian world that I was preaching to at the time was in a righteous uproar about homosexuality and that insidious gay agenda. I was definitely living in both worlds by that time, and I was both shocked and disheartened by what I was seeing from Christians in their attitudes and prejudices, as well as what I was hearing coming from Christian mouths—more and more all the time.

I had thought that our assignment was to go into the world and preach the Gospel to every creature. Sure God was pissed at the fags for their outrageous outfits, but likely no more than he was with any other unchurched group in places like Zimbabwe, Zaire, or Zurich. My understanding was that everybody was lost and deserved to hear the most positive presentation of the Good News that we could provide—

regardless of their sins. I was taught way back during my time in the Navigators that we were all sinners saved by grace. But I was coming to understand that some peoples' sins were so egregious they should just go directly to Hell—do not pass GO and do not collect 200 dollars. So there. And without even hearing the gospel either!

This is probably the point at which I began disliking some of my clerical colleagues and a hefty number of the church members who were throwing money at me to promote my work in China. I was the mole in their midst, and my mind was recording—like a reel-to-reel tape recorder—everything they were saying. I replayed their mean-spirited and crass comments over and over in my mind during sleepless nights while I was still praying about what to do. I could hardly imagine a world outside of the missionary life that I still loved. I struggled with the idea of leaving the ministry, the church . . . and what all that would involve. It would definitely blow up my life and that of Beth and Vincent for starters. But I couldn't even imagine the ripple effect that would result if I were ever to even contemplate actually "coming out." Unthinkable. I was definitely starting to think about it, nevertheless.

It was a slow transition, I have to tell you. If I were to get to the point where I could no longer honestly continue to participate in any more deception, half-truths, and downright lies and bullshit, could I do it . . . and let the chips fall where they may? Not then. Not yet. But it was growing increasingly difficult to deal with what I was hearing more and more frequently from my friends and coworkers in Hong Kong; more still from Christian media, as I was traveling in the U.S. a lot, fundraising. It was no wonder I was getting sick of turning on the TV in any hotel room and encountering Pat Robertson, Jim and Tammy Faye Bakker, and Jimmy Swaggart any time of the day or night—or especially in the wee hours when I was doing jet lag. The day of ubiquitous Christian media, complete with Christian Rock bands and megachurces, had arrived with a vengeance. Hell, I was turned off by it clear back in that little motel lobby in Kabanatuan, but now it was making me nauseous.

I still enjoyed traveling to new and exotic parts of China. I even went as far west as Kashgar, which was still off-limits to foreigners at the time. I kind of stood out, as they likely hadn't seen a gwailo in years out there in the wild hinterland where China, the then-USSR, and Afghanistan converge. I was arrested immediately upon arrival and was whisked right away to the local police station, which was, of course, the local headquarters of the Gung An Bao. I really had no intention of entering the real border zone, which was heavily militarized. I was foolhardy, of course, but not stupid.

Well, they didn't keep me in their jail, but more or less put me on house arrest at the hotel—a kind of mini version of the Dong Fang in Guang Zhou that I told you about. It, like the whole town, was colorless and ugly. I was impressed with the local mosque, however, as the region is heavily Muslim and hardly Chinese at all. Of course, the government was stacking the deck against the population of local Uygars as they were doing in Tibet against the local Tibetan residents at the time. They were flooding the place with Han Chinese and overwhelming the indigenous populations of both S.A.Rs (Special Administrative Regions).

Of course, a simple glance at my passport would indicate that I was a Hong Kong resident. And since they were talking to me in Chinese, obviously, I had been around in the country a while. But they didn't really even need to call Hong Kong; they called Beijing instead and in no time had my number. They knew that I was a religious rabble-rouser and they knew the whole mailbag story—the smuggling and the whole shebang. I didn't deny it. In fact, I was confronted with a weird question that I hadn't seen coming: "Why are you doing this? Do you hate China? … Are you political?" I figured that this must be an opportunity from the Lord, so I just assured them that I loved China and the Chinese people—their culture, their customs, and their language. I even demonstrated my calligraphic skills with a brush and ink. I think they really got it. "My religion requires me to share my faith with all mankind. I am particularly fond of the Chinese, and I am always eager to learn more about the land, the history, and the great progress that you are experiencing at home and abroad." I laid it on kind of thick, and they were impressed that I mentioned an interest in "learning more" about their wonderful political system. That was a cheap shot, but they failed to pick up on my sarcasm or irony. They must have figured that I was basically harmless.

It had taken me ages to make the trip on the train, and I wasn't really looking forward to the return trek; so I asked if I could buy a ticket and fly back to Urumci and off to Shanghai or Beijing from there. The next flight out was in two days, so I knocked around the town till I left, (but the eyes of the Gung An Bao were on me all the time, and in a most obvious way). It wasn't very productive for the Lord, but I got a lot of mileage out of the story on the fundraising circuit later. I did manage to send a quick telegram to Charles from Urumci, and he obviously passed the info on to the consulate folks in HK. I was debriefed immediately upon my return to the Colony (twice :-)

My first trip to Tibet was equally challenging. I was visiting one of my pen-pals who lived in Chung Qing. That was where all the Tibet-bound flights were leaving from at the time. All during the mailbag extravaganza I had instructed the staff to pull out any letters that were written in really good English. There were many, as most were in fact English teachers. Many were older and had taught in various universities throughout the country before the Cultural Revolution, when they had been disgraced for being snobby intellectuals, foreigner lovers, and counter-revolutionaries. Many had been sent to remote parts of the country where they were basically exiled for life. The expression was that they were "sent down" to the countryside to learn from the peasants. Like, oh sure.

This was one of the most tragic stories that came out of that period of national madness. Like other peoples who have gone mad—the French under Napoleon, the Germans under Hitler, and the Japanese under the regime of emperor worship and militarism of the Second World War— the Chinese had gone mad as a people, destroying their own proud and ancient culture in favor of the stupidity and lunacy of Marxism. I met many of these wonderful exiles in my travels, and one of them had been rehabilitated because in addition to great English she also was fluent in Japanese, having studied in Japan before the war.

I mentioned that I was interested in visiting Tibet but that foreigners were not allowed into that distant and forbidden land. She looked at me quizzically and smiled. I didn't think much of it, but she asked me the following day if I would like to join a Japanese mountain-climbing tour that was leaving in short order. She was the interpreter. China was keen to curry favor with the moneyed Japanese by sponsoring such trips. I knew nothing about mountain climbing, but then neither did she. To this day I don't know how she was able to include me on the tour (maybe because Muzzio actually sounds kind of like Japanese sometimes). LOL. Anyway, we had a fine—if brief—trip; but it was an adventure, to be sure.

I did get a chance to talk to her about the Lord; and she confessed that she had attended a Presbyterian missionary academy as a teenager, and was a "secret" Christian. How cool is that? I decided not to mention any details of that trip (other than the mountain climbing part, as anyone who knows me realizes I hate too much physical exertion). Of course, I was careful to make it clear that I was simply hitching a ride with the tour group, and that I did no actual mountaineering myself. Like, duh.

There was one other really remarkable moment that I had when meeting up with another of my pen-pals. This was in Hang Zhou, that wonderful city by a lake. I was keen to meet the guy there with whom I had been corresponding from HK and from other places. He loved foreign postage stamps, so I sent him envelopes carefully covered with nice colorful stamps from places like Belgium, Sweden, and Germany (and the U.S. and Canada, of course). He and I had been born on the exact same day (7-11-51). I was kind of bummed out by his life story. He had been dragged into the Red Guards despite a total lack of interest in politics. He wanted to paint, draw, and learn about new languages and cultures. But that was all quashed when he was tattled on by neighbors and school friends for having foreign magazines and some old English books. He explained it this way: "They taught me a lesson." I didn't have to ask for an elaboration. I got it.

Some years later, Xiao Dong was allowed to return to his home town, since his parents were still living there. He was doing some crummy job, but was reapplying to the University, as even older students whose educations had been interrupted for over ten years were being allowed to reenter school to try to pick up where they had left off. It wasn't easy. And, although he was hopeful, he was as yet unsure. He taught me a trick: when one wanted to talk where the secret police could not hear, a cheap ticket would rent a rowboat on the lake. We talked in hushed tones. But I did lead him to the Lord. He prayed with me. I was unsure where he would end up as I left the next day, but I continued to pray for his well-being. Sometime thereafter all his letters stopped. I never heard from him or of him again.

Back in Hong Kong, the mailbags and the pandemonium was still swirling; but I was losing interest, as it had become a circus. People I barely knew from Springfield and around the world were interjecting themselves into the operation. I didn't care, since I had never considered it "my baby" anyway, as the original idea was undisputedly mine; and that was my satisfaction.

I was getting depressed. I guess we all get blue now and then, but I became increasingly aware of the politicization of the Gospel message by then. Reagan went to church like once or twice a year—for show. The Christian rednecks loved him. I didn't want to go back to the States again to raise money. I wanted to stay with my gay friends in Hong Kong

I had visited San Francisco a few times en route to and from speaking engagements, and began plugging more and more into that world—a world that embraced me for who I really was and not for what I was pretending to be. I don't know when it happened. It was not a bolt out of the blue. But one day I just admitted to myself that I no longer believed anything that I was saying. I did not believe in what I was doing in China or anywhere. And in fact, I really couldn't even dredge up a dying ember of belief in any of it at all. I knew quite truly that I was indeed no longer a Christian.

I didn't rejoice. I didn't run off to tell the world. I didn't write a vignette or a letter. I didn't seek help from a Christian counselor. I didn't feel. I didn't feel anything. I was numb. I quit praying. It seemed so pointless. I was facing a decision that would affect the rest of my life. I was sitting in a hideaway that I had discovered months earlier. I went there for my coffee break every morning at about ten for an hour or so to just sit by myself and think. There was a bar on the top floor of the Excelsior Hotel in Causeway Bay. My office, still inundated with piles of mail, was only a short walk. They didn't serve alcohol at that hour as the bar was closed, but they would always bring a nice hot coffee. I pondered my future. One cloudy morning I sat down at one of those little round tables by the window overlooking the bustling city below, and ordered a coffee. Someone had left a Chinese magazine on the chair as they departed. I picked it up and glanced through it. A certain article caught my eye. It was about a topic that I had never considered before. The title was something like "Seven million persons in China die annually . . . What to do with all those bodies?" I was freaked out. Seven million? That is like the population of a small country. I finished the article and took the magazine back to my office where I grabbed my little calculator again.

This time I was not figuring volume, but numbers of souls. If seven million Chinese die and go to a Christless eternity in Hell every year, how many are being dumped down God's garbage chute and into the lake of fire every day? 7,000,000 divided by 365 days is roughly 20,000 a day. I thought of it in total shock. What kind of a sick and twisted joke was this anyway? I thought of all the missionaries in Hong Kong who hadn't lead a single soul to Christ in years . . . if then . . . if ever. I thought of all the churches that I had preached in, and all the money I had raised, and all the prayers that had been prayed. Yet the numbers don't lie. Twenty thousand souls a day—most of whom had not even heard of God or Jesus or salvation—just frizzling and frying for eternity—condemned because

I had not been able to reach them in their masses. The task was futile, impossible, and stupid. It was beyond stupid. What was I doing here? What was I doing with my life? I knew that this chapter was definitely over . . . but what next? What indeed?

ESCAPE!

Stop the merry-go-round I want to get off!

Thus began my escape. I had to plan carefully to avoid hurting people whom I loved. I knew it was inevitable, but wanted to prevent as much collateral damage as possible. I sincerely did not want to hurt Beth and Vincent. I also had strong feelings of love or affection for many of my Christian friends and coworkers. I knew full well that most were well-meaning types. Most really wanted to bring the blessed Gospel message to the lost and dying souls around us. I also had a great deal of love for most of my pastor friends in the U.S. who stood with us and supported us as we gallantly went forth to the mission field to represent them. I really had not understood how highly esteemed missionaries were "back home." When I began itinerating way back en route to Viet Nam, we were treated like solid gold everywhere we went. Those good people gave money so that we could go forth as their "ambassadors" to a lost and dying world. Of course, that notion is a Pollyanna worldview; but I never resented them. This was part of the reason for my emotional state at this time years later. I was conflicted. I knew that I was no longer a believer, but I did not want to drop the atomic bomb on all my friends and family. This was going to take time. But circumstances were propelling the whole play forward!

I knew that I was going to have to figure out a way to extricate myself from life as a Christian missionary and well-known public speaker, and slide into a self-imposed obscurity of some kind. I was not hurting for money, as a gay friend and financial adviser had helped me invest most of my Hong Kong (tractor) earnings with the Union Bank of Switzerland in the Colony. He had transferred all my accounts in the Colony to Zurich when we learned that China was not going to extend the lease on the Colony past its due date in 1997.

This was in 1982. Margaret Thatcher, the darling of the Religious Right (as she was Reagan's friend and co-conspirator), had gone to Beijing fully intending to write a new lease agreement on Hong Kong. This beautiful place that I loved so much was actually *rented* from China on a hundred-year lease. This was a relic of the Opium Wars of the 19th century. Without going into elaborate detail . . . suffice it to say that HK—as we all knew it—was coming to an end. Of course, the beautiful city and it's world-class harbor would cease to be a British protectorate, but would—as we all learned to varying degrees of dismay—be returned to Chinese sovereignty. Communist Chinese sovereignty, that is. And that was not lost on anybody. Panic ensued.

Everybody around the Colony had known for years that the end was coming. This vestige of Britannia and the world of colonialism was dying a slow death around the world. And we were all actors or players in this performance. The transition that was taking place on a geopolitical stage was likewise playing itself out in my personal life as well. I loved it. I have always liked change and embraced new things with relish. My life, though in transition, was good. Or so I felt.

I felt so alive and happy in so many ways. I was born-again. Yes, I knew what it feels like to lay your burden down. I had been born-again the first time back in college when I had accepted Christ into my heart, and was emotionally free from my dad's dicta. I had felt such a liberation. This was just like that. I was emotionally and intellectually free from the tyranny of Fundamentalism. I knew full well that I would have to play along—to pretend—at least for a while longer. I was going to have to be a mole in the ranks of the Fundamentalist Christians, who were gaining political power daily in the U.S. and around the world. I was still part of them (if in name only). I was still not able to "come out" and be honest. But being a closet gay in a Christian world had certainly taught me how to live a lie. I figured that I could do it a bit longer—for the sake of *harmony.* How very Chinese of me!

Upending the apple cart is not something that I take to naturally. I have always been a seeker of compromise, finding the middle ground, making everybody feel good without hurting feelings unnecessarily. So I chose the middle way. Sort of Buddhist, huh? Of course, I knew full well that this middle path would not last. Surely I would have to take a stand at some point. Like choosing for Christ, one has to make a decision—a defining statement. I knew that I had to put that off as long as possible. And I did. Months went by. I was back in my happy space. Hong Kong was so warm and lovely. We all knew that it was like an illusion—a beautiful bubble that was sure to burst at some point. But it was still so wonderful for the moment. I cherished every minute of my life on my little island between ardent Fundamentalism and gay activism. I knew that I could not simply slide into a quiet new life with the man of my dreams.

Making Love, a film being shown in cinemas in Hong Kong, moved me a lot. I vividly recalled the scene where the husband, played by Michael Ontkean, finally came out to his wife (Kate Jackson). She threw a plate at a wall and it shattered in a million pieces. I wondered if Beth would pitch something at me. I also saw *Cruising*, with Al Pacino, that year. Both had an impact on my life and direction. That particular film showed a dark underside of the gay life, which I was aware of, but had not experienced personally. While I did dabble on the edges of the dark side, it just never was my thing.

Still, I felt that I needed to explore the entire realm of the gay "lifestyle" in a way that I had never explored anything before aside from Evangelical Fundamentalism before. Like most all hard-nosed Christians, I had no interest in other aspects of my religion . . . other creeds or ideas. They were all *incorrect*. I was taught so and I believed so. But that was a choice. I simply chose to have no interest in Catholic doctrines, Lutheran liberalness, or Mormon madness at all. But I was genuinely interested in all things gay. It was not a choice to be homosexual. I knew that from early on. But I was finally choosing to *actualize it*—to realize it. That's different.

I had become like a vacuum cleaner, sweeping up new gay ideas and concepts with the same voracity that I had sucked up Christian memes back in the days of the Navigators. It must be my nature. I am a wholehearted kind of guy. And in later years, almost everyone has told me that that was the very thing that most attracted them to me. I embraced all my new gay friends with abandon. I scrutinized my Christian friends with increasing focus. Well, I was still young and passionate. Still am—in spirit at least :-)

Christian celebrity status is not easily granted to those who are afraid to take risks. I had a secret. I was not a Christian. I was a mole in a Christian world. I was audacious. And the more audacious I became, the more I was adulated and embraced by the Christian world. I had already encountered Christian fakes like Sergei Kourdakov, Marjoe, and "Dr." Colon Wickramaratne—total frauds who fleeced the stupid and gullible. And, being from Oregon, I sadly missed the total whoopty doo of the Bhagwan Shree Rajneesh extravaganza. But I heard plenty. I would have bought a ticket to that fandango!

I understood the dynamic of mass hysteria and madness. I was part of it, but knew inside that I did not want to keep participating in this charade.

It was time to jump off the merry-go-round . . . but how? I honestly rather enjoyed being a Christian celeb. I was treated with deference wherever I went. I hated every minute of hotel life and airports and crummy restaurants, but, all the same, once I was in the pulpit I loved to put on the show. I can honestly say that I understand why certain actors like the stage more than the silver screen. When you perform for a live audience, there is immediate feedback. In the theater, there is darkness out there. But in the world of the religious circus, there is light. You can see the faces of those who are hanging on your every word. I knew that I was feeding them a line of bullshit, but they loved it so! The more I made up, the more they swooned and raised their hands in praise of the great things that God was doing in China (pronounced Cha-nah south of the Mason-Dixon).

I had begun looking forward to meeting up with total strangers in hotel rooms here and there—now and then. *Spartacus* was a real find. I was young and in musth, I guess; and I knew that it would not last, but I kept on pretending and mentally recording all of the things that the devoted "Christians" were saying about gay people. It was not really revenge that I sought. I was getting disgusted with the true nature of the Church (the body of believers) and not so much the organizations, as they tend to be similar, whether they are religious, governmental, or commercial.

My experience with Pat Robertson and his still-famous 700 Club was a case in point. I had met Pat years earlier through a mutual friend from Frankfurt days—a certain Mike Little who had left the military about the same time as I had. He had not gone on to seminary nor into the clergy, but gifted as he was with keen administrative skills, he had landed a job with the 700 Club and had managed to rise in the organization. He was a vice president (of some kind) when we met again in Hong Kong just as the China thing was becoming a big deal. They sought me out. Pat wanted to get into the Chinapalooza. I couldn't blame him. He was a clever showman like Jimmy Swaggart (minus the piano) and Jim and Tammy Faye (minus the makeup :-)

They sent me a ticket to visit their Virginia Beach headquarters. The whole place was tacky in its faux 18th C. American brick facades. It looked like a Benjamin Franklin Savings and Loan (before the bankruptcy :-) I particularly enjoyed the imitation Early American furniture in the lobbies and offices. I think Ben F. and Tom J. and the other founding "fathers" would feel right at home there. LOL.

On my first visit of many I arrived early to participate in their morning prayer service, where I was featured. I had learned to forbid taping or filming, as the Gung An Bao back in Asia could easily make my life difficult if not miserable. I had no need to be on TV in the U.S., blabbering on about all the cool secret stuff that we were doing in the PRC. I did have the pleasure of meeting up again with Tyronne of JCSS. Hadn't seen him since our days back in Britain, preaching, testifying, filming and having a great time in general. He had gone to work for the 700 Club, and it was fun to drag up some old jokes and tell a few stories about the likes of the Nidrey Terror. We made a date to get together for lunch a few days hence. I hung around with Ty for a while after the meeting, and he got me back to Pat's office where he dropped me off. I was a bit early for our one o'clock, so I camped outside his office next to a very attractive guy with a leather portfolio of some kind of work to show Pat and his wife, who had "decorated" the place. We got acquainted. He was an interior designer. Who told? Once we let our hair down about the hideous décor, he mentioned that he had been commissioned to do a makeover of some of the offices, waiting rooms, and the grand foyer, which could only be described as Revolutionary War meets Jesus at Valley Forge chic. We made a date for an after-dinner drink. He thought to bring a toothbrush :-)

This fellow, Ed, had a twin brother living in L.A. I was kind of shocked but pleased that God (who I began referring to as Gawd or gawd) had done so well with Ed that he or *she* had decided to make a carbon copy. Apparently his brother, Ted (Ed and Ted. Cute, eh?), had been living in Southern California for some time. And being so close from childhood, they got together a lot—usually in L.A. where Ed could "party" more easily than in Virginia Beach or Norfolk where he had to take jobs like the one with the 700 Club. We had a good laugh as we changed our tickets to fly "out to the coast" together.

Ted lived in the small coastal gay enclave of Laguna Beach, which I loved a lot. But this was the first time I had actually stayed a while. It was March, as I recall, and the weather was lovely. It was there that I first met Jack, a kind of celebrity around town. Everybody seemed to know him. He owned a cool little collection of small shops all connected together on a small, cobbled walkway called Pepper Tree Lane, as a giant pepper tree was the main feature. It could only be called "charming" and oh-so gay. It was crowded all the time, and Jack had made a killing. He owned the candy shop and the gift shop, and rented out the other storefronts to antique dealers, a bistro, and a small pizza place. Jack was a mover and shaker in the community. He was the president of the Chamber of Commerce and various other organizations that truly did serve the community. He, I found out, gave a lot of money to various charities and good causes—particularly gay-related causes, like homeless shelters in L.A., beautification projects, and civic improvement groups that no Christian would ever support. After all, why give money to making the streets cleaner or build more park benches when you can buy a million Bibles for China?

Ted was sick with some new ailment that I had read about once or twice in *Asian* TIME magazine and *Der Spiegel*. It was some kind of cancer that was effecting a lot of gay men for some reason. It was particularly prevalent where there were large concentrations of gay men ... my favorite places. When I got up to San Francisco to catch my outward flight to HK, it was all anybody was talking about. By that point I had been in "the City," as locals called it, enough to know my way around. I liked the place, but it still seemed like a one-horse town compared to Hong Kong and big Asian cities. "Where are all the people?" I would always muse. I knew I would miss the teeming millions, but was convinced on that trip that I needed to step up the planning of my exit strategy as I returned to the Far East with a lot on my mind. I had finally had enough time to interact with my own kind.

I had met some key players in my life-to-be and although keen to just get on with it, I was not quite sure where to land once I jumped ship off the *HMS Missionary Misadventure*. Things were changing back in Hong Kong, and although it was as cool as ever, I was beginning to put out a few rhizomes into new soil. I could not call them roots . . . tendrils, perhaps. I walked around the busy streets of the Crown Colony in a kind of daze. I was gradually ceasing to be a part of the fabric of this place that I loved so much. But it wasn't going to be like this forever, was it? I began getting irritated with little things about the other missionaries, the church people, and even the government, which was becoming more and more influenced by the powers-that-be up in Beijing. I was sick of preaching and looked for every excuse to get out of it. Travel became my main exit strategy. There were always conferences and conventions where I was in high demand as a speaker and a fund-raiser, so I kept that up for a while. But then the Fundie churches began catching onto something new in the world.

China was starting to get old hat for some in the Christian world, and there needed to be something new, fresh, and exciting. I was entertaining a lot of Christian dignitaries from the U.S. at the time, and was tuning more and more into the things that they were talking about. One thing that really pricked my ears up was the constant references to this new thing they called "the gay agenda." I was unaware of this agenda, so was constantly trying to get them to define it for me.

I was involved daily in gay circles all over the place by then. I had gay friends and sex partners from HK, other Asian cities, the U.S., Europe, and Australia. As HK was kind of a travel and trade hub in Asia, I met an increasing array of men in various related industries where gay people were growing in our comfort level and even visibility. I think that was the thing that the visiting pastors and church officials were trying to put their finger on . . . "visibility." They simply were seeing more and more gay people around them both in person and in the media. We were coming out of the shadows, and it was bothering them. Our increasingly higher profile everywhere was disconcerting to them. I began to understand why.

This holding pattern of mine began to unwind and became untenable for me. I was beginning to fill in the blanks. I had always been aware that the religious world is reactionary by its nature. It is the hardwired circuitry of the religious mind to resist change. Whereas I had always embraced the new and different, I was keenly aware that most of my colleagues were not comfortable with other than the "old ways." I remember my dad commenting once about some new legislative proposal in Congress. As a visitor from overseas at the time, I was unaware of what it was all about. His explanation? "I don't know what it's about. But whatever it is, I'm again it!" He meant "against," but was digging at other conservatives who could not be as clever with the turn of phrase as he. I understood him. I knew how he thought, and had accepted that lack of vision years earlier.

Now I was recognizing that same new anti-everything mentality all around me in the church. Beth assured me that it had always been there, but new circumstances had just brought it out into the open more. And, besides, with the 24/7 news cycle, both in secular media and on "Christian TV," there was a great need for filler. Controversy has always driven the media. Newspapers, magazines, radio and satellite television all loved a good squabble. The Bible is rife with chaos, murder, and mayhem. Christians loved to fight, and had even gradually changed their god, Jesus, from a loving, caring, sweet, gentle savior to a conquering hero—a roaring, raging campaigner for truth, righteousness, and the American way. Just like Superman :-)

I had always known that "Christians" felt put-down, put-upon, and disrespected. I understood this, but it never bothered me . . . kind of like my perception of Jerry back in Viet Nam and his weird relatives (the snake handlers, that is). Anti-intellectualism has been the hallmark of religious thinking since the Dark Ages, when no one could read and write except the clergy. So there's was a perfect environment for social control. The educated clergy could manage the blockheads in the streets and on the farms, whereas "the Literati" were needed to keep society running. Like, who else controlled access to societal needs like weddings, funerals, baptisms—even property issues like deeds, wills, and disputes over farm animals? Everybody needed the clergy. Even if there is plenty of evidence through ancient writings, diaries, and such that the clergy most often didn't even believe the drivel that they were dishing out to the peasants, at least they had job security.

Then came the Enlightenment. Most Evangelicals dismiss this shift in Western thought away from religion and toward reason, as simply a "work of the Devil." Ever since, the clergy and their dummy followers, have resented how "secularism" is fighting a war against "good." And that would be the Church. It was my once-hero, Dr. Francis Shaeffer, who helped define all this for the Evangelicals way back in the 1960s and 1970s. He saw it as a "culture war" for the soul of Western Civilization. And it just points out how powerful and influential a single person can be if he is truly dedicated to his creed.

He used to tell a story, using an analogy that was very fitting in the environs about L'Abrie, Switzerland, where he lived and taught. When I was living in Augsburg and was still in the army, I visited his outpost in the Alps as frequently as possible. He was a kind of beacon—a prophet of sorts who could see where we all were in the history of Western "Christian" civilization. I was smitten. He used a great analogy of humped-back little stone bridges that one can find everywhere in Europe. They are quaint, charming, and photogenic. I have painted many of them, and have included them in many of my artworks that I have sold over the years. These durable, little architectural constructions have lasted for centuries. Roman soldiers and Papal armies had crossed back and forth over them endlessly. Hannibal and Napoleon marched their men across them. Then came the 20th century and mechanized warfare. Tanks and other heavy artillery were simply too much for the little bridges. They were no longer useful or practical. They had finally outlived their usefulness.

Schaeffer constantly preached that the Christian Church would outlive its lifespan if it remained entrenched in a medieval doctrine of monks, priests, scribes, and Popes. It had to change and catch up with the world of science and technology, employing these and new skill sets to bring an ancient message into the modern world. In many ways he succeeded brilliantly. But as time went on, I was not so sure. He was right about the bridges. But as a Fundamentalist at heart, he still was stuck with Biblical baggage that did not translate well in a rapidly transforming and increasingly globalized world.

For one thing, he had a *hobby horse*. Most people have them. These tend to be issues that are important in one's life and world-view. He seemed old back when I was sitting on his carpeted floor in L'Abrie, hanging on his every word with rapt attention. But when you are twenty, sixty-five seems ancient. His success was based primarily on his writings, all of which I read and absorbed thoroughly. But over the years he began drifting in his theology. Like many true born-again Christians he was beginning to be romanced by the "Religious Right." I would use the word "bewitched" here, but that might be a bit too smarmy, even for me.

There was an issue arising in the American consciousness at the time, and it was abortion. The legal medical procedure that had become law in the early 1970s was coming under fire by religious conservatives, fueled on by Right-wing political operatives. The whole of the Fundamentalist world began going mad. Abortion was tantamount to murder, as the fetus was destroyed in the process of the abortion. I neither agreed nor disagreed. After all, it had nothing to do with me— not really, that is. In the Fightin' Fundie world, abortion was simply the easiest of several targets to go after. But I (admittedly) had a hobby horse as well—gay rights.

Shaeffer just happened to be the smartest guy in the room full of Pat Robertsons, Jerry Falwells, and Rex Humbards. All these professional "ministers" had made it big in Christian media. Their empires were built on fundraising, as I was keenly aware. They all owned media machines that had to churn out programming at an alarming rate. And they were all in competition for the donors' dollars. They were also in direct competition with the churches themselves. How many times had I heard the moans and groans of pastors who had to beg parishioners to dedicate church funds in order to fix a leaky roof or a recalcitrant furnace? Why do that when you can give money for a million Bibles for China? Why indeed?

The 700 Club and other television ministries had to compete not only among themselves and with the church organizations that sent out missionaries; they had to fight with the likes of Phil Donahue, Jerry Springer, and Geraldo Rivera—to name a few. The airwaves were chock full of religious programming, and it was getting mean. Of course, these were the halcyon days of the Reagan administration. I have always said that the "great communicator" probably should have become a preacher. His style and delivery were better than that of most Christian loudmouths screaming incessantly for money (who were now being referred to as "televangelists").

It really began with the *Moral Majority*. Barely able to disguise their intent, this Falwellian nightmare was not really religious in nature at all—nor was it evangelistic. There was no great commission or reaching of a lost and dying world for Christ. This creature was political. Like the Roman Catholic Church of the Middle Ages, this melding of religion and politics (plus mercantilism and militarism) had the Papacy written all over it. Yet, it was a Protestant papacy, and the contenders did not have a College of Cardinals to vote on who was to be the top wop. They had to duke it out in the political arena. I had anticipated it in a dark vision, but found myself right up against it soon enough.

The abortion issue was a perfect target for the televangelists. They knew that it could rile up the base (as they were now being called). The Evangelical Christians—particularly in the South—had been pissed off ever since the institution of slavery was wrenched from their cold, dead hands back during the big war. (That's the one twixt the blue and the gray.) But abortion was not the only arrow in their quivers. A totally new issue was handed to them on a silver platter . . . and it was called AIDS.

NUCLEAR WINTER

Life in a total new reality

I was really sick of the Christian Barnum and Bailey dog-and-pony show by this time. I mean *sick* of it. On one of my last preaching (fundraising) engagements of my career, I was the featured speaker and was introduced to the huge congregation as: "the man who has reached more souls for Christ in China than anyone in history." I was actually nauseated. But I went onstage and did my shtick. I certainly understood that "The show must go on!" But this act was not me— not anymore.

After a few more engagements in the Midwest, I made my way to San Francisco via Reno. "Reno?" was the predictable shocked response I got when I reported back to gay friends in Hong Kong that I was moving to a little place in the mountains, called Virginia City, Nevada, with a population of about 730 or so. Was I out of my mind? Of course. But considering all manner of weird stuff that I had pulled off in the years since my first trip into China, how could this really be all *that* strange? I had something in the back of my mind, naturally.

Okay, I admit it. Like a lot of gay men, I had a fantasy of moving to a quaint, charming little place somewhere, marring the man of my dreams, and living happily ever after. I was not content with San Francisco. It was too self-absorbed—too full of itself. Like the Americans living as expatriates in Europe, they saw "the City" as the center of the Universe. Well, the gay universe maybe. But I just could not see myself living in a gay ghetto, and walking my little dog named Toto every night in the rain. Hong Kong has the world's highest population density, so maybe I was just wanting something new and different; or maybe it was temporary insanity that caused me to choose to buy a place in Virginia City. Of course, I was familiar with the town of myth. Kids of my generation had all been raised on the television series *Bonanza!*

I was not wild about the Wild West. Oh, I had visited my share of gay cowboy bars by then, and had rustled a few hot guys in chaps, boots, and Stetsons on the weekends; but that was just a show—like preaching and putting on a religious act. All those guys went back to their accounting and hairstyling jobs on Monday mornings. I'll admit that I had been dazzled for a while with all of the excitement and entertainment of playing gay on the weekends. But I considered it to be a lot like playing church—at which I was obviously quite good. *It's only a paper moon . . . hanging over a cardboard sea* (to quote a favorite ditty). I was not planning to get sucked into the gay world and the gay "lifestyle." But I guess that was unavoidable at some point no matter what.

I bought a Victorian house on A Street in VC. From the upper story bedroom window I could see the Ruby Mountains 175 miles away. I never really adjusted to it, but you have to admit living in a tiny town in the high Sierra was a far cry from the hustle and bustle of Hong Kong. I likened it to jumping from a speeding train and hitting the ground with a thud. Now, Virginia City is definitely historic, but not because of Hoss, Little Joe, and Ben Cartwright. I knew of it from my perfunctory studies of American history in high school and college. I had heard of the Comstock Lode, the world famous silver strike that brought the region to widespread public awareness during the American Civil War in the middle 1800s. But like most first-time visitors, I was not familiar with the finer points of the historical record, which I quickly learned with the purchase of a few books by some Nevada authors at a local bookstore. Well, you have to admit one thing . . . this was definitely going to be different. It was.

Okay, I will admit that there was one specific fact about that little burg clinging precariously to Mt. Davidson (Sun Mountain) that I did not know. It had been host to the birthing of a legend. I was astounded that I had not known that a certain notable author had made his start in these high and dry environs back during that big war. An escapee from the grasp of the Missouri conscription militia, he was young and brilliant and destined to become America's best-loved author ever. He was a wild, red-haired, crazy guy named Samuel Clemens. He fully intended to be a draft dodger, and had no compunction whatsoever about taking advantage of the one card that he could play in that place and time . . . his brother, Orion. It seems that Orion had been appointed to be assistant to the governor of the newly-created Nevada Territory . . . then-called (get this) Western Utah. LOL.

In his much-loved book, *Roughing It*, he begged and cajoled his brother to take him along to the Great West. Well, he claimed, he could be the secretary to the secretary, and could help him fight Injuns, Messicans, and prairie dogs. Anything to get out of Missouri and impending war. I bought a copy of the book and fell in love—not with that cantankerous young misfit, Sam, but with the great guy he became. We all know him today as Mark Twain.

I had been ignorant of the fact that once Sam had arrived in the Nevada Territory, he proved to be totally inept at being a secretary to the secretary. He was disorganized and impatient, motivated but scattered. He was the perfect ADD personality. Though brilliant, he simply could not do the job; so he hit the road to make it big in the silver mines. Well, that was way too hard and boring for a character like Sam. So he took to writin'. He was an avid reader and was keeping up on all the latest political goings-on down in Carson City, the provisional capital of the newly formed Nevada Territory. But he was far more intrigued by the big town up the hill where all the action was: Virginia City. He began sending letters to the editor of the *Territorial Enterprise*, the newspaper of the Comstock. He was pleasantly surprised when he found them in print in rather short order. He wrote more. After accidentally starting a forest fire near Lake Bigler (Lake Tahoe), he skedaddled ahead of the law and found himself in VC. (Actually, that was not totally by accident.) Joe Goodman, the owner/editor of the paper had enjoyed Sam's yarns and had invited him to come on as a full-time employee of the TE. A match made in Heaven.

The story of Sam's triumphant entry into the journalism biz is well-documented by many writers, so I won't digress. I bought a copy of *Mark Twain of the Enterprise*, a scholarly treatise by Henry Nash Smith. I read it and was struck. I was hanging around VC while the paperwork was being finalized on the Victorian sale. So I walked into the Mark Twain Museum in the Territorial Enterprise Building on C Street and talked to the owner, the woman from whom I was purchasing the house. She was getting "up there" and wanted to retire to her own condo down in Reno. Her son John, a very likable, closeted gay guy, was running the paper. He confided to me that he really did not enjoy running a small-town newspaper full of boring articles about fights over water rights, building contract disputes, and high school basketball scores . . . small town news. He did have a degree in journalism from UNR (University of Nevada, Reno) and wanted to get out, see the world, and work for a big time newspaper—anywhere (else). He had grown up in town and felt that it was rather limited in opportunities beyond running a bar, a casino, a bed and breakfast, or a brothel. I had also not known that bordellos were legal and controlled in most counties in Nevada (kind of like in Europe). Totally cool.

So, to make everybody happy, (including myself), I bought the newspaper. Diedra, the mom, got her retirement wish in one fell swoop, and John got his much-desired freedom. I wasn't quite sure how to play it, but like back with TC in the Philippines, I just threw the ball up in the air, fully intending to make up the game before it came down. Of course, I had no *intention* of running a small-town news rag. I was the new Joe Goodman. I was not interested in county politics or local squabbles or football games. But I was interested in bordellos :-) Ideas were cooking. Just buying a house wasn't much more than finding a place to put my furniture, and setting up my drawing table for business. Well, what business? I knew already. I had no illusion that the TE, as the small-time newspaper that it had become over the years, could pay. It was a hobby—something fun. Something that I might enjoy as an outlet for my newfound liberation from religion. But I had to combine that fun stuff with serious reality. I had to make money. I knew what to do—just not how to do it (yet). I had already made up my mind in the abstract. Now I had to think it all through.

* * * * *

On one of my last trips to the City a few months earlier, I was knocking around the Castro District, aka "The Castro." It was the quintessential example of a gay ghetto, where most who lived there, worked there, ate out there, and cruised there were gay. The shops catered to gay men, their needs and tastes. It was a great place to buy leather products or cowboy hats and boots as well as outrageous costumes that could shock your Southern Baptist mother. In fact, I had made up my mind about what to do in VC upon my first visit to a gay greeting card and novelty shop in SF. It had an unforgettable name: *Does Your Mother Know?* It was an experience.

The place was packed with gay guys of every description pawing through various male-oriented "skin" magazines, which were all dog-eared and manhandled. Obviously, the shop owner was not in the business of selling porn. There are plenty of shops of that nature all over town and country, for Christ's sake. There were some hot male posters and some gag gifts as well, but what people were there for was the vast array of greeting cards—most of which were either downright gay, mildly gay, or suggestive. I had never seen cards like those before. I loved them, and spent a couple hours reading and laughing, then selecting and buying.

The handsome guy running the cash register was quite friendly and talkative. He asked where I was from, and I said Hong Kong—a natural reply for me then. I still was not psychologically tuned-in enough yet to say Virginia City, Nevada. He was unfazed. "Oh, we have people in here from all over the world," he said nonchalantly. "Mostly they're from the Midwest and Texas and places like that. Many buy a whole year's supply of cards for all occasions in one visit." While I felt like such a tourist with my six-month supply in the bag, I did manage to learn the shop-owner's name before leaving with my treasures. I knew nothing of the greeting card business, but had decided right then and there to learn all I could about the industry and how it worked, and how to get involved . . . immediately.

I had never paid much attention to cards before, except for the random birthday card or a *Get Well Soon* and the like. I took the owner, Mike, out to dinner a few nights later and came away with an incredible education on the subject of "alternative" greeting cards. His store had only been open a few years at the time, and had been clearly spawned by the then-developing gay market (part of that wicked "gay agenda"). Since he was a retailer—a merchant—he saw my interest as having no conflict with his; since I was interested in designing, printing, and distributing cards to stores like his. In fact, he offered to introduce me around to the movers and shakers of the "paper products industry." That was magical.

First of all, I learned that the greeting card industry was simply an element of the much larger industry—generally referred to as the paper products business, which included calendars, posters, and anything pretty much involving ink on paper. My favorite thing! But the PP biz as I began calling it, was itself part of a much larger gift industry, which was part of the worldwide multi-billion-dollar Gift and Decorative Accessories business. Mike introduced me to an older gay couple named Hobie and Scott, industry representatives who sold the manufacturers' products to the retailers. Their company was called Scobieco, and I met them in their showroom on the sixth floor of the San Francisco Merchandise Mart on 888 Brannon Street, in the City. They were extraordinarily helpful and friendly. They "repped" about twenty card lines of all kinds throughout their carefully prescribed territory of Northern California. I learned one thing for sure: the entire paper products industry was *crawling with* gays of every age, type, color, and description. I could almost hear Pat Robertson screaming all the way from Virginia Beach. But apparently he was unaware of this massive, steaming, bubbling cauldron of Satan (yet).

I extended my stay a few days, and flew to New York with Hobie and Scott to attend the "Gift and Dec." trade fair. Wow. The shindig was a huge production. We walked the carpeted isles of the Jacob Javits Center in midtown Manhattan until I was ready to drop. I had never seen so many cards, calendars, teddy bears, and Santa Clauses and toys and gadgets and gimmicks together in one place in my life. I was kind of overwhelmed. But Hobie and Scott assured me that I only need concern myself with the paper products section at present. Since they also repped all manner of gifts and décor items, they had to "shop the whole show." So I was scooped up by another gay couple—older folks from Palm Springs who were the Scobieco counterparts, repping all of *Southern* California. They took me to the booths of all the vendors that they represented.

I was treated well, but with a wee bit of standoffishness. The reps had already mentioned that this guy from Hong Kong was planning to come out with a new product line based out of Virginia City, Nevada. I am sure they were thinking: This I have to see! Well, they did. The alternative card business was in its infancy. There were really only five companies that specialized in what was becoming a booming industry. Chuck and Bill took to me right away and mentioned that unlike other more developed industries within the greater Gift and Dec. (G&D) world, there was still room for a new guy to get into the ball game. It was by no means saturated . . . yet. I wasted no time.

Back in Hong Kong everyone was aflutter. The grand wah-wah zippity-doo-dah conference of all times, called the *General Council*, was about to take place a few months hence in Denver; and China was going to be the premier, spectacular, extraordinary extravaganza; and I was going to have to get up in front of thousands of delegates from around the country and the world to tell the mailbag story. And with feeling! Oh no! I just couldn't do it. I had my back against the wall. There was no escape. I had to come out and let the chips fall where they may. I could not live in the Christian Circus any longer. I came out to Beth. She did not throw a plate :-) That was good. She had guessed—sort of—and was so grateful that it was not "another woman." We decided that she and Vincent would leave immediately for the States, I would remain and close down the flat in Hong Kong, and we would rendezvous in Portland a few weeks later where I would write my letter of resignation to the Church.

It kind of happened as planned, but Beth confided in a Christian friend who immediately broke the confidence and tattled to Springfield who summoned her back to the headquarters to explain what was happening to Tom, as they had been unable to contact me. I had disconnected our phone and shipped our household stuff with dispatch. I was camping in Reno where the divorce proceedings would take place. As of then—with the purchase of a condo in Reno and the Victorian in Virginia City, and the change of driver's license—I was an official Nevada resident. This was really not the way I had wanted it, as it was going to get ugly. I wrote my letter of resignation (which was handwritten) in the San Francisco airport, and posted from there.

"They won't let you resign . . ." Beth told me on the phone from a hotel room in Springfield. "You are ordered to come back and stand trial." I laughed. So did my attorney. A church trial is only a "something" if you are still into the organization and willing to submit to its dicta. I was not. I simply ignored the whole thing. Beth was adrift and I understood. But I knew that as the "injured party" the church would take care of her, give her a job of some kind somewhere, and figure out what to tell the entire world about Tom. I referred to it as dropping the atomic bomb. I didn't want to do it, but circumstances of the whole adventure in China had been blown so out of proportion already by the whole kit and caboodle of them. I had to bail. My concept had been to quietly get the millions of names and addresses, and send Gospel literature in over time. But the churches, now in bed with the Christian Media, just had to take it and run. Well, they did, but without me.

Beth called from her hotel room the first night of the Denver General Council confab, and compared the whole thing to "nuclear winter." Not only was China not featured; it was not mentioned. Apparently some of the HK missionaries and Church workers had been visited by the Gung An Bao (in HK), and were warned to cool it with all the talk of Bible smuggling and mail ministries and "reaching" China with mass media. It was beginning to look like the PRC was inept and was losing control with all this "cheun-gao" (spreading of religion) going on in the mainland *illegally.*

I had come out to her, but to no one else (except our partner, John and his lover, in Startram). I was not trying to get involved in a gay crusade. The Church had been good to me, and gawd knows they had raised enough money by means of my efforts. But she had spilled the beans to the big wigs when they interviewed her. *Tom is gay.* Likely that was the last thing they suspected or ever wanted to hear. I think that ranked right up there with Tom is no longer a Christian (for at least the past two years or so). But wagging tongues! I had learned years earlier that Evangelicals are incredible gossips. They love to talk. And although I was not mentioned from the podium, *others* were. Some things just had to be addressed.

By that time the PTL ministry of my friends Jim and Tammy Faye Bakker had not only unraveled, but both had been indicted for fraud and tax evasion or something. They were in the news all over the country, and I had been watching that saga play out on nationwide television from hotel rooms for months. Even Jerry Falwell had gotten into the feast as various other Fundi-ministries swooped in to chew on the carcass of the moribund ministry, now in financial receivership. Court proceedings were already underway. There was plenty to gossip about.

I felt bad and so did Beth, but she understood. I warned her to keep the gay thing under her hat, as I had no intention of making a big deal of it. I was simply going to quit the ministry and go into the newspaper business (and the greeting card industry) from a small tourist town in Nevada. But the gay thing was hard to sweep under the rug. I was living high above the Truckee River, on the tenth floor of my new condo in Reno, with a fine view of the snow-covered Sierra; and putting together the card side of the *Territorial Enterprise* publishing operation. I could have just left it there, but the "gay agenda" was constantly in the news.

The term "culture war" was being used freely to describe what Francis Schaeffer had been preaching for years. But, as usual, the Americans could not see that there is a real world out there. Everything is viewed as an American issue. The culture wars, as Schaeffer had seen them, were global . . . or at least Western. The Western World was dying spiritually. It was in a struggle of cosmic dimensions. His protagonists/ antagonists were the intelligentsia, the liberal churches, and secularism in general. He thought like a philosopher. The American clergy thought like preachers (and fundraisers). Those two things always seem to go hand in hand. But the new element in the mix were the politicians. Their teaming-up with the preachers and televangelists had added a new element—a new dynamic: votes. It was not enough to use religion as a weapon in the culture wars, or fundraising for myriad holy causes. Now "the Culture War" (singular) was heating up, as the newly born-again Republican Party began with a new and very simpleminded slogan: *God, Guns, and Gays.* Catchy, huh?

On the second night of the conference I talked with Beth again. I could tell by her voice that she was seeing the irony of this whole laughable folly. "Well, you're not going to believe this!" she said incredulously. "Guess who has just been arrested?" I held my breath. "Jimmy Swaggart was just caught in a cheap motel with a prostitute in Mojave, California!" You can't make stuff like this up.

MARK TWAIN WOULD BE PROUD

Not to mention amused

Virginia City is a weird place. The entire town was aflutter after Dee Schaffer announced the sale of her Victorian house on A Street to some guy from Hong Kong. In fact, I hear tell that she had made a point—simply for clarification—that I was not Chinese. I had lived and worked overseas for years and was returning to the U.S. after a divorce. That seemed to stimulate both interest and concern. Who was this mystery man anyhow? As one so totally accustomed to living a rather secretive life, I was in no hurry to draw undo attention to myself. I sort of planned to move in quietly and begin developing my new venture in the alternative greeting card business. Nothing to see here.

But when she revealed that she and John had also decided to sell the *Territorial Enterprise* to the "foreigner," tongues were wagging and heads were spinning. I had begun working with a marketing firm in the City, so I was mentally getting totally tuned in to the new venture. On the other hand, a weekly publication like the TE had to meet deadlines and publish on time every week. The show must go on. Familiar? I hired some staff whom I had known in Hong Kong, along with a couple of talented guys from Laguna Beach who had worked for Jack. The Victorian was plenty big enough to accommodate all of us (for living), but I had decided that it would not due for working. So I set up my art department and office down in the condo in Reno. I also hired the general manager of a competing card company in New York, and we were in biz.

I met Dale even before I left Hong Kong, when we were hanging out with a collection of friends who were helping me move into my new condo in Reno. I wanted to get fairly settled before I finally pulled up stakes in the Crown Colony for good. I knew that I would miss it so I wanted to have a comfortable place to land. Jennan, our real estate agent, had been working with the "advanced team" of Gene and Joel from

Laguna to get the place livable with stuff like bedding, rental furniture from Levitz, and to provide cable TV and get phones up and operating. Although I was planning to live in Virginia City, I needed a place in town where I could work late if I wanted (or bring tricks, to be honest). LOL.

We went into a campaign to simultaneously train the staff in the art of newspaper and greeting card production. John had agreed to teach the basics of journalism and layout/design as part of the purchase. John Posnan, the guy from New York, had been in the card business for a few years already so knew all about how it worked. I was a quick study; and our first line of fifty cards was ready for the next G&D show in New York on schedule. Hobie, Scott, Bill, and Chuck introduced us to reps around the country. *Territorial Enterprise* greeting cards were on sale from Boston to Bakersfield, from Houston to Honolulu, in no time. But despite the fun and raucous life of the greeting card business, the real excitement was not down in Sparks at the card company office, studio, and warehouse, but up in the high wilds of Virginia City. Well, the word was out in rather swift fashion: The "guys" who had purchased the TE were gay! Oh shit. Now some in town were okay with that, and some nonchalant. But the Fightin' Fundies went into a tailspin. It was a marvelous work and a wonder! They hooted and howled, snorted and shouted; they foamed at the mouth and spit green bile. (Well, maybe not green :-)

I was not really used to small-town life. Well, not since St. Paul, burgs in Oregon when we first started out, but I was always the featured speaker—the missionary—and that called for songs of loudest praise. I have to admit that I was so unprepared for what I soon encountered in Virginia City, where I had spent my teen years. Even then, I never had participated in all that pettiness so I cannot say that I had had much experience with small town small-mindedness before. Sure, Beth and I itinerated in little burgs in Oregon when we first started out, but I was always the featured speaker—the missionary—and that called for songs of loudest praise. I have to admit that I was so unprepared for what I soon encountered in Virginia City. During the previous few years as a Christian celebrity, I had been automatically shielded from a side of religion that I was now walking straight into by owning and publishing a newspaper. I had at first thought of churches as being full of "good Christian" people—all of them sweet, giving folk who loved the Lord and cared about the lost and dying millions in China and around the world. As I lived in the Evangelical culture a little longer, I began thinking of them instead as well-meaning simpletons. They threw their money at stupid causes, but were sure that it was not up to them to judge how their funds were spent. God would give them credit for their contributions in Heaven even if they were squandered. But in the end I began to see the Fightin' Fundies as really fightin'. When I used to talk about them as pugnacious, I was always referring to disputes over doctrines and points of scripture, or ordinances of the Church like baptism techniques. But, for the first time ever, I actually saw the Evangelical Fundamentalists for what they were . . . monsters.

These were not nice people. I figured out quickly that they were not disposed to "live and let live." Just being gay was an offense. Of course, with my preacher background, I was totally aware of the Biblical call for the death penalty against the "sin" of homosexuality. I thought about that a lot, as I was also aware of over fifty other offenses that call for the same punishment as well. Capital punishment, that is. But even by that time I knew that some sins are worse than others, and being gay was the rock bottom worst sin possible. Well, I had, by then begun work on my treatise entitled *The Biblical Mystery Tour*, where I took an honest look at the Bible for the first time without Evangelical filters. Oddly enough, I had to come into this snake pit to spend that much time in the Bible itself. I always had little interest in doctrinal disputes and controversies. I had likewise ignored denominational differences and fractures. I was just interested in preaching the Gospel to those who had never heard, thus giving them a chance to accept Christ and be saved. Now I read the Scripture with a totally new and keen interest. It was amazing. I have to say that I am glad that I had never read it critically before, or I would have never gone into the ministry in the first place.

One thing I had always known . . . the shepherd/sheep model from the Bible was an apt metaphor. The sheep need a pastor to guide them lest they run off a cliff. Of course, that was what I encountered right away when I first met the head monster in Virginia City—William George— a priceless example of self-centeredness and smugness. He was what Mark Twain referred to as "the Christian with four aces." Oh gawd, he hated me. I'd met a few guys like that back in the army: pushy, loud, and unapologetically "Christian." The best man at my wedding, Jim from Salem, referred to those types as never having learned much about living the "crucified life." He was right about that. "Brother" William, as we called him in town, reminded me a lot of Terry Furth back with the Navigators in Frankfurt. I was sure he had never been in the military either (but maybe military school). He was mean, obnoxious, and cocksure of himself and of his Jesus, who was so unlike the Jesus that I had known and pledged to serve. He was envisioning and worshiping a totally different deity all together. His Jesus was an alien personality to me; he was a guy whom I later came to routinely call "Super Jesus."

Well, Super Jesus was a new experience for me, to be sure. He was a bit more like Superman, Batman, the Hulk, or some other "superhero." He was so not the humble carpenter of Galilee. William had managed to intimidate most of the town. In fact, he was the town bully. Not all towns have one, but Virginia City surely did at the time. I avoided bullies in high school and the military. But I was on a collision course with a personality type that would characterize my ongoing experience with Fundamentalist Christians from then on. I was taught that we are to be "ambassadors for Christ" with God making his appeal through us. I was still stuck back on Jesus' admonition to us in Matthew 20: **"Let your light so shine before men that they will see your good works and glorify your father in heaven."** This was going to be a challenge.

Now I can't say that this one particular Fundie Monster—this Christo-jerk—this "minister of the Gospel" without any training, education, or credentials—was the only new personality beginning to influence my personal life at this time. But he was a good start. My old friend Pat Robertson, was by then stumbling and fumbling around trying to explain what had happened to his big mission to China, let alone whatever happened to Tom Muzzio, "the best missionary ever." I heard all of that through the Jesus grapevine. The culture wars had been heating up over the years since Pat, David Wilkerson, and Francis Schaffer got the ball rolling way back in 1970. But with the political situation in the country under our "fearless leader," Ronald Reagan and the Christian Coalition, the Moral Majority, and other sundry political organizations disguised as religious bodies, the conflagrations were getting white hot.

God Hates Fags! Shocking, isn't it? LOL. Actually, I was peripherally aware of earlier struggles between gays and "Christians" that had been kindled by that wonderful godly woman in Florida named Anita Bryant, and by the struggles in San Francisco with the murder of their mayor, Frank Moscone, and our slain hero, Harvey Milk. But these things had not impacted me to the same degree that the new pseudo-religious groups had begun to. I knew Pat, Brother Dave, and the Bakkers (who were far less malicious than Falwell and his kind). I knew Jimmy who-was-caught-with-his-pants-down Swaggart, and so many other minor characters in the grand play that was still in Act I.

Cable television was something that we never had in Manila or Hong Kong. It was actually relatively new even in the States, but was a boon to the Fundimonsters. They loved it. They gobbled up airtime nationwide (particularly in the middle of the night). I had long known that "Christian radio" is a wasteland of ranting, raving, screaming, and shouting. Don't forget, during my days of itineration, I drove all over the Pacific Northwest and California where there was nothing to listen to on the car radio but frothing-at-the-mouth preachers. I could handle that. But as I often took to staying up late or waking up in the wee hours when everybody else was sleeping, to write articles or greeting card gag lines, I encountered a lot of the old "friends" and a whole lot of new enemies in the Religious Right there on the tube.

But as much as I loathed them, they constantly gave me great new material for my newspaper columns for the *Territorial Enterprise*. I began to fight back in my own way. I was nice at first. Well, sort of. As I was writing my treatise on the Bible, I found plenty of material to just toss out to the general public unedited. I wrote many articles addressing Bible anomalies and contradictions that riled the "base." The Right-wing political base, that is. It was great fun. Actually, Mark Twain had done the exact same thing over a century earlier with much the same effect. When I was writing a chapter in my book that involved a great deal of quoting from Leviticus chapter 26, I just published what I had written and printed it directly in the paper, making no assertions or comments. I simply printed it verbatim from the Holy Bible.

A firestorm ensued. Well, not quite. It was more like dropping a tactical nuclear weapon. I began using the word "tactical" (as I had learned to in the military), as those weapons are designed to hit specific targets rather than wiping out whole cities. I had no intention of wiping out Virginia City—just the evil people in it. Like in the story of Lot in Genesis chapter

19, some were spared when God blew up the city of Sodom. Well, I figured, since Brother William was beginning to refer to the staff of the Enterprise as "Sodomites," I would do what the inhabitants of that unfortunate town didn't get a chance to do—fight back.

Poor Brother William. He was so distressed and perplexed. Most bullies of his kind are not used to people kicking them in the shins. He was so pissed at me and the paper that he took to publishing his own little mimeograph rag in rebuttal. It was total pablum. As would be expected from most guys like him, he simply assumed that everybody agreed with him. I didn't need to respond, but I just couldn't help myself. It was way too much fun.

Another weird thing about Virginia City (and all of Storey County) is the aforementioned existence of legal prostitution. I had been intrigued by this cool feature of the state of Nevada. Prostitution was what they called a "county option." Most counties, save for Washoe and Clark, had opted in. Brother William was always seething about that blatant immorality. Before the fags arrived and bought the *Enterprise* his primary fixation had been with trying to "close down the brothels." Well, I loved that. Having lived in Europe where I'd learned that legal prostitution is far better, safer, and more hygienic than streetwalking, I made common cause with the brothel owner of the then-notorious Mustang Ranch. He was a colorful character, to be sure, and took to me right away. I was on his side and gave him and his "girls" (and boys) a lot of ink. Poor Brother W.

Meanwhile, back down the mountain in Reno, the card company was gaining steam and we were roaring ahead in the paper products industry right on schedule. We had been hiring out our photography to local guys who worked by the job, but we really needed a full-time photographer and art director. We needed somebody like Joe Altman, a jovial, bohemian kind of guy from San Francisco. I had noticed his work in magazines like *The Advocate, Drummer,* and other rough trade leather magazines of the day. When I contacted him I discovered that he was also quite a history buff. He knew right away of the *Territorial Enterprise* since he was a Twainophile and knew all about Lucius Beebe and Charles Clegg. Although the famous couple was long gone from the planet, there were still lots of people in the gay community—particularly around San Francisco—who had known them personally.

Joe had lots of those kinds of friends. So when I offered him a full-time job with the card company, he posed only one condition: that he could be the official photographer for the *Enterprise* as well! That was so Joe :-)

Joe, a lapsed Catholic, fell into the whole scene in Virginia City and the newspaper's tangle with the local Fightin' Fundies with enthusiasm—along with our associate editor, Dale DeSautel and our computer whiz, Gene Romaine, who got us into "desktop-publishing" (the first newspaper in Nevada to even know what it was!). We were amazed at the extent of Joe's connections in the City. Of all the great suggestions that he put forth, what really turned out to be a total hit was our introduction to the world-famous *Sisters of Perpetual Indulgence*. Of course, I had even heard of that notorious group of pranksters when I was still living in Hong Kong. He introduced them to us as potential card character models—complete with their own U-Haul full of outrageous costumes—including, of course, their trademark nun drag outfits. We did a whole subline of cards with the "sisters" and brought them up to Virginia City for shock value. It worked. Everybody in town was appropriately shocked. Yea. Hallelujah :-)

Their cards sold like crazy nationwide and in seven foreign counties as well. By then the card company had like three-thousand-plus stores (in the United States) that carried our products, including calendars, wacky notepads, and cocktail party napkins. We paid them standard modeling fees for which they were quite happy. But then, of course, we owned all of those hundreds of images of them. And, naturally, I had an idea (as usual). We began using the sisters' images in the newspaper—for fun. But it was so popular that we decided to pull a Mark Twain, inventing a pseudo-religious organization of our own, which we called *Keep Right and Pure*. It was the Virginia City answer to the Moral Majority and the American Family Association. K.R.A.P. was a hoot, but the Fundies—especially Brother William—were not laughing. Why did that not surprise us? For the longest time we ran a regular column (complete with nun images, including cartoons and captions) detailing the ministerial outreach of KRAP. It was just too good for words, and I only regret that we didn't have the internet back then. It would have gone viral :-)

So life was great fun, but like the Beach Boys sang: "She'll have fun fun fun till her daddy takes the T-Bird away." Life took a serious turn in about 1990 when so many of our friends began dying from Acquired Immune Deficiency Syndrome (AIDS). Of course, we had all been aware of it five years or more earlier, but it began hitting closer and closer to home. I had already lost Jack back in Laguna, and several friends in SF as well. But then Joe was diagnosed as were several other friends in Nevada, including our dear friend and supporter, "Andy" Anderson, the Nevada State Librarian down in Carson City. A kind of black cloud began forming over the Comstock, and the only persons laughing then were Brother William and his following. "God's judgment!" they roared. Of course, by then we knew that it was a virus. But they still gloated that so many gay men were dying. They were so gleeful. You could just see the "love of Christ" shining through in their lives. It greatly pissed me off and I decided to leave the fight in VC and move to San Francisco to get involved in the struggle on a larger scale.

We bifurcated the corporation, selling off the card division to a great straight woman, Patti Wolfe, who is CEO of the company to this day. *The Territorial Enterprise* morphed into the *Territorial Enterprise Historical and Educational Foundation* and became a 501c3 nonprofit corporation with its legal registration in Virginia City. Brother William wrote a book—or so I heard tell—dedicating it to his mother who taught him all about true "Christian" values. I never saw it for sale anywhere, so cannot give a book report. Alas. (sigh)

I arrived in "the City" in June of 1990 and moved into a fifteen-story block of flats on Cathedral Hill. I rented an apartment on the top floor from a wonderful Chinese doctor from Bangkok. It had a view of the Bay Bridge from the living room and of the Golden Gate Bridge from the bedroom. The neighborhood is referred to as "Japantown," but there are shops and restaurants of all sorts of other Asian ethnic groups as well. I was so at home. Our building sat right next-door to the Embassy of the People's Republic of China! Just like home :-) I could stand on the small deck of my bedroom facing north and look down on the enclosed courtyard, watching the embassy staff doing their regular early morning tai chi. Just like home.

But after a few weeks at 66 Cleary Ct., I began to feel guilty as I continued watching those Mainlanders exercising in unison every day.

So I wrote a letter of apology to the people of China for my crimes. I had flaunted their laws and had sought through trickery to deceive them into hearing the Gospel message. I had lied on my visa application multiple times and had engaged in smuggling contraband religious materials into their country. I walked next-door, rang the bell, and was greeted by a very polite man to whom I gave my letter with a brief explanation. He accepted it graciously, but I never went inside the compound. I told him to give it to whomever would be in charge of such matters, and went away and never heard another word about it. But I'm sure they passed it on.

The PRC has a legal system a bit like that of Christianity. It is good to confess your sins and seek forgiveness—which I did. I thought about all those missionaries in far-flung regions around the world, breaking local laws and violating customs in the name of Christ and serving the CIA and other branches of the U.S. government in the name of patriotism. I had been a liar and a lawbreaker. Now I was beginning to enter the world of other liars and lawbreakers more heinous than I. They are called the Religious Right.

LIFE IN THE PLAGUE YEARS

Five friends in five months

The Bible specifically calls for the death penalty as punishment for male-to-male sexual behavior. I had been aware of this way back from my Navigator days. But, as I had never had sex with a man at that time, I tried to ignore it along with all of those other horrible things that I was beginning to discover about the Scripture back then. But I could not. There is always a Brother William out there somewhere, and I found myself reacting to them again and again. AIDS had by now become the cause célèbre of the Religious Right. It was tailor-made for bigots, and we were powerless to stand up to them for the most part as we were fighting for our lives everywhere by then. There's only so much energy one can muster.

Living in San Francisco turned out to be somewhat richer in experiences than I had anticipated. As I had enjoyed visiting the City frequently from Virginia City, or later in Tahoe, I always thought of my visits as kind of like going to the movies. Approaching the Bay Bridge one has to pay a toll. Like buying a theater ticket, one has to pay to enter Oz, the magical city full of wonders and excitement (especially for gay men). It was great and I always wore myself out like the proverbial kid in a candy store sampling all the wares.

After each visit I got to leave and go back to my own home, bed, furniture, and drawing table. At the time I was a resident with an apartment, a parking space, and a new boyfriend, Mike. I had met him within a week of my arrival. We clicked sexually right away and began hanging out together. He was HIV-positive, but by then I assumed that everybody I met was infected. We had all learned what "safe sex" was by then, so I was not in fear of contracting the disease, as there was a test as of 1986 and I had tested negative. Since I never was inclined to engage in "risky sex" anyway, I just enjoyed being with Mike. We got along very well and soon talked about moving in together to save on rent; but our tastes in décor were enough to dissuade us. How very gay, huh? I kept my apartment with my stuff and a killer view—and he kept his, walking distance to the Castro. Perfect. We took turns camping at each other's places, depending on what we had on the agenda. It worked out swell.

Mike, like most of my friends at the time, had little religious training or understanding. I had been kind of an anomaly back in Virginia City, with my crusade against Brother William. Nobody got as riled up by him as I did. They all just thought of him as a jerk, which he was. But to me he was a Christian jerk; and that made a difference. I understood that Christians set themselves up as a "type" of Christ. In other words, they are supposed to live lives of example. We are supposed to see this shining light of life and want to attain it. The theory goes that we are supposed to be so taken with—so wowed with their stellar lives—that we will be drawn to them and ask: "What is your secret? What makes you so happy, and how do I get an 'abundant life' like the one that you have so overflowingly?" Well, it rarely works that way. My experience is that Christians are smug, underhanded, and haughty. Their lives are far from the testimony that they think they are, and most people either ignore them completely or see right through them and run the other way. Mike really was indifferent. He could hear the most horrible, hate-filled diatribes from the likes of Lou Sheldon, William Dannemeyer, Richard Mountjoy (and other local California bigots of the time), and just flip the channel without a comment. I could not.

I would get furious, incensed, and livid. I would start cursing the TV screen and ranting. He would look at me with that "why don't you just chill out?" look. I couldn't chill out. I knew how Christians were supposed to act and comport themselves. And when they did not (in fact, they flaunted everything that Jesus taught about what their lives should be like, and did just the opposite) I was outraged. Technically, I know that was not likely good for my blood pressure. But I didn't worry about my blood pressure back then. I do today though, so I don't watch as much "Christian" media now :-)

It is quite true that one can live in San Francisco—especially in, near, or around the Castro—and still be oblivious to the undercurrents of religious fervor bubbling and gurgling around about in the wasteland of suburbia and in rural parts of the Nation. It was fun living totally apart from the religious freaks that I had grown to loathe so much. But, then there was television . . . I was kind of a TV junkie back then (and still am, but try to keep it under control . . . haha).

CNN was still relatively new, so there was news on the tube all the time, day or night. I kind of attributed my TV-watching to a starvation for real news during my sojourn in Marco's Manila back in 1975 when we only heard and read what little news remained after censoring by the "democratic" government of the Philippines. Now there was nothing but news, and it was investigated and dissected from every angle. I was hooked. Unfortunately, so much of the news was relating to the "gay plague"—AIDS, and the Christian reaction to it. I was right in the epicenter of the maelstrom—San Francisco—so I just couldn't help but be swept up in the torrent.

Back when Jack was first diagnosed with the disease we were all freaked out, as none of us had any idea what it was and what caused it. Of course, even back then the loudmouth Christian televangelists were preaching that it was "just retribution" from God on the "Sodomites," those most horrible and sinful of all people on the Planet. As a card-carrying member of that so-called club, I resented the varying simpleminded explanations. I knew that they didn't know any more than any of us did as to the cause and prevention possibilities. But they were just cashing in on a new thing for the purpose of raising more money. And they did so constantly and with vigor!

I had thought even back then that if I wanted to just make a lot of money quickly and cheaply, I could "come back to the Lord" and go into a *healing ministry* . . . proclaiming that I had been born-again (again) and that I had "dabbled" in the gay lifestyle and found it wanting. In fact, I could imagine a whole big-time traveling show that I could do so easily, especially given all of my contacts. I have no doubt that Pat Robertson and the old gang of money-suckers would love to have me come on the 700 Club (or any show, for that matter), and crawl and grovel, acknowledging my sin and waywardness. Then I could announce that I had returned to a "saving knowledge" of Christ and had experienced a renewed sense of being filled with the Holy Spirit and all that shit. It would have worked easily.

But I just chuckled about such a notion. I was just not that dishonest. Lying on visa applications and Bible smuggling was one thing, but pretending to have a religious experience for money? Now that's just too far. That's flat out wrong. (Smile) I would just leave that to the televangelists. I was so used to the religious fakes that nothing they said on TV surprised me; angered me, yes, but surprised me? No.

What I was not prepared for was something new. It was the rise of "Christian" *politicians*. Now I was aware of certain political animals who used religion as a foil—as a kind of cloak, a mantle. After all, Ronald Reagan was president at the time, and he was the best. He was a total religious charlatan. He never even pretended to attend church beyond the occasional photo op once or twice a year at the National Cathedral. But he learned his lines and could spout the scripture de jour like the pro that he was. He could have easily been a televangelist if he had not found politics even more challenging (and lucrative). I agreed with him on that. Being a religious phony is much easier than being a political phony, as there are fewer press people and even fewer regular pew-sitters ever challenging you. Politicians have constituents, and they have to make promises that they are expected to deliver on. The religious hucksters just steal the money and run. I know . . . I did. Too bad I never got to keep any of that money I raised. My dad even asked me about that. "Couldn't you just have figured out a way to get your hands on some of that cash?" he asked me face-to-face one day. I assured him that I could have, but that I just wasn't all that interested; especially since I could simply sell some more encyclopedias, tractors or electronics in China, and do it without tangling with the IRS or the press. LOL. Besides, my friends were dying, and I was genuinely more concerned about ministering to them than making money.

I watched with a kind of perverse fascination as the preachers on Christian media huffed and puffed and shouted and railed against the fags and their horrible disease (brought upon themselves by sinful behavior); and yet how they were missing a golden opportunity to truly minister healing in the name of Christ. I listened carefully for years, waiting for some Christian minister, preacher, or teacher to ever even suggest that Christ's followers should be ministering to AIDS patients instead of dumping on them constantly. Never happened. In the year 1991 I lost five friends in five months. January, February, March, April, and May. I lost a friend either in SF or Nevada once a month. I went to more funerals than an undertaker. I spent a lot of time in hospitals as well. I drank too much. It seemed like a sort of natural painkiller. It had its advantages personally, I suppose, but didn't make the issue go away. So I began to write. I set up my typing desk right next to the glass slider facing out and down into the PRC Embassy courtyard below, with the Golden Gate Bridge swimming in the fog in the distance—with the great sea beyond. It was a good place to work. There I started to write the *Biblical Mystery Tour*.

Still, I was continually distracted by events of the day. Mike was marvelously healthy for a guy with a 9 T-cell count. But many of my other friends were not so robust. A friend from New York named Dean, whom I met at a paper products trade show in Chicago, came for a visit. He was terminal. I recall wheeling him, ashen and thin as a broomstick, through the San Francisco airport in a wheelchair. He needed to change his ticket or something, and the first thing the cheerful young woman at the ticket office said to him was "Well, and how are you today?" in a most casual and friendly way. "I could be better," he said flatly in reply. He didn't mean to be rude, and she didn't take it that way; I gathered from her conversation that she had sick friends as well. That told me something. During my brief year in the City, I noticed that many women, both lesbian and straight, had somehow felt our pain and had bent down to us like the Good Samaritan to the poor stranger who had been robbed and beaten up by thugs along the road.

During that time, I was constantly amazed at the kindness of non-Christian strangers when I went to a lot of volunteer meetings such as Meals-on-Wheels and other community outreach projects totally apart from religion or spiritual motive whatsoever. I met so many genuinely "Christlike" people then who were not even marginally Christian in name or calling. They just happened to be good decent people who saw their fellow man in pain and did something about it. Meanwhile I watched Christian congregations on TV screaming and shouting and "coming against" the satanic homosexuals, gleefully rejoicing in their disease and deaths. The contrast was not lost on me. I was ashamed that I had ever called myself a Christian. *They* were the thugs along the road that Jesus described in the parable of the Good Samaritan. The monsters . . . the thugs. Ironic, isn't it?

During his brief stay in my flat in SF, Dean died. But it had started a couple of days earlier when I had to rush him to the hospital. It was everything I could do to get him into my van and drive him there, but he was admitted at once and I waited. As I was not a blood relative or of any formal relation whatsoever, I had no say in his treatment or wishes. He had talked about his coming death rather frankly as we drove out one day on Geary Avenue to where it dead-ends at the ocean side.

We sat there in the parking lot watching the Pacific and the nearly empty beach. He had given me instructions. . . "Tell them to let me die."

But I did not get the chance. He asked me to go down to the little shop near the lobby and get him a bottle of Avian water. I got off the elevator on the seventh floor with the water bottle in a small bag . . . and as I stepped into the hallway I heard an announcement come over the PA system: "Code Blue." I didn't have to guess. I walked straight to Dean's room. It was packed with people.

Dean was dead on that hospital bed. A doctor was holding the paddles at the ready. The room was filled with mostly medical students watching. I just stood there as he shocked Dean twice. He came back. Just like on TV. A few days later I found myself at the airport again saying goodbye. He then flew back to be with his family in Illinois. My phone rang a few days later. It was his mom. He had died. "Why didn't you have them let him die there?" she asked me softly, with no maliciousness at all in her voice. "I had no standing," I told her honestly. "Nobody even asked me or noticed me standing there." She understood. I guess that was the first time that I realized how few simple rights gay people actually had. If we had been related, even by marriage, I could have intervened and told them to stop. But I had to just stand there with that bottle of Avian water and watch the demonstration for the class. I didn't resent the doctor or the students. Someday those same students would be medical professionals and would help a lot of people. But I felt powerless no matter. Something needed to change.

Actually, as I realized later, I could have easily just said that he was my brother and they would have acquiesced. But I was too stunned to think that fast. Just as well, I suppose, as I came away from the experience with a deeper understanding of the struggle that we were in—a struggle of life and death. But that would come later, as I would find out. I didn't envision Dean frying and sizzling away on his first day in an eternal burning Christian hell. He was gone and I had to move on. I went back to writing. I began a lifelong project that still engages me today. I wrote a "vignette." I would have used that story as part of a sermon in times past. Stories like that are dynamite for fundraising. But instead I decided to type it out and save it to disk. I found that to be a good kind of therapy for me, as I was just about to go through the same thing again about two months later.

It was July 11, 1991. It was my fortieth birthday, and we had a solar eclipse that day in San Francisco to celebrate. Well, I am sure God really was not celebrating my birth and it was only a partial eclipse—LOL—but I was impressed in any case. Praise the Lord anyway :-) I stood on the balcony of my flat on the 15th floor and looked south. The sky grew perceptibly darker; it was like putting on a pair of sunglasses. Totally cool . . . The phone rang. It was a friend, Ray, calling from the wilds of the High Sierra, miles out in the sticks where he lived with his partner and my dear friend, Lake. He told me that Lake had died in the night. I was expecting it. I drove up the following week to help him scatter the ashes. Meanwhile the Christians raised their hands in praise. Another lost soul slid down to a Christ-less eternity. No one had even tried to reach him with the Gospel. If I still had been a believer, I would have certainly "witnessed" to him. But he just had to take his chances on eternity. I was all out of words.

It was hard at the time to watch religious television for even an hour without hearing of the evils of homosexuality and gay men having sex against God's divine plan. It was then that I began hearing a new Christian mantra: "One Man One Woman." The concept of marriage had come under scrutiny as certain gay men and women were beginning to discuss the possibility of what we have come to call "marriage equality." Not only was I shocked to even think about it, but I was kind of tickled that anybody could be so dumb and naïve as to think that such a thing could ever take place. It had never crossed my mind. But I remembered Dean and how I had nothing to say about his healthcare despite being told by him directly what he wanted. His wishes were not heard, nor did mine consider. Obviously, those fights were yet to come.

During that year I learned a new word from the scientific community that the Fightin' Fundies were picking up on as well: *hypothalamus*. It is a small part of the brain . . . under the thalamus and linked to the pituitary gland that controls a host of human bodily functions like temperature, thirst, fatigue, and various circadian rhythms. A theory had been proposed by a brain researcher (somewhere in California) that the hypothalami of homosexual men were smaller than those of heterosexual men—in fact, were equivalent to those of women. It was perfect for the likes of Rush Limbaugh, who immediately began introducing himself on his daily radio broadcast as "The man with the the world's largest hypothalamus." Of course, the implication was that he was Mr. Super-straight. And that gays were puny, wimpy, and basically no better than women, building upon a traditional male putdown of women.

Along with that soon-discredited theory (hey, there were thousands of gay cadavers around to dissect to verify for sure) came other "scientific" notions that Evangelical Fundamentalists began to glom onto and tout. The great fights with and about science had begun. Of course, the Evangelical Protestant Christians (and Catholics as well) had always had an uneasy relationship with science, as it so often disputed the Biblical account of just about everything from the Genesis flood to Joshua commanding the sun to stand still. But they would grab anything that even marginally adjudicated their pre-conceived ideas and prejudices about gay persons. Of course, I thought to myself, if such a theory were to be true then it would only further the claim that one is born gay. If any guy was simply born with a female-sized hypothalamus, he would turn out gay no matter what; and it was not a choice at all—like we were saying all along. Can't have that! After all, we all know gayness is "caused" by an *overbearing* mother (like mine) and a *distant* father (like mine). LOL.

But that never came up. I heard many a preacher of the day claim from their electronic pulpit: "See! Even science proves that fags are different, deformed, and inferior. They are like women. Gotta hate 'em!" And they did—and they still do. But the cat was out of the bag, and the conflict between Fundamentalist religion and science was moved to the front burner, where it remains to this day.

I was totally aware of the uneasy truce between scientific thought and religion from the time I first opted to accept Christ on faith and just kind of ignore science when a conflict arose. It worked for years. I just didn't pay much attention to developments in the field, as I was more interested in religion and fulfilling my mission to go into all the world and preach the Gospel to every creature. Now science was coming up front and center in my personal life as the religious around and about me were making a big deal out of it. I never believed the Biblical creation story, and so I quietly said nothing, just like most thoughtful, educated Christians whom I knew. We never discussed science much, except for the occasional "Isn't that something?" when we heard of some new advance like cloning or stem cell research.

Those were too vexing for the brains of most of my ministerial and missionary friends and colleagues, so we exercised the theology of ignorance ... and ignored them.

Unfortunately, most of the televangelists and others with a microphone and a camera were not so thoughtful and discrete. They began making pronouncements about science that they never should have. Of course, having been around those types a lot back in China days, I knew that they just couldn't keep their mouths shut. They just had to blab. It's their nature. Evolution had been torturing Christians since way before the Monkey Trial in 1926. The "theory" of evolution, as the TV preachers constantly called it, was absolutely false and unproven. Unproven perhaps—at least on an intellectual level—but, as usual, preachers who make such grandiose claims are not particularly intellectual in nature anyway—are they?

It was back at this time that the age of the Earth was beginning to be a topic of debate. In order for there to be myriad plant and animal species, they would have all had to be created simultaneously by God on day four of the creation process. As I watched brain-dead preachers on television discuss scientific topics way above their pay grades, I realized that such men and women had been dishing out this crap to their congregations for years, but that the difference now was that their bullshit was coming into the living rooms of everybody else nationwide at this point, and their stupidity was manifested more profoundly than ever before. It really depressed me. As I watched beautiful, talented, and sensitive gay men around me dying in droves, I heard in the background the drone of loveless Christian preachers and pundits filling my ears with their hate and ignorance. How could I have ever bought into that? I kept asking myself.

Another Christian travesty began rearing its ugly head around this time as well. It was a further example of the growing power of the Religious Right to insert themselves into areas that they should not, and to exert political pressure in areas that are totally antithetical to their Christ-given assignment—to reach the world with the Gospel message. I wrote a lengthy article for a religious publication at the time entitled *The Narrow Way*. It created a stir. Nowadays we might call it a "backlash." Christians had become so powerful since they had gotten out of the Evangelism business and into the political power biz, that they began forcing their judgments into every corner of the lives of the very people they were commanded to reach. I just never have been able to get over how completely they had abandoned their mission. They had traded it in for political and social *clout!* They had become bullies (just like Jesus). I was appalled.

I lay night after night in my room, looking out and staring contentedly at the Golden Gate Bridge—its red lights flashing regularly in the fog— and listening to Christian media ranting and railing about all manner of contemporary issues. I challenged myself to try to actually find a program that was directed toward the unsaved, endeavoring to preach the simple Gospel to the lost and perishing. I failed. All religious programming had become hostile and downright mean. It had become a crusade. America is dying; it is a pit of sin (all caused by the fags, of course). America must be saved. And if we don't do something about it, God is going to blow the place up (like he did back in Sodom). Damn those sodomites. Damn them. The message was unrelenting.

But right behind the fags and the liberals was another group that was particularly despised by the Religious Right monsters: the scientists. This notion of evolution had stuck in the collective craw of Fundamentalists ever since Darwin first proposed the theory way back in 1859. They just never took to it at all. And with their newfound power, strength, and clout, they set out to beat it to death. Actually, I always figured that they had a case to at least argue for the *possibility* of divine creation of some kind, but they never argued it in any convincing way. They simply attacked anybody who figured that maybe the universe came into existence in some manner other than the six-days-of-Genesis myth. The term "intelligent design" had been born. Way cooler and easier to sell than "creationism" or the later version, "creation science," intelligent design was repackaged as a logical alternative to the big bang and the evolution of species.

The design points to a designer! Wow, what a slogan—what a tagline! What great sermons could have been preached to the unsaved with that line as a jump-off. But did I ever hear that once on wee-hours Christian TV? No—not once. I heard a lot of screaming and yelling about scientists as "agents of the devil" and that the faggots were actually behind it all anyway. That great line alone (and a good "Jesus saves" sermon) could have won millions, sparing them from sure eternal torture in the Christian lake of fire. And, like China, even in the U.S., millions of souls were dying without Christ yearly, monthly, and daily. Yet here the Bible-believing TV watchers in their masses sent their money in to the televangelists to give them more hate and fear and loathing addressed to themselves, no concern addressed to the lost.

I saw this coming way back in Kabanatuan when I recognized the Evangelistic possibilities of Christian television for the first time. "Wow," I had thought, "look at how many souls they can reach by this means." But all I heard coming out of my 19-inch Sony Trinotron was more screaming, shouting, and condemnation. When will they ever learn? I guess they never will.

Anyway, intelligent design was rapidly being lapped up by the vast church audience (many of whom decided that going to church was unnecessary or passé anyway, as now they could simply attend church in their pajamas or sweatpants instead of driving to some building with a leaky roof and a bum furnace.)

And so many of those churches were falling apart due to the fact that their congregations were sending their tithes and offerings in to the TV preachers and "teachers" instead of paying their pastor a decent salary and maintaining their church facilities properly. Yet, I surmised that those same fairweather parishioners would expect a personal visit and a prayer from their pastor when they found themselves in the local hospital with a burst appendix or a gallstone. But they all loved intelligent design. After all, they were all so intelligent themselves . . . LOL.

Of Pandas and People was a little book that caused a great deal of trouble in the decades following its release while I was living in San Francisco. I bought a copy and read it while watching a friend with AIDS sleep quietly in his private hospital room with those oxygen tubes up his nose. He slept . . . I read.

The book was genuinely stupid, written from a narrow Christian perspective. It was a total waste of time in my opinion. It twisted itself in knots trying to disprove Darwin. I just shook my head. "Why is this important?" I asked myself: "What are these people trying to do here? What about preaching the Gospel?" All this time and energy they were expending to disprove a scientific proposition that was already generally accepted worldwide seemed like lunacy. Of course, I was not surprised or shocked at this gross misuse of time and effort running after something that Jesus never charged them to do in the first place. The Great Commission, to which I had so closely adhered for years, was abundantly clear. Go preach, convince, win souls, and live your life as an example. How hard is that? Christ never commanded his followers to disprove anything—especially some nineteenth century Englishman's theories about birds, lizards, and small rodents. The creation story had been fixed in place way back when and every Fundamentalist claimed to believe it word for word. So why waste so much energy trying to get into the ring with the entire scientific community? Well, the Fundamentalists' problem was the same one I had encountered so frequently. Their late-20th Century brains were struggling to maintain Iron Age ideas, notions, and societal structures—like those little humpbacked bridges. Modern science and philosophy were overwhelming them, so this was their way to lash back.

It was during those gray days in San Francisco that I began genuinely feeling sorry for the Fightin' Fundies. Like wild animals with their backs to the wall, they were becoming really scary. Their rhetoric on TV became increasingly hostile and shrill. Even their voices seem to go up in pitch. They were trapped by their own theology, and were pissed that the world out there was (in their eyes) dissing them.

This was the first time that I caught whiff of a new Evangelical attitude and notion . . . they were being "persecuted." I began hearing this refrain on Christian media. At first it was a kind of "poor us" wah wah kind of whimper. Everybody is picking on the Christians. We are so put-upon.

I have to admit that in some ways they had brought it on themselves with their ham-handed approach to so many contemporary issues (like abortion, evolution, and AIDS). They were so "out there" that everybody with a TV set sooner or later ran across some of their genuine stupidity. And late night comics had a field day. I had learned years earlier that— like the Communist Party of the PRC and my dad—to their own peril, people who take themselves too seriously simply cannot laugh at themselves. They were as humorless and dour as their Puritan forefathers back in Salem. Life was no joke, and their religion was no laughing matter. Gawd, how they hated being laughed at. They took it way too personally. When I had mocked Brother William back in Virginia City, he had reacted with rage. Now the televangelists were doing likewise, but on a national stage. They looked stupid. Well, I guess that is because that is just what they were—stupid.

As I watched the Evangelical movement grow and drift ever further away from their original central message (given by Christ himself), the more it morphed into something really hideous. It was no longer a religion of "love," but of hate. *God Hates Fags* appeared at that time— a slogan that was oh so fitting to the mindset of what the Jesus Movement of the early 1970s had become . . . a big ugly monster.

* * * * *

My time in SF ended rather abruptly. My phone rang late in the evening around eleven. It was Mom. Dad was in the hospital. He had collapsed or fainted or something. She was unsure, but wanted to get in touch right away. I flew up to Portland in the morning. We had gotten together some years earlier and formed a family trust, which I needed to come up and deal with right away. Mom confided that the whole situation had stressed him out to the point of creating a health issue. I'll say. He recovered and was sent home with strict instructions (which he ignored like usual). What do those damned doctors know anyway? Yeah, sure.

We had been landlords for years already, renting our property out to real professional agricultural corporations. Despite his dream of being the hands-on family farm owner—out driving his tractor and tilling the soil—age had caught up with him, and he had grown increasingly reclusive and bitter. All he wanted to be was rich. He took to playing the stock market. He had always preached to me that the market was "no different than playing the ponies." I had always disdained that notion, preferring to be more careful and contemplative in my investing. But he was bored. Mom laid out the whole situation to me on that visit and we ganged up on dad, insisting that we put together a family trust into which we placed all the family property, including 250,000 dollars from my Hong Kong tractor and equipment sales in China that had been sitting quietly in Switzerland for years earning interest. So I saved the day. LOL. Yay for Tom! :-)

But it was abundantly clear that I was going to have to leave San Fran and head "home" to take over the family agribiz. I was not worried or freaked. I realized that I would not have to do farm work or get my hands in the dirt. My hands had been plenty dirty over the years, but that was with ink or paint, which I didn't mind at all. I was going to have to be the administrator of the trust, and I walked into the task with eyes open. Piece of cake. I had learned a lot in the card business that translated well into just about any kind of similar economic endeavor. I hired Mayflower and didn't see my furniture and drawing table again until everything was delivered to my new digs on the 25th floor of a block of flats in Portland—walking distance from Portland State University. How full circle was that?

NO ON 9!

The OCA will get ya if you're gay!

But even if you're not . . . beware! They'll get you anyway! That was a clever little ditty that arose out of probably the biggest political battle in Oregon history as far as I or anybody alive could remember. It was an epic struggle between evil Fundamentalist Christianity parading as "morality," and secularism which was being represented by the gay movement—characterized as, of course, the "invading gay agenda." And it took place in Oregon. Oregon! Not Texas, Alabama, or South Carolina—where one could expect or predict such bull-snot—but open-minded, liberal Oregon . . . my home state and such a livable place at that. I came back to begin caregiving for my dad, and was sucked into the maelstrom of antigay politics unlike anything I had ever experienced before. Anything.

The tussles and tangles with the likes of Brother William down in Virginia City were child's play compared to the bubbling cauldron of venom and toxic bilge from the Oregon Citizen's Alliance (OCA). It was a Right-wing group that had relocated from California, setting up shop in the Pacific Northwest as a political/religious movement to counter the (as they saw it) growing homosexual advance on the whole of American society. They preached a doctrine of hate and bigotry as vile as anything I had ever read about happening in the Deep South. I was appalled. Before I even returned to the state, I had read of the group in the San Francisco newspapers and heard of them on the tube. I immediately got in touch with the key players on the gay side of the issue, and volunteered my time, energy, and writing/ graphics skills.

I felt that I had been called for such a time as this! (As in Isaiah :-) I was ready for the fight, and was it ever killer! Fighting with the fossils in Virginia City was actually kind of fun, as they were so genuinely stupid and intolerant (and pissed that the fags had bought the *Territorial Enterprise*). But these people of the OCA were political and had actually taken advantage of the state's initiative feature in the constitution, collecting enough signatures to put a measure on the ballot restricting every aspect of the rights of gay people that they could.

I remember learning about the initiative process while studying Oregon history in seventh and eighth grade at Willamette Grade School in West Linn back in the early 1960s. Actually, I had always considered it cool that Oregon had been the first state in the Union to come up with a plan whereby private citizens—no matter who they were—could vote on any idea or concept that they could collect enough signatures to sponsor. It was originally designed as a way to prevent state legislators from simply making laws of their own liking (or more likely, laws tailored for the lumber industry or other powerful interests in the state). Many other states had adopted the initiative process over the years as well, but now it had come back to bite. It was now being abused by the Christofascists—the Fundimonsters—the haters. And by god, did they hate fags—and their little dogs too!

The chairman of the OCA was a moonfaced, balding, pudgy, middle-aged guy from Fresno or some similar place, who featured himself as a kind of messiah, or prophet, or some other such religious leader type. His name was Lon Mabon, and even to this day his name makes my blood run cold. He hated gays with a kind of psychopathic hatred. Homosexuality, to his mind, was abnormal, wrong, unnatural, and perverse. And the OCA had actually done some legerdemain in the wording so that in addition to the terms sexual orientation and sexual preference there were included those other gay-related traits that we all know about—namely pedophilia and sadomasochism. I considered it brilliant, if not straight from the deep limbic system of a tortured brain. By associating being gay with other widely considered antisocial behaviors, they had managed to paint us all with the same brush. We were all perverse, evil, immoral, and everything else they could think of to demonize us.

I was furious with the wording myself as it just assumed that this was all one category. Being gay was tantamount to being a child molester, sadistic monster, masochistic evildoer, and an anti-religious Communist (and any other negative thing that they could think of). Anyway, it stuck and colored the campaign that followed. Obviously, nobody could get behind outrageous—if not dangerous and illegal behavior —especially in the schools. Clever, huh? It was couched as "protecting our children" from the evil ones. It was oh so Christian! I could just feel the love of Christ exuding and extruding from their very saved and righteous souls. . . saving the very Christian world from Satan and his minions, the fags. The wording was so severe that it had to be fixed here and there in legislative committees down in Salem before it could even be put on the ballot and printed.

I was amazed that I was not the only one (nor homosexuals as a group) that saw how unfair this was. Straight people began coming out of the woodwork to join the NO on 9 campaign. Part of the OCA strategy had been to place as its primary goal to change the state constitution. That is not so easy to do. I still could remember back to 1975 when I was living in Manila and reading about the Equal Rights Amendment, which would have guaranteed equal rights for women. It never passed! There is something sacred about constitutions, and since most state constitutions are modeled after the U.S. matrix (which was dictated directly to James Madison by Almighty God himself), changing them has not ever been simple. Most Oregonians began to see this operation as kind of like tweaking the Bill of Rights or the Holy Bible itself. It was a messy operation—like making sausage. And we all went through the meat grinder.

* * * * *

During this time, I had moved in with two roommates, Dick and Harry. I know . . . Tom, Dick, and Harry. We even used that line on our shared home answering machine. Actually, we had all been in search of housing when we put our heads together, figuring out that it would be cheaper for us to get a three-bedroom apartment and share all the costs than for us to live separately. And since we all worked at separate jobs with different hours, we never ran over each other in the kitchen or dining room. It worked swimmingly. Harry worked for Orkin, the national pesticide company. He was a horticulturist and did all the work on the three balconies in our 25th floor apartment in downtown Portland. He created a garden in the sky. Dick (aka Rick) worked as a computer operator of some kind for a large oil company. I had used the proceeds of the sale of the greeting card company in Nevada to purchase a large art gallery in town. It was soon to become a kind of epicenter for the fight against the OCA and Measure 9. Neither of the two roommates were political, but both kept up with the news.

I became increasingly wrapped up in the day-to-day planning and strategizing, as well as in doing speaking gigs around the state for the No *on 9* campaign. My abilities as a public speaker from my preacher days stood me in good stead. I was still in contact with a large number of churches, pastors, and congregations who had heard of my "demise" (their word). Oddly enough, the only genuinely hateful mail that I received at the time came from total unknowns. Everyone who knew me—and either heard me speak on the radio, TV, or in person—was overtly kind to me. Since the source of the Measure 9 campaign was the Fundamentalist churches, I took a great deal of the responsibility to not only interact with them, but to liaise with them and the "faith community" at large. I subordinated my lack of faith and dusted off my Christian vocabulary to communicate with them. In fact, I even became active in an organization called *People of Faith Against Bigotry* (PFAB). They were doing a lot of good in general, and I just blended in, making common cause. I was pleased to find so many really true Christians in their midst. HOGGING THE SPOTLIGHT. And while I was never tempted to flirt with a return to Christianity, I realized that not all Christians are Fundamentalists. The latter just make the most noise.

I was kind of surprised one evening at an ACLU fundraiser in the East Portland home of a gay activist couple, when I found myself sitting next to a female minister wearing a clerical collar. Our denomination would never ever wear such a thing. It simply was not done. I do recall once, however, in the Philippines thinking that such a practice might really open some doors for Teen Challenge. But I just let that slide. The friendly lesbian pastor of a UCC (United Church of Christ) church struck up a conversation with me over some rather good hors d'oeuvres.

When I came out to her as a former clergyman, she dug right in to find out more. I had been so reluctant since leaving the ministry to ever even mention my background—even to most colleagues that I had worked with in the paper products industry and, later, the art gallery biz. I was ashamed and embarrassed of my background and my former associations. But she wanted to know what my church background was—a simple enough question. She was curious. Finally after much hemming and hawing, she dragged it out of me. The Assemblies of God, I peeped, hoping nobody else would hear.

"Oh," she said in a tone I could not quite determine, "I was raised in the Foursquare" (an equally—if not more radical Pentecostal church organization). Of course, then I was intrigued. "Wow," I exclaimed sotto voce to her, "I sure know all about those folks." The biggest Foursquare church in Portland was the primary driver behind measure 9. We didn't have to go into that, as we were obviously both here for the same reasons. But then she floored me with what she said next. "Why don't you just transfer your papers to the UCC?" she asked matter-of-factly. "We would accept them." Dumbfounded at the very notion, I quickly clarified: "But I'm an atheist!" To which she replied unflappably, "So what? What one believes or does not believe in his own life is not our church's primary focus. *What are you doing for your fellow man?* That's the key." Game, set, match. We became friends after that. But I never served as a UCC minister. Obviously. But you have to admit it is kind of funny in a weird sort of way.

Scott Lively was a regular attendee at the big Foursquare church near Sandy Boulevard in the "Close-in East Side" neighborhood of Portland. If there could be someone sicker and more fanatically antigay than Lon Mabon, it would have to be Scott. He was often called a soulless lizard by many in the gay community, as it was claimed that if you watched him intently on television, he never blinked his eyes. I checked that out. It wasn't true. He did blink once or twice, but his stare of death was frightening. We took to calling him Scott Deadly. He and Mabon made a magnificent couple, and I could see how their lives, dripping with hate, could appeal to a certain mentality of Christians whom I had met during my years in the legitimate ministry. They liked to refer to themselves as "pastors" and "missionaries" though they had no theological training or any ordaining institution behind them. They were just freelancers, charlatans, and fakes like Marjoe and, of course, dear Brother William back in VC. But they had a unique ability to wreck lives around them wherever they went.

I am not sure which of the two was the better mobster, but they managed to wring tens of thousands of dollars out of gullible Fundies during their reign of terror in Oregon during that unlucky time. They took up living in the freeway-side community of Wilsonville (not too far from West Linn) where I grew up. They managed to incorporate the Oregon Citizens Alliance with themselves as its head. I often referred to them as the head rip-off artists, because at board meetings they managed to vote for nice fat salaries for themselves (and the same for their spouses and other family members). As is usual in phony, contrived ministries like theirs, they bought themselves homes far nicer than those of the saps that gave them money to facilitate their bigotry. I raised a lot of money in my day, but never took a drop. Independent ministries like theirs always manage to get in trouble with the law or the IRS or both. They chose both. But that came later. At the time, they were confining their chicanery to the unfortunate state of Oregon.

They didn't actually get "called" to overseas ministry in Africa until they had (so I hear tell) done jail time for tax evasion and fraud. Maybe it was contempt of court, but once they had been trounced by us at the ballot box in 1992, they had lost some of their appeal to the stooge donors in places like Canby, Junction City, and Klamath Falls. Once they failed in front of everybody in the statewide election, they regrouped and tried a watered-down version in various small communities where there were a lot of rednecks. I know, since I had preached in over 200 Christian churches in Oregon myself and learned my way around the bigots.

As an aside, I might mention that they did try the whole extravaganza again a few years later with the similar (if wimpier) measure 13. It failed by a wider margin. Of course, when people like that lose they always blame others and not themselves. And there is always that ancient foe, the Devil—and his devotees, the dreaded homosexuals worshiping at his hoofed feet—to blame. Next time they would have to pray harder. Of course, they claimed that they were doing it all for the children—those innocents who so easily fell under the enchanting spells of gay teachers. And, they continually pointed out, none of this would have happened if "they" had not taken prayer out of the public schools. Actually, "they" (the Supreme Court of the United States) did not take prayer out of the public schools; they ruled in 1962 that state-sponsored or required prayers were unconstitutional. But, as usual, the Fundies wanted to coerce small children to pray (to their god and Jesus of course). As usual, they were spittin' mad and ready for a fight. The "Fightin' Fundies—gotta love 'em. LOL.

* * * * *

I don't know about school prayer in places where the OCA leadership may have gone to school, but I guarantee that we had no such thing in the Oregon public schools that I attended from first grade on. We did say the pledge of allegiance (including the additional phrase "under God," which was not part of the original pledge, but was added in 1956 during the Cold War). It never much bothered me, nor my folks. It was harmless enough, I guess. But the subject of school prayer had stirred up a hornet's nest nationwide back then.

Since the Pacific Northwest had apparently not been hit by the fanatical tornado that was wreaking havoc on the Bible Belt during my childhood, it was not until I was in the military that I was exposed to friends and colleagues—fellow soldiers, that is—who had been raised on mandatory school prayer in their public school systems. I had never heard of such a thing, but as a rip-roaring Fundamentalist at the time, I thought it was a great idea. Thinking back to both grade and high school, I felt that a good dose of "old time religion" might have slapped some sense into the "juvenile delinquents" and bullies.

But most of those who had been required to bow the knee to the blond Aryan Jesus were not so enthused. I had a black friend who was a photo lab tech in Frankfurt. Although I had been assigned to the "Visual Aids" (graphics) section of Document Services, because I had a photo MOS from Viet Nam, I could always fill in at the photo lab in a pinch. One day I was helping out John Fordham, a black guy from somewhere in Texas. As usual, the lab was way behind. During runs of multiple rolls of film, there are long periods of nothingness punctuated by rapid activity—changing chemicals and the like. I asked John about what it was like growing up as a black kid in Texas of the 1950s, the golden age of *Leave it to Beaver* and *Father Knows Best*.

"It was the shits," he replied to my query. "We were always looking out for trouble. Just walking on the streets or going to a park to play ball could turn ugly . . . and it did a lot. You had to learn to fight." So I had come around to my mission—to witness to him like I had so often done in such times in military photo darkrooms. He was not hostile to me personally since he knew me well as a coworker. But his memories of school and, most of all, mandatory Bible reading had left him bitter. His family was Catholic and although they had attended mass on a regular basis, the teachers and principal in his district were Baptists. Oh, I figured . . . I could see the problem: He was still pissed off about having to read daily from the "Protestant" King James Version of the Bible, and having to stand and bow his head at school functions (led by Protestant clergymen)—even at ball games!

I had little experience with ball games, as my time in school was spent studying. But in Texas, high school football (and basketball to a lesser degree) was an almost religious experience. People took the game very seriously and, by god, if you didn't bow your head and play along, you might just get your "ass kicked" by some white Baptist kids behind the bleachers after the game. "We had to just learn to keep in our place," he lamented. I had never been tuned into such issues in my young life. I think back to that day with John in the photo lab and wonder how he is dealing with current similar situations these days.

The approach of requiring people to comply with the dominant religious force in a certain time and place was becoming more and more apparent to me. I had always read about the dictatorship by the Roman Catholic Church during the "Dark Ages" and of the various inquisitions. But I was hearing from the OCA and those quarters of similar contemporary "tests" for religious purity. The school system, they reasoned, had been infiltrated by the gays as part of the larger "gay agenda," and there should be some sort of interview system put in place to ferret out undesirable teachers.

This topic was debated a lot back then, and one of my really dear gay friends who was a first grade teacher was a prime target. I was often called upon to engage in these types of debates. Because they were most often sponsored by the Religious Right, they needed a voice on the "opposing side" to make for a real debate—which they were not. But I did enjoy the fight, and as with dear Brother William, I attended a lot of "town hall" style meetings around the state at the time, as the "bad guy." I was hissed and booed at a lot by loving Christians. But I must have grown accustomed to it, as I could get in my digs (due to my religious training and background).

* * * * *

I was at a town meeting in a Central Oregon city where I had preached years earlier. The crowd was hostile from the get-go. By then I was learning how to handle the slings and arrows of the "Christians" who always showed up for such events. These meetings were usually held on an "off night" like Monday or Tuesday so as not to conflict with church services, Bible studies, or football games. The topic of the meeting/debate was: "Should gay teachers be allowed to teach our children?" Even couching the topic in such a way was stacking the deck, but I expected that. I would have posed the question like: "Should all gay teachers be fired?" Anyway, we went round after round as usual and everybody was screaming—just like on the *Jerry Springer Show*. As I looked out over the crowd of over a hundred angry faces contorted by hate and shrieking at the top of their lungs, I tried to envision them the previous Sunday evening shouting and praising their god with hands lifted toward Heaven. It was a way I had learned to cope with such venom and bile. Deep down inside those black, ugly, Christian hearts was an inner Jesus just needing to come out. But they rarely could get over their prejudices to let him shine through.

Anyway, that particular evening, things turned out as normal. No one was converted to a different point of view. Everybody went home just as angry and frustrated as when they arrived—only even more so. As I was walking to my car in the dark parking lot, a disembodied voice came out of the darkness: "Brother Muzzio!" It was the pastor of a church across town that I had preached at some years earlier. He came up to me and offered to shake my hand. "I still remember," he began, "when you preached about China and your concern for the lost in Asia a couple of years ago." His tone was even and I could not guess where he was going with that. I had no reason to be aggressive or negative. "You really spoke to my congregation. God really spoke through you in a powerful and wonderful way." His vocabulary began to become Evangelical, but after several years and a lot of grief, I had not forgotten the lingo, nor did I need an interpreter.

Actually, for years I had dreaded a meeting such as this with someone from my past—a former fellow clergyman, a pastor of a church that I had preached in and received an honorarium from. Such honorariums were referred to as "love offerings." And they were kind of different from offerings specifically designated for our ministry only. These were indeed love offerings, as they could be put into our personal account for us to use for stuff like buying food, clothes, rent, gasoline, and other necessities.

Eventually his voice took on a kind of somber, almost sad tone. He told me that he did not agree with most of the people (the screamers) in the room that night. He did not hate gay people; nor did he hate me. He had what I would call a mature Christian theology. He knew that we are "all sinners saved by grace" and that no one sin is any worse than another. Gay sexual sin is no different than any other, such as gossip, backbiting, or gluttony. He knew that sin is a "condition"—a place we are all in due to the fallen nature of mankind. I was with him.

BTW, this idea of calling gay sex a "sin" is very Catholic. Every Protestant who has ever warmed a church pew or graduated from seminary (or Bible school) knows that Catholics have a notion that each individual act in itself is or is not a sin. But over the years Protestants have systematically slid into this doctrine, as it is way more effective in arguing with people you don't like, or people who are sinning in a way that particularly offends you. All fags are going straight to Hell had become the battle cry of the Religious Right for years. That is not good theology, as the Bible clearly states that everybody is destined for Hell—everybody, regardless of whether they are gay or not. The only escape from damnation is salvation through Christ. Deep down they all know that, but their hatred for gaydom and particularly male-to-male homosexuality is so compelling that they have to become pseudo-Catholics to emphasize how the "sin of Sodom" is somehow worse than all other sins.

"My congregation is full of people like those who were here tonight. They really are being so un-Christ-like." Then he said something from his heart that touched me . . . "In so many ways I have failed as a pastor. I have failed to teach them better." I almost wanted to give him a hug. He was obviously in pain . . . some kind of internal struggle. Then he said it: "My son is gay." I remained silent. Waiting . . . "I love him so much, and have loved him with all my heart from the day I brought him home from the hospital." I thought of my straight son, Vincent. I loved him in that way, so I related to what he was saying. He went on . . .

"He was daddy's boy from the very beginning. He and I did everything together. We played catch, we went fishing. And he especially loved our father-son campouts in our own special spot over near the Metolius River. Then a few months ago he came out to me. He told me that he was gay and that he had always been. I never knew nor suspected." I realized that using words like "gay" or "come out" was hard for him. After all, he was the pastor of a church full of people (his flock) who would crucify his son if they knew his secret.

He didn't have to ask, but I knew that he wanted to talk to somebody who might understand. I was obviously that guy, standing there in the cold dark parking lot that night. He was sort of asking *What should I do?* Without coming right out with it. He was a man in pain. Kind of like the pain that gay people feel when they are rejected by their families. It hurts.

So I asked him the logical question: "Is he still a Christian?" Of course, that was the main worry that a Christian parent would have. *Is my dearest boy going to hell?* Obviously, he had been thinking about these issues a lot. I felt genuinely sorry for him. "Yes, he loves the Lord as much as ever," he said with a kind of tone of relief. "But I know the congregation will never accept him, and may fire me if I stand up for him." I flashed on that movie, *Sophie's Choice*, where a mother had to choose between her two children. Save one and let the other be swept away, forever gone. He was staring at a choice between his son and his calling—his congregation—whom he had dedicated his life to serving and leading as their pastor.

I drove away from our meeting in quiet despair. Why did he have to face such a choice? Why can't Christian people act more like Jesus? Why are they so mean, cruel, and unconcerned? I felt so sorry for the pastor as we shook hands and parted. I gave him my address and phone number (this was before email) and told him that I was open to dialogue with him or his son any time, but that I had lost my faith and could not be counted on to do any "Christian-style counseling." He was cool with that. But I already knew that he was not going to abandon his son whom he loved so much.

About halfway back to Portland I noticed a funny light shining into my rear view mirror on that empty road leading back to "civilization." I stopped to observe a big, round, white, paper-mâché moon coming up in the east. I so wished that I could still believe. I wanted to pray. So I did anyway . . . in my own way.

Why are Christian people so dense? Why can't they see that they are the Pharisees who Jesus called out constantly to stop being so evil, judgmental, and mean-spirited? Where is the love of Christ that is "shed abroad" in our hearts? Where? I still don't know. But I did find out some months later that his son had finished high school, left town without a scene, and was now attending a "liberal" seminary back East. His dad was so proud of him. And I rejoiced . . . (in my own way).

LIFE AND DEATH WITH DIGNITY

The sky is falling . . . The sky is falling

Abortion. One of the epic struggles of the last fifty years—and I don't really have a dog in the fight. I have never felt the need for such a procedure personally, as most gay men don't. Lesbians have to work to get pregnant, so I doubt that many of them feel particularly passionate about it one way or the other either. But I do have an opinion and strong feelings about it, because many straight couples feel the need to support gays in our ongoing struggle for marriage equality. It is a matter of human rights, and I am on the side of those whose rights are being threatened.

I was only marginally aware of the struggles to legalize the procedure in the first place back in the 1960s. I was too self-absorbed; getting out of high school early and into college where I took as many courses as possible to avoid tangling with my dad; and I was getting saved. That was a lot on my plate. But I was aware of the anti-Vietnam-war protests and certain other political movements of the time. My sister dropped out of high school and disappeared for like twenty-five years into the "drug culture," and I wrapped up the decade in a combat zone (the kind with rockets, mortars, and land mines). So abortion was really kind of low on the radar screen when things were first formulating. To me the struggle appeared to be a Catholic deal . . . and as you know, Catholics were just hell-bound sinners to me by the time I even heard of Roe v. Wade in 1973.

My first serious encounters with Catholics were in Europe during the Jesus Movement and its spawn, called the "Charismatic Catholic" experience, when RC folks (particularly in Southern Germany) were singing, clapping, and praising God in a most Pentecostal style. And they spoke in tongues! OMG! I was very conflicted about my attitude toward the Church at the time. Part of me wanted to embrace these seekers—these wandering sheep (almost in God's fold, but not quite). That was rather quickly pounded out of me during my trips to Northern

Ireland where the chasm between the Protestants (the Orange) and the Catholics (the Greens) was intense to the point of open warfare in which people were shot in the streets every day and night. No talk of abortion there, for sure.

Then the Philippines and alive in the Catholic sea! My work with some sweet nuns in the Vietnamese refugee camps there had melted my hard Protestant heart anew, and I genuinely enjoyed working with crossover Catholics in the Teen Challenge ministry too, as we were all united in the fight against drug addiction and the crime that grew out of that misery. But then came my first skirmishes with the antigay bishops, pastors, and priests. My attitude was changing again. I began to see the growing abortion struggle as akin to the gay struggles into which I had plunged myself by merely coming out. I began seeing the antiabortion priests and bishops (and the Pope) as true personal enemies, so I paid more attention to what the "reproductive rights" struggle was all about.

My fights with the Roman church and its clergy were infrequent, as I had my hands full with the likes of the Brother-William-type, hardcore Protestant haters, and caring for and ministering to the real lost and dying during the AIDS crisis, which was by no means over even though there were hopeful signs and more and more friends were living longer all the time. But I began seeing antigay Catholic priests, bishops, and writers appearing on the *700 Club* and other religious media outlets. Arm in arm, embracing dear ol' Pat, arose a new crop of televangelists and a new cesspool of bad ideas—FOX News. Now these most unlikely allies were forced to team up against the united satanic forces of the "rabid feminists" and the "gay agenda" at the same time. OMG, for that alone, come soon Jesus!

My involvement still wasn't personal when I first saw that famous anti-abortion commercial on TV. It was a classic with far-reaching impact on the whole movement. It had been created by the son of my old favorite Christian philosopher and teacher, Dr. Schaeffer. I had met Frank Shaeffer Jr. in Switzerland when he was still in boarding school and I was in the U.S. Army in Augsburg. We were   only a few years apart in age. I thought of him as kind of a hippy-type, young guy who had grown up in a super-advantaged Christian home, but who was squandering his aces on riotous living and rebellion. I was kind of judgmental back then, huh?

He was on leave from school, and we didn't connect on any level. If I had met him in a different environment, I might have tried to "witness" to him, trying to bring him back to a more meaningful "walk with the Lord." Such a Pharisee I was . . . at the time. I am sure his good parents did worry about him, but in the end, he had come back into a rather good symbiotic relationship with his father and his dad's world-famous ministry. His dad had gotten involved in the anti-abortion fray, and Frank Jr. had followed. Apparently, they were a very well-coordinated and simpatico kind of team. If the anti-abortion ad was any indication of this, they must have been formidable. But the ad in question was Frank's "baby" all the way. Of course, having his father's wide range of contacts didn't hurt.

The first time I saw it on the tube I was in Virginia City. I was totally wowed. The Surgeon General of the United States, Dr. C. Everett Coop, was standing in what looked like the Bonneville Salt Flats in Utah. Surrounding him was a sea of plastic dolls symbolizing aborted human beings (fetuses)—babies, children, lives lost forever, never having had a chance to live, grow up, and thrive (and accept Christ). It was killer. Even I was moved.

But even on the very first viewing I noticed something wrong with the ad. I considered it dishonest and deceptive. Why? Because all of the dolls were *white!* I was well aware—even then—that approximately seventy-five percent of all abortion procedures in the U.S. are conducted on young, unwed black women! The ad had kick-started a national surge against abortion in general, and an appeal to begin the process to undo Roe v. Wade and make all abortions of any kind illegal. All abortions. I had never thought that they could pull such a thing off up to this point, as a very high percentage of the American populous favored a woman's right to choose. But after that ad I was not too sure.

Some years later when Frank had renounced his Fundamentalist life and deeds (much as I had done), I contacted him by email about the doll ad. He was genuinely shocked and said that he had never considered the *racial* component before I brought it up. I believed him (still do). He hadn't considered that seeing a sea of *white* dolls (snowflake babies) speaks a certain message to the congregation at Dallas First Baptist and Tulsa First Assembly of God that a sea of mostly black or brown dolls would not.

He saw my point. I had learned years earlier that down inside most Fundamentalist Evangelical Christians is a secret racist, like that guy from North Carolina in the Doc Services Department in Frankfurt who professed his Christian faith but trashed and made sport of John Fordham, the black photo lab tech, behind his back. The abortion issue had grown into a kind of "whites only" issue. I had come upon plenty of antiabortion literature by that time in the mid-1980s. They were put around everywhere by well-meaning Christians who saw themselves as saviors of the unborn. And the vivid images of aborted fetuses were always always always white. Those poor little white embryos—never getting a chance at life, liberty, and the pursuit of happiness and accepting Jesus (and voting Republican :-)

At about that time I had managed to pull out a filling with dental floss and had made an appointment with a dentist down in Reno to get it fixed. While waiting for the appointment a few days hence, I pulled out *another* in the exact same way! "Well, if it isn't the Mad-flosser!" was the dentist's opening line. I guess he couldn't resist. But I laughed. What I did not laugh about, though, were the Jesus posters on the ceiling conspicuously staring down at me—captive—with my mouth wide open and full of cotton packing. His waiting room was awash in anti-abortion propaganda from various "Christian" organizations as well. I took one of each as reference. As a qualified graphic artist and ex-Christian, I always picked up samples of well-done religious brochures of any kind. But the abortion fracas had begun to make me consider the more theological issues involved in such an epic struggle as that which it had morphed into by then.

Why are Christians in general—both Protestant and Catholic—so vehemently opposed to the medical procedure that we call "clinical abortion?" I am still scratching my head, as I have over the years asked that question of my Christian friends (and enemies as well). What's it all about? The reply seems pretty universal . . . "It's murder!" Murder. Killing the unborn by the scraping of the uterine wall is murder pure and simple. "How else can you look at it?" But what is the source of this concern for the killing of unborn embryos—fetuses? Ah, there is where the change has gradually been taking place. "Those are not just embryos or fetuses," the Fundies chant. "They're babies, little people, and human beings. And they deserve life— not death!" Okay, I follow. In fact, I can agree—sort of. But what gets me is that their actual source of such concern always seems to be the same thing . . . the Bible! What?

Hey, I know something about the Bible, and there is no mention of abortion—of zygotes or stem cells or any such thing. The God of the Bible is very arbitrary in his attitude toward all human matters. But, as usual, the 21st Century mind (even a Fundamentalist one) is quite unlike the Iron-Age minds of the Scripture's authors. Even so, I had learned years earlier that one never gains any ground arguing with minds as closed as steel traps. I too had a closed mind once, so I have tried to reach out and have someone—anyone—define for me why a fetus (even if it *is* a potential person) is not better off aborted than born under the curse of Adamic sin. Just being born assures a life of endless misery, toil, and pain—God's curse upon all the living from that moment in the Garden when mankind "fell." And along with that guarantee comes the accompanying assurance of eternal hell and damnation in an eternal lake of fire . . . unless one is spared such doom by accepting Christ.

I have always wondered—since all persons are *born* "in sin" and condemned from the first breath of life to die and fry—what is wrong with sending those sweet little unborns directly to a blissful eternity with God, Christ, and Mother Mary anyway? I include Mother Mary in this question, as it is really something that did not escape the early Catholic scholar's centuries ago. I am not the only guy clever enough to think that if a person is condemned to the furnace at birth, then birth itself is in fact worse than a death sentence. It is guaranteed searing heat, screams, wailing, and gnashing of teeth, pitch forks and the whole lot. So why not forestall that gruesome outcome by simply aborting the fetus—thus sending that precious little soul immediately into the presence of God? . . . Praise his name forever . . . Hallelujah!

Putti. Sounds like the answer to a Jeopardy question, huh? "So, what are Putti?" They are bodiless souls of dead children as perceived by medieval Italian artists. Usually depicted as little heads with wings sprouting out of their ears, these "angelic" little flying creatures adorned the caskets of dead babies, not only in medieval Europe but way earlier in ancient Babylon and Assyria as well. Let's face it, infant mortality has been a gut-wrenching subject for men and women since the dawn of human history. The loss of a child is so grievous and painful to a mother (and father to be sure) that a priest, monk, pastor, or missionary is hard-pressed to explain what happened, what it means, and what the status of the departed little soul is. Believe me, it is not easy to do funerals as a clergyman. It is hard to console anyone for the loss of a loved one; but a child lost in infancy, at birth, or worse, stillborn, calls one's spiritual underpinnings into question no matter what. So how does this relate to abortion?

Well, bless those Catholic scribes, authors, thinkers, and artists; they solved these issues centuries ago. But do people still believe any of it today? Apparently they do. The Bible speaks frequently of cherubim, little putti-like angels floating around the mercy seat of God Almighty. Cool, huh? I can see all those millions of sweet little baby souls fluttering around God and Jesus at his right "hand" like a flock of pigeons :-) Can't you just see it? Doesn't it make you just want to go there as soon as possible? I personally can't wait. "Heaven" is the ultimate Christian reward. It's what the good Christian witness promises to those whom he seeks to convert. "Wow, imagine what Heaven will be like," they breathlessly proclaim. (Hey, and I did it too.)

Heaven, the great reward for an exemplary sinless life (not for fags, of course), is eternity with millions and zillions of itsy-bitsy, teeny-weeny souls buzzing around like flies praising God (in the highest)! That sounds so exciting, I might even consider giving up gay sex for that. Well, maybe not today. When one considers the sheer number of souls of dead infants, along with the stillborn and the unborn, it nearly makes one wet oneself in pure anticipation, huh? Praise God, the Republican Party has taken on the cause of the unborn, who they claim are all "real persons" from conception! Imagine all those zygote and stem cell souls floating around the Throne of the Lamb for all time (and eternity).

Sounds downright microbial! Forget the flies. If one considers the number of fertilized ovum that are detached from the average uterine wall in the bodies of women around the world every day, it is more like an image of krill or even microscopic bacteria. (Pentecostals may sing in tongues at this point!) It is no wonder, given this vision, that God had so little regard for newborns, infants, and toddlers when he commanded Joshua, for example, to slaughter every inhabitant of the city of Jericho when he took it. (Remember when the walls came tumblin' down?) Yahweh specifically mentions killing "infants." Of course, a quick reread of Joshua chapter six will confirm that all the "sinful" animals were to be wiped out as well. Gotta love it.

I had an experience of a personal nature with this subject during the two years between the OCA failed Measure 9 fiasco and the "Son of 9," or the equally tragic Measure 13. My roommate Dick had a delightful friend named Heather. She was often over to our flat for dinner or a game of Scrabble. One day she called and asked to come over, as she had a big favor to request of us. She wanted to seek an abortion at a clinic in Northwest Portland and asked if we would accompany her, as she would have to run the "gauntlet of hate" (meaning the toxic Christians waiting outside the clinic who would be seeking to stop her). We agreed, and on the appointed morning, right at 11:00 as planned, we sought entry to the building.

On that day there were only about five devoted campers who were sitting or pacing on the sidewalk a certain distance from the door. One old geezer in his lawn chair had a sign reading: "Please don't kill your baby. Give him to us!" What? I read it a second time. Huh? Questions popped into my mind. Actually, I was curious what they wanted with an unborn fetus themselves, so I distracted them all while Dick and Heather slid past and into the office on the second floor. I played it cool and just asked about the sign.

At first they were hostile, but I decided to pump them for information and tactics, feigning real interest in their motives. They surmised that I was not with the two sinners who had just gone inside, so we talked. I told them that I was a trainee volunteer and wanted to learn what I should do when young women wished to enter the clinic. Come on— after all the wild tales I had told in China and all that, this was a cakewalk. I knew their language and dished it out in spades. I figured that it was pointless to engage them in a debate, so I flipped and played the rube—the young enthusiastic new Christian from Albany or somewhere not too far away—and talked to them for over forty-five minutes.

Their motives were pure, if simpleminded. They were not thinkers. They could spout Bible verses—but then so could I (by the pound). I was trying to find out where they were getting their information and motivation from in order to sit and or stand out there on the wet sidewalk day after day, confronting young women in distress. They kept focusing on the "babies"—how they were killing their babies. That was their message. It had no depth, no forethought, or really any great appeal.

Their pastors and televangelists had challenged them. Most of them were retired and living on pensions or government assistance (welfare). Hate that socialism, huh? I ascertained right away that they were not really fighters. They did not want to harm the "mothers." They wanted to help them. Their desire was for them to carry the pregnancy to term and then give the newborn up for adoption to a devoted (straight) Christian couple to be raised in the fear and admonition of the Lord in a loving Christian family. I didn't find that motivation all that unreasonable. Adoption is clearly preferable to "the scrape." But I wondered if they would be so anxious about finding suitable homes for black babies being aborted over across the Willamette River in a less affluent neighborhood. But I didn't say anything. I was kind of transported back to my first days itinerating in the small churches in rural Oregon. The people were simple but not vicious. I came away with "mixed emotions." (I hate that term. It just means I was unsure of how to react to those folks.) But although the abortion issue would go on and on, a shocking, new political wave was about to crash onto the wild Pacific shores of Oregon that same year. It was called Measure 16, and it was destined to rock the country. It did. And I was at the very epicenter.

* * * * *

We called it "Death with Dignity. The medical community referred to it as "physician-assisted suicide," and the Fightin' Fundies had lots of other names for the famous ballot measure—the first of its kind in the entire nation (and in most places in the world). Now the idea of suicide is not new. In the Bible we read of various folks who offed themselves for various reasons. Native American tribes had a long tradition based on the notion that once a person was no longer able to pull his or her own weight and became a burden, it was his duty to go off and die. I always have found that kind of a drag personally, but I had a friend early on in my gay journey who had every intention of ending his life at some point when he felt useless. I lost touch, so never knew if he carried through with it.

The Japanese had the most elaborate suicide practices I can think of. The scenes in the movie version of James Clavell's classic *Shogun* are particularly riveting—and disturbing to our Western minds and sensibilities. It is hard for us to wrap our occidental brains around the notion that it is better to kill one's self than to live with shame caused by some gross breach of protocol, etiquette, or behavior. But our current abhorrence of suicide in any form is a Catholic concept by origin. For over a thousand years, the Church was the instrument of social *control* in medieval Christian Europe. Anything that would allow an individual to walk outside the constraints of Mother Church was discouraged, including a taking of one's own life. What right did he (or she) have to commit such a sin? Catholics have been quite adamant in disallowing anyone from making such a decision on their own. In fact, a Catholic follower could count on going straight to Hell for the act. Not only that (and the theme of countless horror films), such a person could not even be buried in a Catholic cemetery! No hallowed ground for anyone who feels he knows better than God when his life span is over!

But the Protestants—particularly in the last many years—have become quite Catholic on this subject. This was oh so true during the fascinating days leading up to the 1994 election cycle in Oregon. Somehow a motley collection of rabble-rousers had managed to gather enough signatures (thanks again to the initiative process) to get a measure (Number 16) on the statewide ballot for a vote. The churches went apoplectic. "How dare they (or anyone) play God?" they shrieked. And I mean shrieked. The churches were universal in their condemnation of the measure, and dumped millions of dollars of otherwise good mission's money into TV and other media ads to defeat it. And, of course, they knew what God (or Goddess) thinks about all this, right? As usual, they were just reacting to something new and different, but could smell the money that could be raised. And the usual suspects jumped into the fray with all four feet. Money came flooding into Oregon from every corner—from the Catholic Bishops, to the Mormons and the 700 Club. Nobody was safe if a sick and dying person were to simply take an overdose of a sedative and a half a fifth of vodka and simply check out. That was unthinkable! Outrageous. Forbidden by God . . . and by those Catholics losing social control.

Some years earlier and all during my time in San Francisco, I had struggled with this issue. My friends were dying and the clergy were lying. I had to face a grim reality clear back to when Jack had first been diagnosed with AIDS. What would he do? And as time went on I had to broaden that question. "What would they all need to do?" I had so many friends who had to deal with their own mortality. I was not there for Jack's passing, but those who were there said that he went peacefully. Joe had left Nevada like so many others, since the state had basically zero interest in helping the dying. California had a more complex and advanced welfare system. When my roommate Mike (Mike in Tahoe) was getting really sick, his doctor down in Reno had advised him to go and throw himself onto the front steps of San Francisco General. He did something like that in the end.

But Les, a friend of Joe and Andy in Carson City, had been thinking seriously in advance of how to end his own life and had asked for my help. Unlike Mike, who just let fate overtake him, Les was a far deeper thinker and a dedicated researcher. I had mentioned that I was driving up to Oregon to visit my folks sometime after my fortieth birthday (the one with the eclipse). He asked if I would do a really big favor for him and stop in Eugene on my way north to buy him some books at the *Hemlock Society*, which was located in that pleasant college town where I had so often preached during my itineration years. I did. I bought several books including *Final Exit* and *Jean's Way*. I had read all of the books and pamphlets and brochures that I had picked up during that trip, so as I drove back down to the City I had many hours to ruminate on all of the various aspects of the deed to which I had pledged myself.

First and foremost, I learned that helping anyone die in California was illegal. Not just illegal—grossly illegal. One cannot simply help another person intent on self-deliverance, by collecting and hoarding like thirty Seconal, or going to the local liquor store for them to buy alcohol. Of course the patient would have to do that. It is pretty easy to shop around for doctors in various towns and cities who will give a prescription for sleeping pills or pain pills. I discussed this method with Les when I got back to San Francisco. He assured me that I need not chase around with him to procure a sufficient number of pills, which would surely do the trick if mixed with alcohol. It is a surefire way to check out. In no time he had secured a stash of Seconal or some such substance oft' prescribed as a sedative to relieve tension—a relaxant to induce sleep. He had put his affairs in order as most such organized personality types are wont to do.

He was one of those really kind and thoughtful persons who make friends easily and keep them. His life was ending way too soon, but he had taken it philosophically. "I had planned a long and productive life for myself," he told me. "But it wasn't meant to be. Of course, any of us can just walk out into the street and get hit by a car. At least I got a chance to spend time with all my loved ones and my friends and family. I had to make it clear that they could not accompany me on my last mile of the way." Because it was so illegal, nobody could be present—or even anywhere nearby—when he took that final dose. He had brought the Vodka a week earlier and in a different neighborhood so as to forestall any investigations. He had all his pills on a small table by the bed. I brought a box of Ritz crackers to settle his stomach and prevent nausea and possible vomiting. I had to be miles away when he was "discovered." I was planning to just get in my van and drive to Lake Tahoe to spend the weekend with friends (far from the City).

I hugged him, and after we cried, I said goodbye and closed the door to his apartment quietly and drove away. I read his obituary in the BAR (Bay Area Reporter) two weeks later. *Apparent suicide.* It was over for him, but not for me. Unbeknownst to me, up in the cool green Pacific Northwest, unrest was afoot. Trouble was brewing. I had negotiated to purchase a large art gallery in Portland with the funds generated from the sale of the greeting card business in Nevada. The gallery was enormous, and it was fun to work with the artists and staff. We all had begun hearing rumblings about the success of the signature-gathering operation for Measure 16. It had been vetted by the elections commission and all other legal bodies, and now there was verification that they indeed had sufficient valid signatures of thousands of Oregon voters, and that the proposal to legalize physician-assisted suicide was indeed going to be on the November ballot.

The flood of preachers, teachers, televangelists, and sundry Christian kooks that descended on the quiet state of Oregon that year reminded me of the flood of religious hucksters who had descended on Hong Kong for the big hoohaw "opening of China" to the Gospel, that I remembered so well. But there was a difference. When the religious world had become aware of Tom Muzzio and the mailbags and other "spectacular" events of that time ten years earlier, I had been adulated, sought out, and praised. This time around I was vilified, called names, and threatened. The sting of the OCA loss in Measure 9 two years earlier had not been forgotten by the Fightin' Fundies in Oregon and around the Country. I had been a little too high profile for my own liking then, but now with this new campaign to legalize suicide—well, I was most unpopular.

I still had friends in the clergy, but their attitudes were different toward me this go-around. They had, for the most part, understood how Measure 9 was evil and mean-spirited. They didn't all just jump on Lon Mabon and Scott Lively's bandwagon. But suicide? How can that be a good thing? Well, of course it is not a good thing. It can be a necessary thing if one is living with a death sentence and is doomed to die a horrible, painful, lingering death. But I struggled to explain how and why I felt so obligated to get involved in such a movement. The slippery slope argument was the order of the day. Surely if society removes the legal constraints preventing people from taking their own lives, where does it stop? Of course, they already knew: Euthanasia. That is where it stops— or more accurately, ends.

No Youth-in-Asia. I still remember the sign carried by a religious protester at the gay pride parade in Portland in June that year. I chuckled, recalling a similar sign carried by another bumpkin back during the No on 9 campaign. The sign had read *No Special Rights for Homosexules* (pronounced homo-sek-shuls)! A local Channel 8 reporter had interviewed the guy with his sign. "What special rights are these people seeking?" the reporter asked professionally. The guy had to think. Well, he finally said: "They want to have a special parade! And they shouldn't be able to." Whoa. No parades for fags. Here we were having our very own disgusting parade through the city streets of Portland; and the guys with the signs and bull horns were pissed about it. So there! But this year they had a new gripe against the homosexuals and their evil agenda. They claimed, we wanted to bring in "death panels." What in the hell are death panels? I had to ask.

The argument against any kind of suicide—even physician-assisted, somehow scares people in general and fundamentalist Christians in particular. In their minds, of course, anyone who commits the terrible "sin" of killing himself will certainly go straight into Hell—the eternal lake of fire. But ironically, I never quite got how it was that they could hate us so much and secretly (or overtly) cheer on our deaths by AIDS, and yet were bound and determined to prevent us from doing so. Huh? And all during that time—those several months of conflict between the religious and the irreligious (regardless of the sexual orientation of either side)—they never articulated very well just why they were so opposed to PAS. Kind of like my dad who did not claim to understand certain legislation before the state's House of Representatives or Senate at any one time . . . If it was something he didn't understand, he was "against it."

Millions flowed into the campaign to stop Measure 16, but all the polls indicated that it just might pass. The issue was eclipsing everything else on the ballot—even the Governor's race, the Secretary of State, the State Treasurer, and the local school board. All anybody was talking about in the run-up to the election was Number 16. It was mightily polarizing. And the night of the election was drawing nigh. Nobody working on the campaign seemed to know where the lot of us should have our "election night headquarters." I was kind of shocked that such a key element of the whole show had been overlooked. So I volunteered my art gallery. Everybody thought that was a totally cool idea. Unlike the regular party campaigns that always rent a ballroom or conference room in one of the downtown hotels, the Measure 16 progressives were going to sit through election night in an art gallery! I figured it was great publicity for my business, but was totally unprepared for what transpired on the night of the vote-counting. Like the day I opened GPO box 6840 in Hong Kong and found it stuffed with mail—when I arrived at the gallery a full hour before anything was supposed to start, I was shocked. It was packed!

Satellite vans—complete with those big dishes facing skyward—were parked all around the gallery, as far as three or four blocks away. I was glad I'd walked instead of trying to drive and find parking. Not only were all of the local TV stations camped squarely in front of the gallery; there were news crews from as far away as the Netherlands and Japan hovering around, microphones at the ready. I was so glad that I had thought to nudify the gallery; stripping it of anything one could easily walk off with, putting such valuables in our storage room. The place was crawling with reporters. I recognized several as local, but the rest—from California, New York and DC—were a total surprise. And who did they want to interview? Duh, me. By the time of the election, it had become clear that not only would Measure 16 pass, but by a huge margin—maybe twenty points. So, the angle they were searching for was "Why an art gallery?" Most of the local TV types already knew me from the No on 9 campaign two years earlier. I have never been camera shy, but I explained that I couldn't do on-camera interviews, as the topic was such a trauma for the Fundamentalist Christians and their ilk, that I had no doubt whatsoever that bricks would come flying through my large gallery show windows if I were to even show my face on TV. I declined, doing some radio interviews instead.

All their stupid arguments just sounded so lame to me and to the voting public. I wish I had had the courage to go on the tube and talk about losing friends and how much I detested the Religious Right constantly carping . . . and always wrong. Always. But I kept quiet and we passed the first such measure in the U.S. to the shock of the entire nation. "God's punishment" . . . divine retribution against the whole state of Oregon was on the lips of every frustrated Fundamentalist for weeks. Over twenty years have passed since that night in November 1994. No death panels ever materialized. The sky did not fall, and after all this time only a couple hundred souls in pain actually followed through with their suicides. Yet the Christians still scream and yell and curse. They forget their dire predictions of certain doom. They threaten earthquakes, hurricanes, and mass destruction. They still hate fags and fear our growing acceptance. Too bad not one of them ever even tried to reach us with the Gospel message. Not one.

GAYS IN THE MILITARY?

OMG... We simply must redesign those dreary uniforms!

I was an original gay in the military. For that reason I followed this ongoing debate in the U.S. Congress and society with great interest and undivided attention for years. I also participated as a gay military veteran in numerous organizations, events, and debates for decades after leaving the service in 1972.

There have always been "homosexuals" in the military, clear back to antiquity. For instance, both the ancient Greeks and Romans—who were unencumbered by Pauline Christianity—figured that if men loved each other they would fight harder to save their buddies. The Sacred Band of Thebes, the most famous of all historical homosexual military units, were (so they say), an exclusively gay organization . . . and a most formidable fighting force. That may or may not be so. But, in any case, one thing I can definitely say for sure: living in an all-male environment is great for male bonding :-)

Remembering back to my first encounter with the Army recruiter in his office in the Pioneer Courthouse building in downtown Portland, back when I was studying at both Lewis and Clark College and Portland State University, I was keenly aware of the need to conceal any possible hint of my inner self—my gayness. Actually, that was not difficult, as I had already faked my way through both grade and high school, and college as well. But I had my guard up significantly on the day that I met with the sergeant whose job is was to "recruit" me. I had already been recruited as a born-again Christian, and now I was being recruited by the U.S. military. The funny thing is that I was never *recruited to* be gay. The irony of that didn't really strike me at the time. But now, when I hear Evangelical Christians whine and snivel about how the fags are out to recruit their children, I shake my head. Think about it. Duh. Their prime *directive on* this planet is to do just that: to recruit. Their supreme commander, Jesus Christ, sent them forth with the Great Commission—an order to recruit men and women around the world into a "Christian lifestyle."

Too bad they are so lousy at it. The Department of Defense recruiter was much better at his job than most Christians are at theirs. Go figure.

On that day of my military recruitment, I took a battery of aptitude tests. But in addition to proving that I had a brain in my head and a healthy bod, I also had to attest to my stellar character. There was a form that I had to read and fill out carefully. It asked very personal questions about who this potential soldier for the U.S. Military machine really was—like, way deep down inside. It was easy to answer questions such as "have you ever used illegal substances?" or "Do you enjoy camping?" (Note how skewed a question like that is.) Why not just come out and ask the real question: "Would you enjoy *camping out* in the jungles of Viet Nam?" I parried that one. But I couldn't escape question #62: "Do you have homosexual tendencies?" This I knew was a deal-breaker, so I quickly lied. I checked the NO box and went on. I actually wanted to go into the military . . . and I really needed to.

In later years when I was involved politically in various *Gay Veteran's* groups, I was astounded to hear the variety of conflicting emotions that all of us had felt when we encountered that question for the first time. I wondered—even at the time—how so many guys (gay and straight) could be so frustrated by that one little question. It struck me then (as now) how easily a guy could get out of military service and fighting in a war zone by simply saying YES to that one simple question. But I suppose that straight guys, unaccustomed to lying about their sexual interests, couldn't even bring themselves to play gay for a day and get a free pass out of the military. All the marching, chanting, and draft card burning were really unnecessary, as the Armed Forces offered a perfect dodge for the "dodgers." But few took it. Hmm.

I did, however, have a gay friend in San Francisco years later who went into the draft board in 1968 fully aware that he was going to be truthful and simply "admit" to being a bona fide homosexual, come what may. He did. He told me that when he had finished his questionnaire and had stripped for the physical, he was called out and given a (get this) pink card to carry around throughout the rest of the process. He was not humiliated or embarrassed as was likely the intended purpose of carrying that "pink triangle" around. He simply went through the motions, knowing that he did not want to be a soldier or to go to fight in South East Asia. He was a fag, and he lived in San Francisco—so there—end of discussion. When he was finally rejected as unsuitable for military service, he walked out with his rejection papers as proof that he had lawfully appeared for "induction," but was turned away. Wah wah, he was so sad. He told me that he simply walked out, stood on the steps of the induction center, lit up a joint, and walked away.

Looking back now, with over forty-five years more experience (thirty-plus as an "out" gay person), I see that my time in the military was rife with potential male-to-male sexual encounters. I may or may not have misread cues here and there, but being a born-again, spirit-filled, Evangelical, Fundamentalist Protestant Christian, I ignored or carefully rebuffed them all. I was quite aware that working side by side in the Graphic Arts department with other "artistic" types, probably at least half had "homosexual tendencies." I faked along as usual, but it was very difficult, as I often spent hours alone with my buds in the darkroom or on night shifts, or even on guard duty where anything could have happened unnoticed. But nothing ever did. How could it? It was unthinkable. From the onset of WWII, homosexuality was considered a "disqualifying trait" for military service; and we were clearly informed so during our induction week of basic training. We were required to watch all manner of black-and-white DOD films produced to indoctrinate us young recruits—most just out of high school. Along with such exciting and interesting subjects as dental hygiene and field sanitation, we watched several films regarding the military's legal system called the *Uniform Code of Military Justice* (the UCMJ). Along with all the other missteps that could "trip up" a young soldier boy and result in hospitalization (psychiatric), imprisonment, and a dishonorable discharge, the worst thing was "fucking your buddies." Everybody laughed. I took note.

During my Navigator Bible studies in Viet Nam I first ran across that famous verse in Second Corinthians (12:7) where Paul confesses: **There was given to me a thorn in the flesh, the messenger of Satan to buffet me.** I just figured if the Apostle Paul could be buffeted by such a tormenting thing that was a constant irritant—and overcome it—then so could I. But it was hard. Being young and around other young men—often in various stages of undress—I struggled, but managed to "pray through" and look the other way.

I lusted after several of my comrades, and was approached myself more than once (to my shock and embarrassment). But when I reached Frankfurt I encountered another shock. Our company clerk, a spic-and-span black guy with an athletic body and a million-dollar smile, was openly and obviously gay. He didn't even try to hide it! Now what was that all about? I quietly asked the guys in Doc Services. They told me that he had won the silver star for bravery in combat and several purple hearts in Viet Nam by saving his platoon in a very bloody firefight, and was kind of off-limits to the UCMJ because the military didn't want to kick out such a decorated "war hero" for being gay. I saw the implication. Like, how did he ever get into the service in the first place, and how could such a screaming queen do anything so heroic as to save the lives of his straight buddies? "They just want to let him ETS (leave the service on time) quietly and without incident" I was told on the QT. Made sense to me. But I kept clear of him, lest he pick me up on his gaydar.

I left the service and went into the ministry. But the situation of both gay men and women in the military began changing even as it was simultaneously transforming in the civilian population. More and more people began knowing gay persons . . . a friend, a relative. We were getting more and more attention both good and bad. The more the televangelists pilloried us for causing diseases, the destruction of the family, and jock itch, the more people in the general public (the GP) began thinking that we were getting a bum rap. By the time we were getting "wrapped" in knots by the likes of the OCA, the more we were gaining acceptance as normal people like everybody else. The military was facing a decision. For years the main expressed reason for kicking gays out of the armed forces was that we posed a "security threat." Very typical Cold War thinking, that. The notion was that if hot, young, Russian, female beauties could seduce straight soldiers into divulging secret information, how much more so could hot young Russian men seduce gays in the military? It was obvious. We were more vulnerable to seduction because we did not have the necessary discipline to keep our hands to ourselves and our dicks in our pants. Why would that be obvious? Especially since there were supposedly no gays in the military anyway. Hmm.

After the OCA collapse and the passage of Measure 16 in Oregon, the landscape was changing a lot in the U.S. Army and in other branches of the service as well. The "close proximity" argument began to sound hollow and contrived. Poor straight guys might have to bunk near gay guys and be "uncomfortable." Wow, since when did the military care a whit about the comfort of its service members? I was told to just suck it up and follow orders and do my job. I never got to choose who I was to bunk with. Admittedly, I managed to get along fine with three years' worth of roommates and bunkmates, but two particular groups managed to perpetuate that myth for years: The Chaplaincy and old doddering U.S. congressmen and senators (Dick Army and Jesse Helms leap to mind). I still wonder how the GP in their states could continually send such horrible people to Congress to represent them. Well, they all claim to be "Christians," so that must be the reason why. Sad, huh?

Don't Ask — Don't Tell (DADT) was a compromise policy that came out of a tremendous fight in the U.S. Congress and in the cities, towns, and villages throughout America during the early 90's. It was a time of intense debate and often warfare as the evolving and strengthening Right Wing in the U.S. began fighting every progressive idea or concept abroad in the country at the time. Spurred on by the Religious Right and their massive multimedia empires, more and more new issues crept into the milieu. But the rise of the Right-wing militias and their lapdogs, the Christian militias and the Christian Identity movement, went hand in hand with the ongoing struggles in the real military. Once the "warriors for Jesus" took to wearing camouflage uniforms and carrying assault rifles, I knew I had made the right decision years ago to get as far away from Fundamentalist Christianity as possible.

Since when did Jesus carry an AK47? Since when would he even have needed one? Since when would his followers need assault weapons? Yet there evolved a clear and inescapable trend within American Evangelical/ Fundamentalist Christianity across the country, which stemmed from a total Jesus makeover. From my conversion and decision to follow Christ in 1968 to standoffs between armed Christian camps and the FBI, the IRS, or Federal Marshals in 1998, the mainstream perception of Jesus of Nazareth had changed. His image had morphed from the humble carpenter from Galilee, teacher and savior of mankind by his death on the cross, to "Super Jesus," that bold hero and leader of whom they so fervently sing: "Onward Christian Soldiers . . . Marching as to war . . . With the cross of Jesus . . . going on before." Hey, I sang that one too. But I was deluded. I realized how I too could be so easily swept up with the singing, clapping, shouting, and carrying on for Christ . . . and against his enemies—of which I was obviously one by now.

* * * * *

Jesus says: "Love your enemy," but modern Evangelical Fundies can't do that. They simply can't. After all, they are hardwired to hate. I speak of what I have experienced. Now, as I have said, my dad was a man of hate; however, he was an unabashed hater. He hated equally everyone *unlike* himself. He was the dictionary definition of a bigot. Modern Fundamentalists hate to be called bigots, but that is precisely what they are. They talk of love, they sing of love, and they preach about love; but rarely exercise it (except to people within their own four walls). I noticed this early on in my Christian sojourn, and it distressed me greatly.

The first time I heard a Christian minister say that "they should crack a few hippy skulls" back in 1969 in Viet Nam, I was dumbfounded. But I got used to it. They couldn't really mean that, I reasoned. They have Jesus in their hearts. They are just upset. Kind of like the battered wife who makes excuses for her bully husband as she covers her facial bruises with makeup, I made excuses . . . for a while. But the fact remains that modern Christians are more like and have more affinity for the monster god of the Old Testament than the mild-mannered Jesus of the New.

Their concept of God is that he is a bully, and they are just like him. Christians are bullies. Though they feign the victim, it is just a show. I also learned that show early on. When I was a "young" Christian, I began hearing the word "persecuted" in relation to modern Christians. Of course, I was aware of the early Church and its real persecution by the Romans—the lions and all that. Everybody knows that. But as I looked around, I noticed nothing that could remotely be considered real (even slight) persecution. I was living in a society that was (and is) overwhelmingly dominated by Christian culture, religious images, references, and customs. Christmas lasts for over a month and even I get sick of it. It is the "dominant" culture in the U.S. But not just in the U.S. At least a third of the world's population is under the general umbrella of "Christianity" in some form or another. Persecution is a myth, and I realized it, and I still know it.

I did not suffer bullies in high school. I was way too sure of myself and focused to even imagine getting beaten up after school by the tough guys. But I know that most high schools have such monsters, and they are dangerous. I have had enough friends over the years (particularly gay ones) who have suffered at the hands of bullies. Why do they do that? Why do the stronger, more dominant types pick on the weaker kids? I can't tell you. I really can't, because I am not inclined to pick on weaker human beings. In fact, as a Christian I was very much inclined to want to help the poor and the weak as Jesus taught me in the Bible. But nowadays I see such a paradox with the Evangelicals that sometimes I think my head will explode.

When I was in the military, I was the sole born-again believer just about everywhere I went. I dealt with that, and "girded up my loins" to live my life as a Christ-like example—and to witness for Christ with my life and with my voice. But now I read constantly in the media of new recruits at the Air Force Academy being coerced to join "Team Jesus" by military superiors who punish those recalcitrant Jews and agnostics who don't want to worship "the Lord" as they do. I do now believe that the U.S. military has been infected with the Navigator spirit that I once sought to propagate. The military is now full of the result of our own Evangelism. Terry Furth, that guy back in Frankfurt, was right. I was not a team player. I would never make myself over into a carbon copy of him. But obviously there were lots of guys willing to do so. They are now the captains and majors in the U.S. armed forces who are preaching their brand of religion to the troops under their command and *control.* It is frightening.

The bullies in the military establishment are a cancer on the whole of the body politic, meaning the armed forces themselves. But their counterparts, the "pretend" soldiers or weekend warriors, are actually more dangerous and toxic. The second amendment of the Constitution provides for a well-regulated militia. Gun nuts like to jump to the conclusion that guns are a "sacred right," and that all red-blooded American "patriots" should not only own guns, but carry them around as well. Bullshit. That is just sick. I was required to qualify with an M-14 and an M-16 (and later a .45) during my time in the U.S. Army. I did so. I did not enjoy it. I did not like it. But I was required to do it, and I did. I have not touched a firearm since then, nor do I plan to anytime soon. I think they are poison; and I think that most gun-owners and gun-lovers are wrong. Having lived in Europe, a continent relatively free from such personal weaponry, I feel that the only Americans who should have access to rifles, shot guns, and pistols are the military, the police force, and trainers of dangerous animals in zoos. Who else really needs such evil implements of destruction? Of course, that is a pipe dream. But I can dream, can't I?

Onward Christian Soldiers—with guns ablazing. Marching off to war—with the Muslim world, the colored of the Earth, and of course the fags. "Kill the fags" . . . "God hates fags" . . . "Slay the gay." The sickness is just below the surface in the collective minds of the Right Wing Christo-monsters. But, of course, I learned years ago to avoid such people. The bullies. Their motivation for their gun mania is usually couched under the general banner of "protection." We have to fight them over there so we don't have to fight them here. Crap. The Taliban are a collection of medieval-minded males with a Bronze Age mentality who, although they beat up and shit on their women, pose no immediate threat to Omaha, Nebraska. The idea that some whackjob in Kellogg, Idaho needs an arsenal of sophisticated weaponry in case they might invade Moscow (not the one in Russia) is ludicrous.

I always find it so paradoxical when I am visiting Eastern Oregon, Idaho, or other such rural places, and I see a massive pickup truck (usually with a lift-kit), a gun in the back window rack, and a Christian slogan on the bumper. How did Christianity get so wrapped up with militarism and local paranoia? Well, when we think back to the first time Christians en masse went on the war path, we see the Crusades. *Onward Christian Soldiers.* There were four Crusades in all, and in the end they were kind of a flop. But they did manage to bring back a bunch of loot that you can see in the Vatican Museum. But why now and why in America? The medieval minds of our time and place see the culture war as a crusade. Like when George W. Bush referred to the national struggle against Islam as a "Crusade" . . . to them it is. Billy Graham began using the word crusade years ago and it stuck. It is not popular elsewhere in the world, I assure you. Americans are such willing crusaders.

As I have so often noted, Americans see the U.S. as the "world." The rest of the nations and peoples on the Planet are like moons and asteroids and satellites and other UFO-type stuff spinning around out there somewhere. We are the world. We are insular and self-absorbed. So, when I talk to most Americans and refer to facts, like that most of the rest of the civilized world does not allow private gun ownership, their response is usually: Fuck them. Who gives a shit about the pansy-ass French, British, or Belgians? Who really cares? And they genuinely do not care about the "outside" world. It has distressed me for years. We see the "others"—those black and brown peoples out there living in endless conflicts and wars—as less than human. Mud People. But modern American churchmen think we should continue to supply them with arms to continue their conflicts and to try to "civilize them—to bring democracy to them" . . . why? I have always thought that the missionary notion of all the English-speaking peoples drives politics on a limbic level in the brains of Christian politicians, clergy, and even the guy in the street. But I think a lot of it is just pure greed projected by pure old-fashioned Capitalism (which is so un-Jesus-like to its core).

The NRA and the famous "Gun Lobby" have conspired to package their product of death as a really good thing. Guns are good. Guns protect us and our families. Guns save lives. If you kill that weird-looking, foreign Japanese exchange student on your front porch who is lost and ringing your doorbell, that is a good thing. After all, he may be trying to break in and steal your widescreen or rape your wife. Better to shoot first and avoid danger. Christians en masse buy into this thinking. I know, as when I was preaching around a lot I became aware of the number of born-again gun nuts there were in the churches I visited. I asked them why they needed guns. They would look at me like I was kind of off my rocker. "Well, we have to protect ourselves!" They would constantly reply . . . like, what planet are you from?

The word "gun control" is kind of like sulfuric acid. Why oh why do modern Evangelicals feel the need for personal weaponry when they have God to protect and keep them? I can kind of expect those "need of protection" arguments from the Rogues at Ruby Ridge or the fools at the Branch Davidian back down thar in Wacko, Texas. But otherwise-sensible American citizens equate firearms with safety. Christian citizens are all for guns as a means of keeping the wolves from the door. Mix that with their loathing of gays and you get a letter to the editor like one I received back in Virginia City from an irate "brother in Christ" who threatened to blow my head off (in Christian love, of course).

* * * * *

If a man lies with a man as with a woman,   it is an abomination. (Or as Jimmy Swaggart always says: It's a *bomb-nation* :-) LOL. As long as we are talking about guns and gays, let's consider the proof-text that gay-hating Evangelicals use to prove that God hates fags (Lev. 18:22). Give it a rest. I am so sick of an entire mass of people in their millions who use one verse of scripture to shape and color their entire attitude toward the behavior of one particular minority. I always used to feel that I could just go along with that kind of shit and ignore the idiots and their rants until I began to identify with the very minority that they were screaming about. Once I came out to myself I began listening more carefully to the calls for the dispensing and destruction of all gay people (in the U.S. at least), as that is all that really matters anyway, of course. Like, who cares about fags in France, Finland, or Fuckifiknow out there somewhere?

After the exit of the OCA from our midst up here in our Pacific Northwest habitat, another breeder (of hatred and discord) arrived in our midst by means of her radio and TV talk show. Her name was "Dr. Laura." She was a real creep. First of all, it was revealed early on that she was no real doctor of any kind—not even an "honorary" doctor like my old friend "Dr." Alf Crawford, with his treasured honorary doctorate from the Bangalore Bible Institute in Southern India. Dr. Laura had a talk show—like Rush, Hannity, and Mike Huckabee. She, like most "abominationists," ranted and raved about how fags upset God—you know, her Jewish God who commanded the cinderization of Sodom and Gomorrah— those hotbeds of ancient homosexuality. She constantly referred to that particular verse in Leviticus and another even more telling line of scripture that is never mentioned in polite Christian circles . . . **They must be put to death.** (Lv. 20:13).

I wrote her a letter that summed up my feelings at the time:

Dr. Laura Slessinger   October 10, 2000
Paramount Studios
Los Angeles, CA 92132

Dear "Dr." Laura,

I have been following with no small interest current events and
controversies swirling around your radio and now TV shows. Your
recent religious conversion to Fundamentalist Christianity and your
use of Biblical references interest me. I am a former ordained minister
of many years with a large Fundamentalist denomination, namely, the
General Council of the Assemblies of God.

Some years ago I resigned from the ministry because I am gay.
Nevertheless, suffice it to say, I have some theological background.
Owing to your constant use of the Holy Scriptures, I can only presume
that you have religious training as well. With this in mind, I would like
to ask you to address a Biblical issue that perplexes me especially as it
relates to you personally and to your adoring Fundamentalist
supporters as well—regarding the subject of homosexuality.

I rarely have the pleasure of taking in your program, but I admit
that now and then I give you a listen in the car. I don't think I have
ever listened in on a program of yours that doesn't talk about
homosexuality in some way, shape, or form. It appears that you are
fixated on the subject.

You and your acolytes seem to base your entire attitude toward gay
people on a particular verse of scripture from the Old Testament. It is
to be found in the Book of Leviticus, chapter twenty, verse thirteen.
Please allow me to quote it for the benefit of your followers, as I am
sure you know it already: **If a man also lie with mankind, as he lieth
with a woman, both of them have committed an abomination . . .**

However, you and your Christian friends never finish the verse. There
is more and it goes like this: **They shall surely be put to death. Their
blood shall be upon them.** (Lev. 20:13 KJV).

This whole verse has always troubled me greatly, as I consider the ramifications. I ask you to consider them with me, as well as the questions that arise from a reading of the entire verse.

Do you advocate capital punishment for being gay? If so, how would you determine who is and is not gay? And what of bisexuals for that matter? Would the death penalty only apply to "admitted," "practicing" homosexuals, or to those suspected of having those inclinations too? Would lesbians be exempt, as the Bible never mentions them at all?

The big question that I have always asked myself, which I hope you can answer for me and gay people everywhere: By what means would these millions of executions be carried out? Lethal injections? Perhaps electrocutions? Hangings? Firing squads— ovens? Would we get trials first?

And what of those of us who live in states with no provision for capital murder? How would we be transported to states that do? Box cars perhaps? And then, how will you house us in our millions awaiting our deaths at your hands? The Bible's *final solution* is a grim one indeed.

In closing, I recommend that you and your supporters read even further in Leviticus twenty—to the end of the chapter. My last question is: Once you have dispatched all of us homosexuals, who would you suggest be next?

Sincerely,

Thomas Muzzio (Rev.) resigned

BTW, I sent a cc: to George W. Bush, Billy Graham, and a motley collection of other Evangelicals, but no one wanted to field that question, I guess. Sigh.

The death penalty is one of the Fundie's favorites. Christian people are not only hopelessly pro-gun, but they are likewise very pro-death as well. Ironically, for those who whine and carry on about the "murder" of those innocent little embryos, fetuses, zygotes, and krill, they are all rip-roaring enthusiasts of the various forms of dispatch used to rid the world of *other* killers. Killing in war is okay, killing an "abortion doctor" is okay, and killing an inmate is okay. But killing a fetus? That's not okay.

When I was a Christian I guess I supported the death penalty—at least halfheartedly. But when I began reading my Bible with new understanding and not viewing it through the proverbial rose-colored glasses, I was horrified. Not that I didn't know that the God of the Bible demands death for faggotry and adultery, for cursing of parents, and Tarot card and palm reading; but for working on Sunday and more. Of course, I ignored those passages as do most modern believers. They simply read over them. Kind of like reading over all the bloopers in Genesis, the massive slaughter of everything in the big flood and the firebombing of Sodom. How could I have missed all that? Selective reading and recall, I guess. We all recoil in disgust when we read of "honor killings" among Muslims. And there are those in the U.S. Congress who daily rail against Sharia Law—which is basically the exact same brutal set of strictures coming right out of the pages of the Old Testament. And when one with a 21st Century brain calls this out and to the attention of the Fightin' Fundies, they just ignore it all and keep screaming. Tone deaf? No. Just plain deaf.

Well, the DADT policy ran and was in effect way into the Obama administration, and I followed it closely. Just like with measure 16 (Death with Dignity), the Evangelicals in unison chanted: The sky is falling . . . the sky is falling! No straight soldier will ever put up with having to sleep near or even in the same room with a homosexual. Well, as when President Truman racially integrated the U.S. Armed forces in 1945, the chain of command kicked in and the generals ordered their officers to instruct the men—and they did. There are some good movies, including *Hart's War*, that deal in-depth with the topic of military integration; but by the time I began my stint in the service, the idea of segregation had been long forgotten. I fondly recall interacting with all manner of new racial combinations and with guys of every racial hue that I otherwise would have never encountered in my life. Before then I had had little experience with blacks, save for some in Benson High School. I was fine with my Hispanic buddies, and very fond of my Asian friends too. But the military introduced me to other groups as well for which I am a richer person down inside. I had never met an Apache, a Navaho, or a Blackfoot Native American before; nor Cubans, Puerto Ricans, Hawaiians, or Guamanians. The army is richer as a racial stew, and adding gays into the mix has just made it more diverse and interesting.

If the military was encountering massive disruptions due to the presence of gay soldiers—believe me—Rush, Hannity, and dear ol' Pat Robertson would be crowing "I told you so!" from the rooftops. Heard any gripes from within the ranks? I haven't either. After the repeal of DADT, when the sky did not fall, the military some years later now seems to be getting along just fine with a new infusion of gays. After all, we've been there all along. But at least now we will get credit for some of the great art, designs, and even cartoons that we have contributed to sparkle up military life along the way. Now if they will just let us redesign those hideous uniforms :-)

FAMILY VALUES?

Our values are better than your values!

I have always loved the lyrics from the theme song of that classic 1970's TV show *All in the Family*. It was the first of a series of reflections on the changing American social and cultural scene that had our Fundamentalist friends, family, and neighbors in a state of utter befuzzelization back then. They just couldn't stand all those neck-jerking changes that were portrayed weekly on the sacred airwaves so carefully controlled by the conservative FCC. Those of us who grew up as children in the fifties (baby boomers) and as teenagers in the sixties, were young adults by the time the seventies rolled around. Our time was coming, and it was a marvelous time to be young and open to all sorts of new things.

Well, not all of us were open-minded and willing to look at the world so differently from how our parents had imagined it. I was personally conflicted a lot during the 1970s. Although I could see forward, like through a glass darkly, I also wanted to cling to certain stuff right out of the 1950s. The first wave of nostalgia for the fifties was so brilliantly portrayed in the classic film *American Graffiti*, which came out in 1973. I loved it. Of course, ahead of my time, I had converted to Fundamentalist Christianity near the end of the sixties, and was being pulled backward constantly by the older generation of ministers, missionaries, and other religious associates who were indeed fossils— even then. Oddly, they didn't see themselves as "Archie Bunker," who was a metaphor for conservatism and unwillingness to change and adapt. I was trapped in kind of a time warp. I had committed myself to a reactionary mentality—Evangelical Christianity—firmly rooted in the past—but with a world moving ahead in all sorts of new directions. I tried to embrace both. But it was hard.

It was doubly difficult, I think, because, as a result of living in progressive Europe during my formative years as a young adult, I was bombarded with all manner of social and sexual challenges from the society at large. America and Europe are so different when it comes to attitudes toward politics, lifestyles, and sex. A brief explanation of why this is so may be in order here, since it impacts all of us today as much as before—or maybe more so. Before the United States of America became independent from Britain during the Colonial period, we not only had a king (dear old George, the crazy), but we had a "State Church" as well—the Church of England (the good ol' C of E). We were required to support the Church with our taxes much as the Brits still do today. BTW, many other European countries support their state churches in similar fashion. The Catholic countries of Europe subsidize the mother church in many obvious and less obvious ways. Countries in Scandinavia support their kings and the Lutheran church as well. For that reason, it has little competition and is largely ignored. Oh, but not in the U.S.

When we ditched the monarchy back during the Revolution, after we won the war, we not only kicked out the monarchy but the State Church as well. Jefferson wrote convincingly of the wall of separation between church and state. There was and is to be no state church. For that reason, we have a free-for-all religious mulligan stew instead. All churches are free to do their thing—no matter how stupid. It is pure social Darwinism—survival of the fittest. All religious bodies in the U.S. are locked in competition with one another. It's a dog-eat-dog world out there on the religious scene . . . or haven't you noticed? There is no government funding of any religious group, sect, or church. Of course, the Fightin' Fundies constantly campaign for such state sponsorship of a church . . . yeah, *theirs*, of course.

But in addition to church-to-church competition (for donor dollars), there are the "independent ministries" (like Teen Challenge, the Navigators, Campus Crusade for Christ, and the OCA) all scrambling and scrabbling daily for money to keep their organizations afloat. I guess you have picked up on how important this is—fundraising. Of course, the *political* circus that is U.S. politics is likewise beholden to donors in order to survive. As long as there is so much "money in politics," we will have endless primary elections, debates, and mudslinging. But I have watched that from afar for years. My participation in the "get the money" religious struggles have left me cold and sick of it all.

But it goes on. The themes change or morph into other things, but the quest for bucks does not change. The biggest two fundraising themes of the Far (political) Right and the Religious Right have been abortion and homosexuality—surefire topics to unloose the emotions of the religious and to unloose their wallets as well. I spent years in those wars, as you know by now. Of course, those topics won't go away anytime soon, but I am seeing some cracks appearing in the Fundamentalist overarching concept called "Family Values," or, to be more accurate, "Traditional Values." For years, the term has been floating around in Christian circles —and not just Evangelical circles. Just about everyone can get onboard with the vague notion of values . . . often called "morals" by moralists :-)

But what exactly is morality? Who gets to define the term? God, the Bible, mankind, the dictionary? I vote for Webster's in this case when searching for definitions. The dictionary definition is: *a belief in or practice of a system of ethics apart from religion.* What? It specifically defines the word as a right or wrong behavior according to standards of society. The word is not found anywhere in the Bible! Oh shucks. And yet it rolls off the tongues of Bible thumpers as if they invented it. Hah! If we are just seeking to define the word so that we are all talking about the same thing, then the God of the Bible is clearly not the source of the word—the Latin language of the bloody Romans is! I can hear the televangelists screaming right now. It is clearly a term invented long after Yahweh dished out the Ten Commandments and other great orders like "Fags must be put to death" (and the like). It is further defined as virtuous conduct, being in accord with the standards of right or good conduct. A knowledge of right and wrong behavior and conduct within a society. So, if morality is a collection of right attitudes of any given society—I figured out long ago—those who claim a "divine morality" are just flat-out wrong. They invented that concept to adjudicate their own attitudes about society as they envisioned it (and for years enforced it). The Puritans are a fine example of enforcement, huh?

Even though I have not been a member of the Fundamentalist clergy for years now, I still know full well that in the religious mind there exists a clear (though false) definition of what morality really is. I have recognized for years as well the appeal of some kind of universal knowledge of right and wrong that is known to all. Christians often refer to this as a *divine spark* . . . Deep down inside we all know what is right and what is wrong; but some of us simply ignore it and do whatever the hell we please. That really pisses their god off—and they are likewise mad at the immorality of others unlike themselves. Not long after I escaped from Fundamentalism, a friend said to me: "Tom, I feel sorry for you, no longer having a divine moral compass. It must be very frustrating and uncertain . . . always living in a world of shades of gray. Give me absolute blacks and whites any day!" I understood her. To many (especially those given to religious dogma), absolutes are preferable to variables. But I had to ask: "And where then do you find the source of your fixed moral compass?" Like I didn't already know. "The Bible, of course!" she replied, looking at me as if I had fallen off a truck, and bumped my head, and couldn't remember that obvious fact.

But this notion of a universal morality that "everybody knows about" puts them in conflict with the other peoples of the world. You know . . . the ones that they are commanded to reach with the Gospel. The problem of their god-damning all those who have never heard their message, along with the real horrible sinners (you know who you are), really left me cold. Still does. But since they alone possess the key to understanding, the problem of the damnation of those outside the fold of Christ (regardless of whether or not they have heard the message) escapes them completely. For them it is not an issue. Mankind is fallen. That is a given. *No it's not.* Who says so? They do . . . so their argument is valid. *No it is not.*

But the modern clergymen and politicians who constantly reference the divine spark or a certain universal morality don't really spend much time preaching about the morality of God; no, they take it to the next level with the use of a word you hear even more often falling from the lips of those in front of the TV cameras these days: *Values!* Once the words "morality, moral, and morals" are accepted as a kind of universal, then the next step in their mental process is that by extension there are certain "values" that they possess and that others shun. They may be right on this, as I have often simply said to the screamers who tout their values: "Well, fuck your values." I will admit that I used to really hate it when nonbelievers would basically just reject my witnessing and preaching out-of-hand like that. Really. It hurt, since I took it as a personal offense against me and my Lord.

During the past decade or so—as I have mentioned—the Protestant Evangelicals have been becoming increasingly Catholic in their theology of of hate. But I know my theology, and I have for years said that I think it is hopelessly immoral of Pat Robertson and Christian Politicians to link arms with Catholic clergy and politicians in a common-cause hatred of gays. They should instead be preaching salvation to us (and those Catholics), warning us that we are going straight to Hell. As I say to this day: What was I doing in the Philippines if not warning Catholics of their impending doom? But they all have family values, so they link arms and bow their heads and pray that their God will rid the world of faggots. I guess that anybody can at least try to "pray away the gay." But the hypocrisy is overwhelming.

Of course, to some degree I understand Catholic teaching as well, and those guys with such firm family values see their Protestant allies in battle as being lost as well. Sad, huh? But they all have what they claim are "Traditional American Values." We need to be a bit more specific about what values in general are, and, later, about what American values are (as compared to—say—Chinese values, Japanese values, or Mexican values). But we will get there. The wild-eyed wackos of the Religious Right honestly believe that they are morally superior to the rest of the inhabitants of planet Earth. I know this as I felt that way myself. Of course, I would condescendingly look down at the immoral sinners and tisk tisk tisk. . . . Poor sad folks. Their lives are shallow and meaningless, as the only meaning in life is Jesus and nothing more. Very narrow-minded, huh? But this attitude colors how these people view the world around them. They sing: *"This world is not my home; I'm just a'passin' through. My treasures are laid up somewhere beyond the blue. The angels beckon me from heaven's open door. And I can't feel at home in this world anymore."* I really used to love that tune. But it is such a lie. This world is definitely the Fundie's home, and he wants to make it over in his way. And if he has to force others to do things that make him and his god happy, he will. That is why I continue to argue that if these monsters were not so bound and determined to make the world over in their image, I wouldn't be so upset.

I have for years referred to these as the TAV set. Traditional American Values. They have values, and the rest of us in the world do not. And when I hear the televangelists, Right-wing politicians, and Fox News pundits preach and carry on about a return to these ill-defined values, I wonder if they have ever even asked themselves what these "values" are. Well, I have concluded that there are three areas that delineate these values for them. The first has to do with behavior (what one does)

The second deals with thinking (what one believes), and the third deals with virtues (what one is like).

The behavioral aspect is based on a list of dos and don'ts. Those who are in accord with the list act in a certain way—to some degree anyhow, as not all Evangelicals (Protestant and Catholic) are reading from the same list . . . the same sheet of music, as they say. Although they are all singing a different tune regarding TAV behavior, there are some behaviors that they tend to agree on. Let me take a minute to point out a few of the most obvious.

Abstracting from years of personal pew-sitting, I have isolated a list of things that most people probably consider to be true American values. For instance, one does not commit murder. All Fundies likely agree on this. (Well, with the exception of abortion doctors, of course, such as a wicked evil guy like Dr. James Hill in Florida; because that's saving the unborn, and is okay.) One likewise does not commit adultery in any case and under any circumstances. One Man One Woman forever, amen. One does not rape. I'm fine with that. One does not fuck another man's wife or a member of the same sex. You are losing me; but for the sake of harmony, I think it is fair to say that most Evangelicals would agree so far. Do not take drugs of any kind (including pot). Do not smoke cigarettes or drink any alcoholic beverages (even those with the cute little umbrellas). It's the Devil's brew. We may be losing some Catholics here. But for the most part let me point out that I know loads of non-Christians who do not contravene any of these prohibitions in any way. So what makes our pious Christian Aunt Mildred so special?

When I was first introduced to the real world of Fundamentalist holiness (coming up on nearly fifty years ago now), I learned a few more that might cause a "new Christian" to stumble. No going to places that are unseemly . . . like movie houses, pool halls, and— above all—dancehalls. (I think even referring to them as discos is now rather passé.) When I was a new Christian myself I had to sneak into the movies lest I be seen as presenting a bad testimony. But when was the last time you even heard of a "pool hall?" Really. These antiquated terms are straight out of the American Temperance Movement of the early 20th C. And that lovely holy notion lead to the 18th amendment to the Constitution forbidding the sale, transportation, or consumption of alcohol . . . the war on drugs of its time. And we all know how successful that was. LOL.

But herein lies the moralist's dilemma. He wants the world to adhere to his list of don'ts because mankind is "fallen" thanks to those two naked kids in the garden. But these moralists look around and are disgusted that the world is full of wicked sinners. And though they are screaming that the sinners should change their behaviors, nobody appears to be listening to them. That pisses them off. Of course, their doctrine should inform them that their job is not to change the behaviors of the sinners. They should live exemplary lives so that the sinners will cry out: "Oh, look at those holy, righteous people! Tell us your secret! We so want to be just like you!" Doesn't usually happen that way, does it?

The second value area is what one believes. This is important, so pay attention. First of all, God exists. No proof of any kind is necessary. It is just so. The Jewish god of the Old Testament, Yahweh, is the creator of the Universe; and no other possible explanation is acceptable. All other gods are false. Period. The Bible is the inerrant word of God and is the very foundation for these much-touted traditional values. I leave out the word American here, since Christians throughout the world believe likewise, so how can these values be exclusively American? Well, since the USA is the center of the Universe, it is just so. So many phony politicians who take international junkets all the time (at taxpayer expense) should know better. But they are singing with the choir. These are American values—Texas values! I just threw that in. LOL. I've known a lot of Texas Christians, and they often think their Christian values are "better than yall's."

One must believe in the U.S. government (but not too much, of course) and the Constitution, which guarantees them the right to their firearms (for protection, and to repel invaders) . . . the U.S. military—its courageous fighting men (and women) who are out there in *I-rak* killing commies for Christ. . . I mean, Muslims. And one must believe that flag-burners are particularly heinous sinners, as opposed to just your regular garden variety sinners. Capital punishment is an American value. It is moral. It is "commanded of the Almighty." One must believe wholeheartedly in the death penalty for a whole slew of crimes—like abortion, of course. I heard Jerry Falwell with my own ears some years ago (before his untimely death) preach that the penalty for having an abortion should be death by injection. I remember thinking that it was "injection" that precipitated the need for an abortion in the first place. Sigh. (Well I thought it was funny :-)

There are endless other belief-based values that our friends and neighbors, the Fightin' Fundies, tout as their exclusive domain. A lot of people I hear from the Religious Right do not know why they hold these views—only that they are the politically correct ones de jour. We all know from the headlines that these issues divide the Nation. And I have noticed that when pinned down moralists can't say why they actually believe these things. They just spout another shop-worn cliché: "God makes the rules. I just read them and follow them." Amen.

Then come the third area of values: namely, the virtues. In my opinion, these are the only real values after all. The first values are a list of arbitrary rules that some obey slavishly while others do not. None are exclusively American, and many are stupid and ludicrous (abhorring dance halls leaps to mind). All cultures have their rules and attitudes about what is right and wrong behavior. Americans are not the only moral people on Earth. (Shh . . . Don't tell them.) The second are just attitudes toward contemporary issues, which can and do change in time. Go back a hundred fifty years, and the debate was whether or not it was moral to own slaves. Go back another, and the issue would have been whether witches should be burned at the stake (or hanged). These values, though traditional, were certainly not chiseled in stone.

I will concede, however, that the third area that the traditionalists point to as being values are indeed just that. Honesty, thoughtfulness, thrift, diligence, kindness, hospitality, and helpfulness, are real values— to be sure. These are matters of the heart, which in turn govern our behavior and our attitudes. It is my opinion that without these virtues-of-the-heart, the first two are rather hollow and empty. In fact, they can be destructive. Even Jesus said that a man can follow all the rules yet hate his neighbor. And he did not call that a virtue, but, rather, hypocrisy. Remember the Pharisees? . . . Yeah them. The Fundamentalists of their day. Swell folks, huh? But to this list of virtues, please allow me to add two that I consider super important: open-mindedness and tolerance. Oddly enough, these are not considered virtues at all by the modern Pharisees. They brag, in fact, about being intolerant of sin (other people's sins that is). Hmmm.

"Universal" might be a better handle for these more real types of virtues, since they are honored and lauded worldwide. The Chinese language is rife with poems and adages extolling honesty, diligence, patience, and goodness. Likewise in Japan, India, and Africa, people everywhere seem to agree that these virtues are indeed their values as well. By claiming that those unlike ourselves are uncivilized, wicked, or sinful, we are saying that they lack or do not accept these virtues as true American values. In fact, just about every culture I have experienced around the world (or read about) enshrines the exact same basic values. So, to refer to these values as "American" is ugly and pretentious. But pretension is not an exclusively American fault either.

I recall leaning over the back fence of my house in Ober-Wöllstadt, Germany (when I was working for Teen Challenge), and having a long and enlightening conversation with the older man whose yard backed up against mine. He was originally from Breslau before the war. He was ranting and raving about the decline in the morals and traditional values, which were to him so much more apparent in 1930s Germany! I was nonplussed. To most minds, Germany in the 30s was the epitome of terror and darkness. In his mind, however, like our modern moralistic friends, people "back then" were more moral, civilized, and patriotic than today. They were honest, hardworking, and thrifty. They were God-fearing and dutiful. And, I might add, mass murderers (but only to people unlike themselves). Sound familiar?

To the TAV set, the word "tradition" is extremely important. I had to go back to Webster's on this one. Tradition, it defines as: *A story, belief, custom, or practice that has been handed down from generation to generation, which has the effect of becoming an unwritten law.* Then it specifically mentions as an example of unwritten religious codes those of the Jews, the Muslims, and the Christians. The contemporary Fundamentalists in The USA claim that the world is "going to hell in a hand basket" or some variation of that meme. I have heard the same lament on the lips of Chinese friends and acquaintances that I heard from my German neighbor. I heard the same thing from my father. I hear it from Pat Robertson, and those whining words are still ringing in my ears from Jerry Falwell and Francis Schaeffer. This longing for the past—its glories, its goodness, its traditions—is universal. One can read the writings of the ancient

Greeks and pick up this same moaning spirit of despair . . . The past was so great, the present is so terrible, and the future is unthinkable. Wah, waah.

I think there is a difference between plain old nostalgia and this more deep-seated longing for the past. I still love the music of the sixties and still think of that as a kind of magical time of awakening and excitement and energy. My father saw it as the beginning of the end of civilization. Were the 60s really such a watershed? When I listen again to that music, see the films and look at the styles, I find it all a bit quaint—even tame. But most of the "Traditional Values" people point right to that time as the beginning of the end of values. It was a sinister time of long-haired hippies, unruly black people, and unfettered sex. That bad, huh?

Well then, should we hearken back to the "fabulous fifties" instead? Is that period more likely to hold the answer to Dr. Schaeffer's famous question: *How shall we then live?* There is, to be sure, a great deal of nostalgia for the 50s. Those were the good old days of black-and-white television, "I like Ike," and ever-expanding tail-fins. Who could find fault with the philosophy of *Ozzie and Harriet, My Three Sons,* and *Father Knows Best*? Who indeed? Many modern Americans look back to the 50s as the "best years of our lives." There is a good reason for that. Right after the Second World War the United States was the only country left on Earth with a viable economy. The rest of the world was in utter ruins. Germany and Japan had been virtually flattened. The rest of Europe and all of Asia were impoverished. And the Soviet Union was spending itself into oblivion, building an atomic arsenal, which opened the door to what we should remember now as mutually assured destruction (MAD).

Americans were on top. We had not only survived the war with all of our infrastructure intact, but had actually benefited. I talked at length with European friends who remember the 1950s with a shudder. For most it was a grim, gray time with no frills . . . and a lot of fear. But I remember that we were afraid too. I still have vivid memories of air raid drills in school—duck and cover (hide under your desk)—as the Russians might bomb Portland at any time, and the fireball might reach us out in West Linn. Polio was terrifying our parents, and who can forget the McCarthy era witch hunts? OMG.

Francis Schaeffer often spoke of the decline of Western Civilization and traditional values. He liked to draw a line somewhere around the turn of the 20th century as the actual beginning of the end. I believed every word he said back then, and always sort of thought of everything before 1900 as more civilized and Christianized than before the airplane, the automobile, or electric lighting. Ah, those were the good old days! I had my doubts. Still do. The horse and buggy, and life by candlelight—oh so charming. The TAV set of folks preach about hard work and pride in one's work.

This emphasis on pride and fulfillment, which resulted from the so-called "Protestant work ethic" has been eroded and diluted by labor unions and child labor laws. Their America, which they lovingly envisage, is a time of real family values and social order. Funny—I see instead sweatshops, dirty factories, and dangerous mines. I see people being chewed up building railroads, working intolerably long hours, and dying on the spot, as the rest pushed forward and left them behind, buried by the side of the tracks. Ah, the American frontier and manifest destiny. Now that was truly a time of real values, huh? I really don't see the 19th C. as a golden era like most conservative, reactionary Republicans do. And shall we go back further to a more enlightened time? What do we find there? Chattel slavery!

A few years ago the *Christian Broadcasting Network* did a special series claiming that the origin of traditional American values could easily be traced back to the halcyon days of the "Pilgrim Fathers" (note the male bias). In this theatrical reenactment of the Puritan's life of faith, healthy, well-scrubbed extras dressed in neat, tidy, modest costumes of the time, portrayed the ideal life in 17th Century New England. (BTW, that series was originally my idea/proposal as a tool for subtly preaching the Gospel in China—appealing to their thirst for TV programming on their burgeoning provincial TV stations at the time.) Those cheerful Christian folk were shown planting crops, harvesting the Earth's bounty, cooking on open-hearth fires, making their own cloth, raising wholesome families, and attending simple churches (where attendance was mandatory. But that was not mentioned.) Right. But the point was made that this was indeed the ideal model society as God himself envisioned it. Too bad I don't read it that way.

Unfortunately, my vision of early colonial America was not nearly so cheerful and sanguine, in contrast. The accounts of the period in most unsanitized history books paint a far different, less salubrious picture. I see grim, dour people struggling in a harsh and forbidding environment. I see a narrow-minded, closed-in group trapped in a small region of rocky, cold real estate between the sea, endless dark, and foreboding forest, which they feared as the domain of the devil and his minions—the native Indians. These people of faith and values are remembered not really so much for their cheerful demeanor and loving spirits from the Lord, but for their famous witch trials and tortures, hangings and burnings. They were a frighteningly mean-spirited lot. Theirs is a study in hysteria and the consequences of contravening "traditional" values. I have often said that if the Republican's wet dream of a Christian utopia is Salem, count me out.

So, to quote that great question posed by the 1970's rock opera *Lonesome Stone*, "Where do we go from here?" Into the Sea? Back to Europe? Where? I am not so sure I want to go back any further in search of real traditional values. I hear modern Right-wing politicians speak of Western Civilization and those overarching values of the "Judeo-Christian" universe. What a crock! If you are going to go in that direction, there is no choice—back to "Christian Europe." After living those years on the Continent, I have some indelible mental images and impressions. Among those that come to mind are the dungeons and rooms of torture in palaces, castles, fortresses and cathedrals throughout the Continent. When one stands by a rack—and can imagine bones and cartilage popping and breaking, or imagine the pain of the thumbscrew or the taste of the whip, the song of the ax, and the whisper of the gallows—one should not forget in whose name such misery was perpetrated: the Lord Jesus Christ (by his followers).

No, I don't think we should keep going back. It just gets worse. Should we stop? I would. But I have heard countless Fundamentalists make references to "earlier times" whereby they demand that we all return to the traditional values of old. If they insist, we should look back ourselves before we go there with them. It gets fuzzy and hard to define as the centuries are peeled away—as it melts into a blur of antiquity. In my clerical career I have actually (and rather often) heard

Christians sigh nostalgically for "Bible times. "They are sure that things were better then. . . I don't think so. Recently I heard a former California congressman on *YouTube* lamenting the rapid spread of gay sex, the gay agenda, and same-sex marriage. He wailed that "The Roman Empire fell because of sexual promiscuity like this. Every great civilization has fallen because of that!" What?

Amazing, I thought. Since when have Christians and the TAV set considered the Roman Empire such a great shining moral civilization—whining and sniveling at its downfall? I seem to remember the Christians gleefully taking credit for its demise. Well, I figured, if the Roman Empire should be held up as an example of values—the loss of which is to be mourned—perhaps we should consider readopting some of those old Roman virtues, values, and practices after all. Maybe we should just bring back the lions! :-)

ONE MAN, ONE WOMAN—ONE CROCK

It has always been this way . . . Oh yeah?

Perhaps due to the fact that I have been married and divorced, the desire for "gay marriage" really never has been high on my To-Do list—until I did it, that is! :-) As the culture wars rage on in America, one topic of particular fierce dispute is marriage equality, also known as "same-sex" marriage. For years the preachers and politicians on the Right have chanted the same mantra: "The Bible says marriage is between one man and one woman." Both the radio and television preachers, with voices like braying mules, shout and scream, snort and blow from pulpits across the country: One Man One Woman. The gullible and uninformed lap it up or miss it completely. For those of us who have actually read the Bible, it says no such thing.

I have never known for sure about the preachers and priests who spout this untruth. Either they are knowingly lying or they need a Bible content refresher course. The politicians can be forgiven up to a point, as they will say anything to get reelected. And the redder the district they represent, the more likely they are to just spout the lie by quoting their favorite cleric du jour. In unison they proclaim: "It has always been this way. For centuries—yeah, for thousands of years— indeed, since the beginning of time. It has forever been so." This is absolutely not true. The One Man One Woman marriage model is a modern Western adaptation. It is a relatively new cultural concept, in fact. The actual Biblical model could best be explained as the following: "marriage is between one man and as many wives as he can afford." Yes, folks, polygamy is the Biblical order of the day.

All of the Biblical greats had more than one wife. From Abraham to Zedekiah, they were polygamists. Some years ago when I was letting this get under my skin, I googled "Biblical polygamy" and found several useful sites. My favorite is called *BiblicalPolygamy.com*, strangely enough. It contains a directory of the names of forty well-known male characters of the Bible called Patriarchs, although some are prophets, kings, and sundry clerics of Biblical renown. Each man's name can be clicked on to reference his number of wives, their names, and even their sons' names from multiple wives. The corresponding Bible references are helpfully provided in each case. Look for yourself.

My favorites are Abraham with his three wives, Sarah, Hagar and Keturah. Then there is the great King David of sling shot fame who had eighteen wives (and a male lover, Johnathan). Moses had only two— Zipporah, who circumcised him so Yahweh would not kill him, and an Ethiopian woman. Moses got a lot of flak for that one. I wonder if race might have something to do with it. Solomon the wise and powerful had something like 700, give or take—not to mention 300 concubines.

In most cultures, male-to-male sex drives straight men crazy. They cannot fathom it, as for some reason it calls their own masculinity into question. Yet, oddly enough female-to-female sex often turns heterosexual males right on. Go figure. For years the pro-marriage-equality folks have argued that it is not just about sex. It is about love and rights. But the wild-eyed preachers and loud-mouthed politicians have long had the advantage of numbers on their side, and have often been able to win elections on this issue alone. One Man One Woman continues to ring out from churches and legislatures around the land. But that is changing . . . history is on the side of progressive thinking and will win out in the years ahead. Of course, the repressive regimes of the Earth (mostly Muslims, alas) that prescribe the death penalty for gay people will likely never change. But I have hope for us. So next time you hear that old saw, just consider the source. They speak not only out of hatred and bigotry, but sadly—alas—mostly out of sheer ignorance. What a crock!

My divorce was long and drawn-out. Well, not so much the divorce as the property settlement. That is not uncommon, but Beth and I got over it. We remained friends after we split up. I went on to Virginia City as I told you about, and Beth was given a job with the Church back in Europe. And I really had not much thought of marriage again for many years. Then I began hearing rumblings about places in the more liberal quarters of Europe that were considering allowing gays and lesbians the right to marry. So what? I asked myself. What's with that? Well, I began tuning in and paying attention.

I quickly discovered that in Europe, like in the U.S., the marriage contract brings with it a whole host of "special" rights that single people were not afforded by any law. What a rip off! I began encountering a lot of folks—primarily women at the time—who genuinely wanted to tie the knot. Once, when I had lunch clear back during the OCA period with a lesbian (attorney) friend in order to discuss strategy, she mentioned something about "marriage equality" and I stopped her. "What's that all about?" I asked rather lamely, as I probably should have been more sensitive. She actually had a list in her briefcase. She let me take a read. I was shocked out of my wits. There were like 60 rights that married couples had, from inheritances to joint tax filing, that single people simply were not entitled to. I knew all about the denial of visitation rights of the dying during their hospitalization. Unless they were a family member or spouse. Remember when Dean died back there in San Fran General? Well, I had no standing to stop the resuscitation—despite knowing full well that that was his wish. A spouse could have easily intervened.

After lunch I made a copy of her list and began my own research on the subjects. There were not a lot of books available, but I read the ones I could find and got all wound up with indignation. And the more I researched the issue and scratched at it the more I found the answer to my most burning question. Who is so opposed to marriage equality and equal rights for gay people? Of course, I had my suspicions. And guess what? I was right. The Evangelical Christians were the primary obstructionists—the people who were behind the efforts to deny rights to their traditional enemies—the fags. They have always hated gays with a purple passion, and this was just one more way they could think up to throw stumbling blocks in our path. At the time I had no dog in this fight. But I jumped in anyway and would have borrowed one on a leash if necessary. LOL.

I learned that there are three basic religious objections made to gay marriage, so I looked at each in turn. As usual, the reasons that the Fundies were so twisted out of shape could be traced rather quickly back to their dumb blueprint for living—the Bible. The first argument against two guys or women marrying and having the exact same legal rights that straight people have is reproduction. I had heard that stupid argument as far back as I could remember in Christian circles. "They can't reproduce" (meaning the fags), so why should they be afforded the rights of those who can? I flashed back to the ministers meeting in my living room in Hong Kong, passing around that latest edition of Asian TIME magazine with the "Gay Agenda" as the cover story. "Well, maybe they will just die out" was the typical un-informed and generally ludicrous responses of the clergymen sitting on my furniture that evening. Although I didn't resent them or their opinions, I was shocked at their ignorance.

Of course, gay persons can reproduce if they (we) want to. It may not be in the conventional way (penis in vagina) but there are plenty of ways to get around that if two persons are of a mind to :-) Of course, given my nearly thirty years as an "out" gay man, I have a lot of experience with this subject. When I first came out, most of the guys my age had situations in their lives similar to mine. We all had grown up in a time when homosexuals were invisible—hiding from society. We were right there in plain sight, but nobody was aware that we were in their midst and listening to their every word. We blended into society and looked and acted like everybody else. In overwhelming numbers we got married. We referred to that as being "straight married." Though certainly not straight, we married women and had children in the conventional way. Piece of cake. Now that I am a grandfather, all my friends my age are as well. So the notion that. We are going to die out cuz we can't make babies is dumb and idiotic. I mean, when I hear modern politicians and preachers blabbing about how we are going to die out, I just have to laugh. They are not only genuinely stupid, but delusional as well.

Of course, for younger guys—be they of Generation X like my son, or Millennials like my spouse—the need to breed is far less pronounced or desired. Most of the younger guys with whom I have contact feel little such compulsion. So maybe there will be a certain amount of that biological fall-off so longed for by the Fundiemonsters.

But the second glaring fact that dumbfounds the Right-wing fools is that every homosexual person on Earth (in our millions) is the product of a heterosexual relationship. Though it is true that when we fuck we are doing it for pure enjoyment, when straight folks do likewise they produce pregnancies—wanted and not. It is always a throw of the dice. And whether or not they admit it, like being born left-handed, about 10% of all male offspring on the Planet are born "different" or gay-inclined. About 5% of all female babies are inclined to be lesbian at birth as well. We are not recruited. No. We are born out of the bodies of heterosexual people. Period. So as long as straight men and women are so inclined to rut, they will continue to produce us.

It is becoming increasingly pronounced as more and more of us come out and live our lives honestly and openly. I remember back during the Jimmy Carter administration when a reporter asked Miss Lillian (the President's mother) if she knew any gay people, she replied in a rather shocked-but-firm fashion: "I'm from Georgia. We don't have any homosexuals in Georgia." LOL. Some of the biggest and finest gay bars and other establishments that I have ever visited are right in Atlanta. Don't look now :-) I am so glad that I have lived to see this all come to pass. When countries as diverse as South Africa, Argentina, Spain, and Iceland can all have marriage equality, I say the world is just getting better and better. Hallelujah. Hah! Of course, this is contrary to the Christian massage and worldview. They believe that the world is devolving. It is getting worse. It is just plain screwed up. But I disagree. If anyone is fucking up the planet, it is they and those like them (their Fundamentalist Muslim brethren) who view the world as corrupt and degraded as well. I say that it is their worldview which is degraded and tired, not ours.

* * * * *

Having been "straight" and married, and having been through the wringer of divorce, the desire for "gay marriage" was never high on my bucket list. Of course, like a lot of things that we contemplated back in the early days of the gay movement, the word "unthinkable" frequently leapt to mind. I was always reminded of Tevia, the reluctant hero of the play *Fiddler on the Roof,* as he was confronted with the reality of the marriage of his five daughters, one by one. Each in turn had fallen in love with a man whom Tevia would never have chosen. He sang out his lament to God. *How can I consent to allow my daughters to just choose whom they love and will marry? Unheard of. Unthinkable!*

I have to admit that back when gays were being victimized regularly by police, local thugs, parents, and fellow churchmen, the very idea of marriage to a man never really crossed my mind. When I entered into a full-time monogamous relationship with my partner, Dale, the idea of solemnifying it with a ceremony in a courtroom, let alone a church, was totally whacked-out. The word was never spoken. It never even came up.

Of course, by that time I had met many guys who had been living together in harmonious relationships that had been on-going for decades. But they were not only not married—the very notion of a white wedding, lifelong commitment, and equal benefits with heterosexual friends and family members never even entered our conversations . . . that is, until it began creeping into our collective mindset. And the origin of this radical concept came not from us—the crazy, creative fags—but from the lesbians!

Having been through the marriage frenzy that women encounter (many from as early as childhood), I could understand how much more important that the wedding dress (and cake) was to women than to most men. My own wedding (as I mentioned earlier) had been a kind of "on the fly" affair in my fiancé's home church in Los Angeles. We had been watching as so many of our mutual friends in the ministry were getting married, so we did kind of get wrapped up in the spirit of the thing. Most of our friends at the time were planning large elaborate weddings with matching everything, flowers for days, choirs of angels, doves flying overhead, and all sorts of cool stuff right from the pages of *Blissful Nuptials* or *Bride* magazine.

Actually, neither Beth nor I had any desire for a big, flashy, showy wedding extravaganza. We were just on a short leave from our work at Continental Teen Challenge back in Europe, and even getting our hands on affordable return tickets was a feat of no small measure. I guess that living in Europe during a down-dollar cycle when everything was outrageously expensive "on the economy" overseas, had made us both very frugal. We decided to just declare our intentions to wed the week before Christmas, pull off a quick honeymoon somewhere as yet undetermined, and grab a cheap flight back to Frankfurt before anyone got too wound up with all the details.

Jumping forward like twenty years or so, and living as an "out" gay person, there were so many political issues on the front burner in the gay community that marriage was rarely even brought up. But, when it was, it was amazing to note that most of us were not whining around because we didn't get to do the big la la wedding gig like our straight friends could. Nor were we all that jealous that they got to kiss in public, show off their wholesome families at the PTA, or even adopt children or leave theirs on a whim. Oh, we were jealous, for sure. But our big gripe was not about the fact that we couldn't march down the aisle of the local Baptist (or Assemblies of God) church, but, rather, was about the inequality of rights.

Even if we were not allowed a state marriage license, we could still live together as partners for years and years . . . even if we could not "have our own" children, which of course most of us not only could but did. And not only could we not have a traditional white wedding . . . oh, but we could, and did! I had attended lots of gay weddings of all imaginable types long before marriage equality became a legal and political issue, but they were all lacking in one key element. In the end we still had no rights.

The internet and Google afforded us all access to information that we didn't have easily available before. We could do a fact-check and see what rights the marriage act bestows on those who can simply say "I do." The first time I read a website or two outlining the over-sixty rights and privileges given to straight couples who marry, I was pissed. Even though I really had no great desire to go through the whole marriage thing again, I knew a lot of people who did. I made up my mind to commit to helping them no matter what. But, I can't say that my zeal to work for and help promote marriage equality was simply a matter of civil rights alone . . . There was another factor involved. My old friends, the fightin' Fundies. Once they caught a whiff of the talk of gay marriage, or "same sex" marriage as they began calling it, they went into a collective spasm of projectile vomitus. Like Linda Blair in her starring role in *The Exorcist,* they barfed up a veritable boatload of gruesome green bile. The venom and vitriol spewing from pulpits across the Nation and around the world was breathtaking! I can even imagine some heads spinning as well, but I missed that pleasure.

At first came the predictable sarcastic Christian catcall: "God created Adam and Eve, not Adam and Steve." How clever, I thought. So dripping with the love of Jesus. But it got worse. How could it? The entire world was hanging in the balance. The Devil was laughing with delight the day the marriage died. Actually, this issue, at the beginning, was made to order for the televangelists—all of them. It was perfect, as it so glaringly spotlighted the difference between the outrageous and unthinkable notions of the "perverts". . .

Even thinking of soiling the sacrament of marriage and the holy institution of sacred "Christian" marriage itself. But, from the get-go, it was not just the wild-eyed preachers and money-grubbing evangelists who began the chant One man One woman! . . . But Right-wing politicians came out of the woodwork to jump on the sure-thing bandwagon. Every whacked-out, wild-eyed, and money-grubbing politician suddenly became a preacher as well, and they were all off to the races! What a show! And they even started sounding like preachers too.

Well, my thoughts went right back to our good 'ol friend, Tevia, again when the first chants became a dull roar and, finally, a mighty choir of angels all singing in unison . . . "Tradition! ... Tradition!" Both the radio and television preachers with voices like bagpipes or out-of-tune pianos and the Right-wing politicians with voices like preachers, took up the incantation. "One man ... one woman! That's the way it's always been!" The uninformed and the gullible sucked it right up! After all, they know that it's the Bible way, God's way, the American way!" But, having read the Bible once or twice, I knew full well that this is simply not true.

Surely, I figured, pastors, ministers, priests, and rabbis would know that One Man One Woman is not in the least the "Biblical model" for marriage. I was dumbfounded that no one was challenging this obvious falsehood that was being bantered around as if it were the "Gospel" truth or something. As I've said many times, either these clergymen or politicians were knowingly lying, or the lot of them could use a Bible refresher course. "It has always been this way. For centuries—yeah, for thousands of years . . . since the beginning of time. It has forever been so!" Wrong.

The modern marriage model is a current Western adaptation; it is a rather new cultural concept. The actual Biblical model could best be summed up this way: "Marriage is between one man and as many women as he can afford." Yes, folks, polygamy is the scriptural order of the day. Actually, the Mormons got this one thing right clear back in 1830 something. And I flashed ahead some years in my mind when I first pointed this out to some born-again friends. I foresaw a day when gay marriage would actually become socially and culturally okay, but when the next issue on the agenda would become the return to the Biblical norm, polygamy! Oh, I can't wait for that. It's coming. Take my word on this.

So, am I for polygamy? Hell yes. Why not? It's right out of my favorite book, the Holy Bible. Once I had reached the end of my tether with Republican politicians bawling against gays marrying based on their vast understanding of the Bible, I predicted that their next fear would be of polygamy. Of course, I knew they were right on this. For years they had been predicting (stupidly as usual) that granting gays the right to marry would simply usher in polygamy, along with marriage to children and animals! Of course, some knew how preposterous this was, as marriage is a mutual contract and both partners must consent. But, as Biblical literalists do believe that snakes and donkeys can talk, perhaps a mule could also say "I do." So I will give them that one. Maybe they could marry an ass. (Supply your own joke here. It's way good, huh?)

Well, I recall sitting and waiting for a friend about ten years ago in a small restaurant in Palm Springs, reading the local newspaper. I was shocked and flabbergasted. For years I had been thinking that we should be taking those to court who were denying us the same rights as straights, since it was discrimination pure and simple. Somebody as smart as I had figured that out, and it looked like some forward-thinking folks in California were about to do the same thing. When my lunch partner arrived, I showed him the article and proclaimed that we should not only sue in the Golden State but in all fifty of them.

Having been through a two-year divorce and many lawsuits during my tenure in the Gift and Decoration industry, I knew full well how expensive lawsuits are. "Let's start suing for equal rights," I recall saying a bit too loudly, as my friend was a bit hard of hearing. He picked up on the whole concept of the thing and took to ranting and raving a bit too boldly himself—causing the very Christian-looking couple at the next table to evacuate posthaste (in a huff). Haha. Too bad. I knew right then and there that we were onto something, and I was right. It was the very same idea that we pulled on the Russians back in the *Star Wars* days. Spend them into oblivion. Make them spend their money until it hurts. I knew good and well that gay lawyers across the Country would take it on as a true mission and work tirelessly and for free, whereas the various governmental jurisdictions would have to pay their lawyers exorbitant fees.

Well, that was then and this is now. Despite the legal and political twists and turns along the way in these past ten years, we now have our legal rights. Praise the Lord! LOL. Of course, as predictable, the Fundiemonsters are kicking and screaming. I love it, as they have made us scream for so many years. Of course, the battle is not over. But it is now having to shift to new areas of dispute. They have rather abruptly changed from being the aggressors, denying us our rights. Now they are playing the victims. Poor us, the put-upon little Christians—the persecuted ones. All their feigning of being the underdogs sends out the signal—projects the image—that their weak, wimpy god can't protect them. They have for years called down God's power and wrath upon the godless, satanic fags; but their prayers seem to have gone up into thin air and vanished, huh? I know how that feels. For years I too prayed to the Christian god for "healing." Please, Dear Father God, in Jesus' name, make me straight. Remember I told you all about that? Well, now let them call down fire and brimstone. See what good it ever does?

They will, for sure get all wound up in church, "coming against" Satan's bootlickers, the U.S. Supreme Court. The televangelists will continue to rant and rave on late night cable TV. The preachers will shout from the pulpits around the country. But once the services are over and everybody goes home to cook dinner, they will have to come up with something better. Oh, but they already have . . .

"They are taking away our religious liberty!" Is rapidly becoming the new battle cry of the Religious Right. With the granting of gays the right to marry, their rights to discriminate have been infringed. It is the exact same argument that they used when they fought allowing gays in the military (but with a twist). I was talking to a Christian friend in the ministry who had served with me back in the Army, about how gays should be allowed to serve the country like everybody else. Of course, his point was that doing so would be discrimination against his religious liberty. I heard: "If fags can serve in the military, it cuts into my religious liberty to hate—to discriminate." I hear the same thing now. If fags can marry, it cuts into my religious liberty because I want to discriminate! They shouldn't have to force me to do something I don't want to do. Like bunk with a gay guy. . . Now that that is no longer an issue, the new wrinkle on that old line is: I shouldn't have to be forced to perform a gay wedding!

This sounds so realistic and plausible to so many with no ministerial experience. They lie to their congregations and constituents. "With this ruling, pastors and priests will be forced—compelled to officiate at gay weddings." Talk about a fucking Christian lie. All pastors and ministers (and priests) can marry whomever they chose to and decline to whenever they feel it contravenes their "deeply held" beliefs. It has always been so and will not be changed in any way. But it really stirs up the haters. No Catholic priest has ever been required by any law to officiate at any wedding. In fact, I still remember an Italian Catholic priest who refused to perform a wedding unless a certain young woman in the congregation put on more appropriate attire. I think he was well within his rights to do so, as even I think a tube-top is somewhat out of place in church. If Beth and I had wanted to get married in a Mormon temple, we would have been surely denied. Lacking any standing in that "church" totally disqualifies any non-Mormons their marriage ceremonies. And on it goes.

Likewise, no Christian school is required to teach scientific truth. They can teach of talking donkeys, the moon turning to blood and the sun standing still if they damned well please. They are not compelled to teach anything but what their doctrine allows. But this argument is presently the best thing they can come up with. It is called the First Amendment to the Constitution, which guarantees the "freedom of speech and religion." The poor, wimpy, beat-up Christians have always had these freedoms, which are not in jeopardy because gay people can now marry. They just don't have the right to deny gays and other groups those rights any more. They have to give up their bigotry—at least in public. A good friend of mine put it this way: "They still have the right to be a bigot, but they just can't act like one."

Actually, that is not quite completely true. They can act like a bigot in their homes and churches, but once they cross the line into the public sphere, they are walking out on thin ice. Their leaders and politicians know this. That is why they are trying to stake out the high ground on the "religious liberty" issue so quickly. They are making it personal. Welcome to my club, dear Fundamentalist person. I have been taking it personally for years—ever since I sat quietly listening to you degrade and humiliate me unaware that you were doing so. I listened to your bullshit for years. I took it when you trashed me and "my kind," not knowing that I would remember your un-Christ-like crap for the rest of my life.

The poor little Chreeestians have their feelings hurt. Tough titty. My feelings have been hurt for years. You never gave a shit about my feelings, did you? Well, no, cuz you forced me into a closet not of my making, and you had no idea that I was recording your every word. Now you whine and whimper that the gay gestapo is preventing you free religious expression under the First Amendment. What a crock! But what should I expect? Consider the source.

Well, wouldn't you know it . . . so predictable . . . some "Chreestians" in the holy state of Tex-ass are threatening to secede from the United States over gay marriage! Really? Gee, we are all going to miss you. But, since you're all thinkin' about it, why don't you just take Alabama and Mississippi with you when you leave? Perhaps some other states might feel more at home in Jesusland as well. Good luck and sayanara.

FRONTLASH

As opposed to backlash (What's next after gay marriage?)

Of course, now we are heading into uncharted territory. Since this is a memoir (so mostly dealing with events in the past), and since I do not claim to be a prophet of any kind, I will stick to my personal narrative, and opine as usual. But I will try to speculate a bit about what I think is coming. Given my years of experience with our dear brethren, the Fightin' Fundies, I think I can say with a relative amount of certainty that they are not going to take this lying down. They are going to try to figure out another way to deny gay people their rights; not to marry— that is—but to live as married couples are wont to do: free of discrimination and harassment. And, as you will see, this goes way beyond the topic of marriage.

I knew that once the big court case in California had been won in the US Supreme Court, Oregon would quickly follow Washington and other progressive states to knock down the unconstitutional state ban on LGBT people being allowed to marry; thus giving us the same rights as other "regular" (normal) people. LOL. Yeah! For the first time we get to be normal too. Smile. Yeah!

So the backlash began. It started innocently enough. A lesbian couple wanted a conventional white wedding. And now they could have one. Unlike the thousands who flocked to the Multnomah County courthouse in downtown Portland the day that the Oregon State Supreme Court down in Salem ruled and pandemonium ensued, they wanted to wait, plan, and "do it up big." That was fine and dandy. At least now they could. So their planning involved ordering a wedding cake—how normal! But not so easy. They went into a small bakery in a rather non-descript strip mall out east of the city in Gresham. They found a bakery called *Sweet Cakes By Melissa* that advertised custom wedding cakes. So they went in to order a cake. But little did they know that the owner was a born-again Christian bigot. Her name was Melissa Klein, and she refused to provide service to the couple. Why? Well, she was a Chreeeestian. Of course. And providing a service that she advertised and had a business license to provide notwithstanding, she claimed that she had the right to discriminate because the "lifestyle" of the prospective customers offended her (and her god, of course). Well, the lesbians were hurt and embarrassed. I would have said, "Well, fuck you and the broomstick you rode in on" and left. But they sued. I guess I have more experience with Fundamentalists and their warped, closed minds than they did, because I really don't think it is worth the hassle to waste my time and emotional energy on narrow-minded, self-righteous fools like that. But it made national news. I was impressed (and sent the couple an encouraging email). I also tried to contact the bakery. No luck. They were whining and sniveling on national TV (read: FOX News) by that time, claiming that they "had been forced out of business by the fags." So I couldn't get in touch. Pity. I really wanted to witness to them. I wanted to remind them of the words of their Lord and savior, Jesus. They really needed to hear them.

They had become kind-of Christian celebrities and were talking about hosting their own reality TV show or something—last time I checked. LOL. But they spawned many copycat cases in various bigot bakeries around the country. Of course, bakeries were just the beginning. Photographers began likewise choosing whom they would and wouldn't serve. If you are a fag—forget it. But this had begun to become a business issue. And believe me (one who has been in biz)— your license to do business with the GP is a sacred contract between the owner and the public itself. It is a trust, and people like Aaron and Melissa Klein breached that trust by their discrimination, and deserved it when the State Labor Commission yanked their license. But, by then they had a *gofundme.com* page and the dollars were flowing in . . . The mission's dollars that could have gone to building an orphanage in Haiti, funding a school in Bangladesh, or starting a Teen Challenge Center in Mindanao went into their greedy pockets. Pastors and missionaries, you can just wait at the back of the line.

Of course, all this is related to the gay wedding issue. But it couldn't just stop there, could it? Some "Joe the Plumber" type in Michigan—a devout Christian—proclaimed that he would not serve faggots—no way, no how (under any circumstances). He would not serve any gay person at all ever—period. Fixing cars has nothing to do with weddings or any of that. He just hated fags and wouldn't fix their cars even if his business license required that he do so. Oh, wait. Come to find out, he didn't even have a business license (in Michigan or anywhere). He was just fixing cars and advertising his services, taking money and not paying business income taxes. But he is a *Chreeeestian,* so that is alright. Damn the government and all their rules and regulations. He doesn't believe in any of that, so he just doesn't feel that he has to comply and follow the rules. Remember the "God's laws are above man's laws" meme of the Bible smugglers? Their excuse for their malfeasance and lawbreaking was that it was in China, and the laws of the PRC didn't apply to them. Well, a guy like this is flaunting the laws of the State of Michigan and the U.S. in general, cuz his god is bigger than the "gumment," so he does not have to pay his taxes like everybody else. Talk about Christian arrogance (and privilege)! But there is more to the story. Not only would "Mike the Mechanic" not pay his taxes (earned from his illegal fix-it shop); but if a gay person were to insist that he work on their car, he would sabotage it! What? Don't you just see the love of Christ shining through his life? Doesn't that just make you want to fall to your knees and cry out "Oh Jesus, save me. I want to be just like that man—your good and faithful servant?" Me neither.

And this is the new wave I see coming. Why? Because Evangelicals are a kind of "tribe" and their tribe is threatened. The most outrageous, audacious, and courageous of the tribe will sally forth and fight for the tribe. It is their duty—their calling. They see themselves as threatened (and they are). They are threatened by modernity. They are threatened by the 21st Century. Their Bronze Age rules from the Old Testament and the Iron Age mindset of the New are like those little humpbacked bridges of Francis Schaeffer fame. They are antique . . . out of date. They cannot stand up to the heavy traffic of modern science, philosophy, and—well—life in general. They are fossils—dinosaurs. They don't know it, but like any wild animal that is cornered and threatened, they will lash out and fight back. Expect a lot more of that in the years ahead. Tom's prediction. (It's free :-)

I have a lot of experience with this tribe . . . the Fightin' Fundie tribe. It's an extremely diverse tribe. A better word for it might be "scattered" or "disorganized." You could also say "conflicted." Due to the fact that they don't have a Pope or any visible leader with any authority over them, people like Melissa Klein and Mike the Mechanic can do whatever they want—even if it is totally in contradiction to the doctrines of the faith or scripture. After all, they get their instructions directly from the Almighty. God speaks to them and gives them a "word of knowledge" (like the dear lady back in Springfield who saw the letter "F" on my tongue). But she was a simpleminded sweetheart. Mike and Melissa are clearly simpleminded; but they are definitely not "sweet" (although Melissa claims that her cakes are). LOL. I doubt it. I'll bet they really taste like hate.

* * * * *

Lunch-counter legislation. I've heard that cool new term floating around lately. Back during the 1950s and 1960s (particularly in the Bible- thumping South), lunch counters were segregated. White only black only. Sort of like one man one woman. Minds that can only deal with a choice of two are kind of limited, huh? Actually, all across the country, congressmen and senators on the state level are conspiring to legislate their hate. And, I might add, they are succeeding in many cases. The Religious Right have managed to infiltrate many state legislatures to the point of total outright control. This is not good. But they love being in power (despite their constant whining about being victimized by the mean fags and their evil gay agenda all the time). Hah. Power fits them in their own minds, as they rejoice in the Lord for bestowing the reins of government on them so that they can enact holy legislation. In most Southern and Plains states, the Republican party—the GOP (God's Own Party)—have connived to make abortion clinics ineffective for everyone seeking their services by forcing the doctors to be appendages of local hospitals, which are beholden to the religious power structure that they represent. They have succeeded swimmingly in shutting down all but a few clinics in states like Mississippi and Texas. This means that women's health issues will only be addressed if they can afford to travel to another state or get a hack-job like the good ol' days. Praise the Lord!

The proliferation of guns in the United States is tragic. It's like a national sickness. And although not all Christians are gun-toting maniacs, all gun-toting maniacs are definitely openly and proudly Christian. I remember discussing this phenomenon with a preacher friend of mine over lunch one day when a deacon of his church was joining us. I knew them both well, but knew that the deacon was quite a gun nut, so I broached the subject of why Americans feel the need for so many guns in the society when other countries did not. "Oh, you mean the French!" interjected the deacon right away, as if on cue. "They aren't worth two cents!" I was shocked. "We send missionaries to France," I said. Like that was supposed to mean something to him. Now, this guy was not mean or malicious (usually); but this really got under my skin. "Well, they need it," he said authoritatively. This was back when I was beginning to note that all my religious friends were gradually becoming more outspokenly pushy about politics.

God, guns, and gays was the Republican slogan of the time; and it was definitely working on this guy, who was gradually becoming less and less of a friend all the time. I wonder what he would have said if I'd brought up the subject of homosexuals. He probably would have freaked, and I wouldn't have been able to finish my lunch. I still knew better at the time and kept cool. I was still formulating my exit strategy, and tipping my hand would have been foolish. Suffice it to say that America is armed to the teeth, and I see a bad moon a risin'. In recent years we have all seen various standoffs between the government and armed militia types in Texas (Wacko), Idaho (Ruby Ridge), and Nevada (Cliven Bundy illegally using BLM property for his own personal use to run his cattle). There have been plenty of documentaries floating around about the various armed "Christian" militias around throughout the country; and it is very scary. I hear tell that it is legal now in Texas to carry a firearm anywhere in public—including Safeway, church, and in taverns. OMG. Or as Bill Maher so rightly said: "And what could possibly go wrong with that?"

But the latest I have heard: our guns have to be at the ready to repel ISIS. This is a relatively new wrinkle in U.S. politics and world events. The Islamic State in Iraq and the Levant (ISIL), more commonly known now as ISIS (Islamic State of Iraq and Syria), is an Islamic Fundamentalist organization hell-bent on creating a pan-Islamic Caliphate. What the heck is a Caliphate? I could say: "You really don't want to know." But I do know, so I will tell you. Since the time of Mohammed in the 7th Century CE, various areas in the greater Near East have been—from time to time—run by a Grand Poobah called a caliph. Kind of like the king of a vast domain, he is the top dog—kind of a successor to the kingdom of Mohammed (only with worldwide aspirations). Anyway, the last real Caliphate went extinct in 1924 with the collapse of the Ottoman Empire after World War I. So various Muslim groups have been dying to recreate such an Islamic kingdom ever since. Well, in 2014 they saw their chance and took it. The newly self-appointed Caliph has a totally cool name: Aku Bakr Al Bagdadi. I always remember that as: "Aboo Baker All Big Daddy."

These guys, notorious for their treachery and meanness, have taken to beheading folks of just about every tribe and tongue (including American and other Western journalists). This has made them very unpopular in these parts. They have so scared the Republicans shitless—especially in places like Oklahoma—that legislators have sought to pass laws to prevent them from getting a toehold in "Merika". How are they going to prevent that? Well, they have been seeking to ban sharia law. (Stop laughing.) Yes, they are so weirded out by the threat of ISIS invading Tulsa that they are going to prevent it by forbidding those hideous barbaric Islamic laws. What fools! They are so unfamiliar with their own hideous barbaric scriptures that they fail to notice that sharia law and the Mosaic laws of the Old Testament are nearly identical in every way. Duh.

Well, the latest wrinkle—of which we have certainly not heard the last—is that several of our homegrown terror groups, called "Christian militias," are fixin' to raise a mighty army to go forth to the Holy Land and fight ISIS "over there" so we don't have to fight them over here. This is just another Fundamentalist Christian pipe dream—a delusion typical of poorly-educated dunderheads in this country who think they can drive over there to fight ISIS in their Hummers and Dodge Ram Pickups (with lift-kits). The Christian fixation on fighting A-rabs goes back a long way. As mentioned, the main objective of the Crusades of the Middle Ages was to recapture the "Holy Land" from the Muslims, who took it over in the 7th Century, right after the death of Mohammed in 632. They wet their pants thinking about fighting for Jesus (with real guns). *Onward Christian Soldiers! Marching as to war. With the cross of Jesus—going on before!* Ooo. I just want to go out and kill a Caliph for Christ. This bellicose spirit on the part of the Fightin' Fundies is rooted in fear and loathing. They fear and hate the Muslims (always have). Why? Well, back in the Middle Ages, those towel-heads just came in and took over Jesus' town (Jerusalem); and Christians have been pissed ever since. The Pope sent the crusaders out to get it back. But these modern Christian crusaders in their camouflage fatigues and imitation bush hats are just itchin' to shoot something—somebody . . . For Christ, of course. They would really like to storm in some Saturday night and shoot up a gay bar. But that could be messy. I mean legally. So they dream their dream and their congressmen scheme. Meanwhile, their presidential candidates threaten and posture. "By God, we ain't gonna take no shit off no A-rabs and no commies neither!" So there. Of course, even though this Christian bravado—this chest-thumping—is not new, it is definitely different. Gone are the shields with crosses, their chain-mail, and their swords; now they have Uzis and AK47s (just like Jesus). Much more effective. Well, maybe. We'll see.

But that is only half the backstory. The main story is about Israel. (Iz-rull for the Southern fried Fundies.) The "holy" land of milk and honey. The land of the Bible! Ooo. Dig it. I'm getting goosebumps just imagining it. It is big mojo these days to love Israel. When Beebe Netanyahu came to the U.S. to drum up support for himself and his similarly Right Wing Likud party in Israel, the Republicans—to a man—swooned and fawned all over him. He had them eating out of his money-grubbing hand. It is so American, so "patriotic," to stand up for Israel and their occupation of non-Jewish lands that one is downright Satanic to doubt the veracity of those wonderful folks. But I know something that the Jews don't. I know something that even the average pew-sitters don't. Guess what? The Fightin Fundies love Israel . . . not the Jews who live there. They love the "Holy Land." They see themselves as a "type" of Israel of old. The present occupants of the state of Israel are interlopers—Christ killers—and doomed to frizzle and fry in a burning Christian hell along with all the Catholics (including Rick Santorum and Jeb Bush, BTW), as well as all non-Fundamentalist Christians, and the rest of humanity.

Of course, as I have already pointed out numerous times in my trip down memory lane here, hard Right Fundamentalist theology states that Jesus is the only route to eternal bliss in a Christian heaven; and, apart from that, everyone can just go straight to Hell. Well, they are going there anyway, you know. Actually, the modern American (and some other Christian Fundies in other countries around the World) see the Jews in Jerusalem and Tel Aviv as nothing more than targets for Evangelism. Unless they convert to Christ—fall on their knees and accept Jesus as their personal Lord and savior—all of them are totally and forever damned. Now, that's pure theology and their actual doctrinal position. Many dunderheads in the pew know this. But they hate Obama, liberals, feminists, and fags so much that they find themselves excusing the Catholics and Jews (who agree with them) temporarily (until the rapture, that is), when they will be left behind with the rest of the unsaved . . . those with the mark of the Beast, that is. Nanner nanner nanner . . . you're all going to hell, and we're gonna watch! Gotta love those born-again Christian folks, huh? They care so much about the eternal fates of men and women around the world they send out missionaries to reach them, don't they? Well, they used to. Now they just give media the job of evangelization. Yeah, sure.

And they have a point. If you watch the big crusades and the telecasts from the many megachurches across the country and around the world (especially in Latin America), you will be convinced that the Evangelicals are growing like crazy. Look at those tens of thousands with their hands waving in the air, screaming and shouting for Jesus. Makes you want to take off your shoes and just dance in the spirit for Jeeezus, huh? Well, cuz that's what a lot of those throngs are there for . . . the dancing. The show. I was talking to several folks whom I know from mega-churches in Texas, where my son lives. I pick on Texas a lot (but they deserve it!). LOL. Joel Osteen is the pastor of the largest Protestant church in America, the Lakewood Church, located in Houston, Texas. I visited the church a few years ago and was in culture shock. Now I had visited lots of mega-churches in Korea and other places around the planet, but they were full of actual Christians. Lakewood Church was more like a rock concert. It is in a former sports stadium and totally wired for sound. Nobody brings their Bible to church (supposing any of them actually have Bibles, that is). The "sermon" was projected on an arena-sized jumbotron, and all anybody had to do was follow along on the screen. I got kind of a kick out of kids with earbuds watching the screen. I guess they had the sermon coming in on some channel or other, or they were listening to their own music selection instead. It was very impersonal and soulless.

The nice thing about a big church is that there is no real commitment. No one knows your name. I talked to a lot of people out in the lobby during the latter part of the presentation by the pastor, who could not possibly know even a small fraction of the congregation. It was too big and impersonal. Anyone could come and go, and never get involved—sort of like I did. Nobody said boo to me. I filtered around, listened to the "sermon," which was really just a collection of anecdotes. I didn't fault Osteen for that. Apparently that is what the crowd liked and wanted. Stories. The formula is simple. I had heard him on TV before, so I knew his presentation—his delivery. It is smooth, professional, and la la. Everybody sang and clapped in true Pentecostal style, reading the prompter for the words. I picked up on the tunes right away and sang along. It just wasn't any fun though. But if that is all the crowd expected, that's what they got that day. Joel has done a lot of interviews and I find him a pleasant enough fellow. He is certainly not a fire-breathing Fundimonster or anything like that. He preaches a very palatable message for the masses—a feel good Gospel. And I have nothing against that. Most Catholic and Episcopal churches I have attended are similar. It was long on show and short on message. I think it may have something to do with people's attention spans these days. Generation X-ers and especially Millennials have been raised on the Internet, and are used to jumping from one topic to another at the touch of a screen. I don't know how any pastor could really keep their attention for long. But I will say this for sure . . . there was zero challenge to go forth and make disciples.

Rick Warren of the Saddleback Church in Lake Forest (Orange County) California is another superstar pastor of an enormous church. "A place of family, community, and hope" . . . Wooo. Their website is very professional. It is a perfect example of what I have begun calling "corporate religion." Like all things modern and globalized, it is a massive corporation that has systematically swallowed up its smaller rivals. The little brown church in the wildwood may still be around in backwater towns in rural America, and that's likely not going to change much—if ever. But as most folks around the World are increasingly exposed to the same food, clothing, entertainment, and social attitudes, the more the old, white Evangelical Christians are losing out. They are dying out. This is not unusual. If you look down over the centuries, religions and sects do in fact go extinct. When a religion and its message become obsolete—like the little humpbacked bridges of Europe—they may remain as a charming reminder of the past, but their utility is no longer viable. They just can't stand the weight of modernity.

So, why are there still megachurches? How is it that we can sustain Lakewood Church and Saddleback? Well, we can't, and, like the great cathedrals of Europe, they will someday be empty too. The main feature of the megachurches is that they grow by "sheep-stealing." It is a very old word in Evangelical circles and is self-explanatory. Big churches, like big companies, grow from absorbing other smaller units. The Food Chain. The small fish gets eaten by the big fish and the big fish gets eaten by a still bigger one. We see huge megachurches developing in places like Brazil, Argentina, and Panama. But they are not creating new Christians from scratch. They are simply doing what I was doing in the Philippines. That is —they are stealing Catholics. The massive growth of megachurches in the U.S. is largely a product of sheep-stealing as well. When I visited Lakewood and other big churches (and some of the huge churches in California and Colorado where I actually preached years ago), the story was the same. When you asked the average Joe-the-plumber type (aka, the lunchbox crowd), the same basic story emerged. They came—for the most part—from other churches. They were attracted to the big church by all the "programs" . . . the bling. They like the interest groups—the gun club, the hiking club, or the gymnasium. Years ago, the originators of the megachurch concept realized that the church should be a "community" (which is cool). A person's life—and that of his children—should revolve around activities in the church. "Something for everybody" it seems. Heck, some big "liberal" churches even have a sort of gay- friendly atmosphere! And believe me, fags love to play church!

My experience with modern Fundamentalist Christianity is way different now than when I first started out on my journey back in college when Glenn personally led me to Christ on that rainy day in April of 1968. If any of us could have leaped ahead fifty years and seen a megachurch, we would have either keeled over in a dead faint or run the other way. I have often thought about this and am really not sure what I might have done. I still think I did the right thing at the time. But one thing I do see about the people back then and the newer generations is that the nature of human beings has not changed much. We all still make choices based on what is best for "me" and what is in it for me??? in the end. And most hot religions always have something to offer . . . in the end.

For years—yeah, even centuries—the "Church" of its time has promised rewards in the great by and by. The Muslims get seventy-two virgins, the Mormons get their own planets, and every Evangelical born-again Christian gets a mansion just over the hilltop! For all these various religious folks, dying really has its perks, huh? A few years ago, Pastor Rick Warren of Saddleback fame, wrote a book entitled *The Purpose-driven Life*. It has been a big hit and has really managed to put some purpose into the lives of otherwise rather flat-line Christians. Every few years a book hits the Fundamentalist playlist and everybody goes gaga for it. It is just one more religious fad. And believe me, I have lived through many in my day as an ordained Evangelical clergyman. Well, I did try to read the thing, but gave up in disgust and sheer boredom. What a crock! Like most books of that type, it is just a pile of platitudes and nebulous challenges to live a rich, full, and abundant life in the Lord Jesus Christ. Nothing wrong with that, I guess, but it is just so dull and predictable.

Born-again Christians' lives are not at all driven to any higher purpose. For the most part they pay lip service to the Gospel's admonitions to good behavior and good deeds. Although helping the needy, the infirm, or the castaways in society is all well and good, it should be left to professionals like Mother Theresa or Teen Challenge. A donation now and then to a charity is usually sufficient. The Bible challenges Christians to "go into all the world and preach the Gospel to every creature." I was heavily invested in that task—as assigned by Jesus back in the day. And, yes, I guess that in many ways I was living a purpose-driven life.

Christians say that they want to serve their Lord—and that sounds fine to me. It always did. But what does that mean? Giving to the poor, helping the sick, and feeding the hungry are noble undertakings, to be sure; but in a rare moment of honesty, most believers would likely admit that they are in it for a reward in the hereafter. I call that the "Reward-driven Life."

Most know that their altruism is not something to which they are naturally inclined. They have to work at it. Some do quite well and others just fall flat. They can't even pretend to care about the "eternally lost souls" around them in their tens of thousands a day. So why do they do well? Because they know that in the end they are going to get something for it. They also believe that their efforts are cumulative and that there is a storehouse in an imaginary realm far away "beyond the blue" where their treasures are "laid up." I can't wait, can you?

The rub for modern Christians is that not all good deeds are of equal worth. Some things count more in the afterlife than others. Sure, feeding the hungry is a good thing, but anybody can get behind that. Heck, even liberal, non-religious, and Socialist governments can give away free stuff to victims of famine, earthquakes, and civil wars. But convincing another human to convert, change his mind, and take on a whole new worldview, accepting Jesus as his personal savior. . . Now, that's real good mojo. The best. The rewards keep piling up and, wow, are they ever great.

When I was younger and seriously into "winning souls for Christ," I was not really that excited about all that promised bling so often sung about in churches far and wide. I never was all that jazzed about wearing some big clunky crown. I am still rather unimpressed with a mansion just over the hilltop . . . and besides, I never even learned how to play the harp either. Too bad, huh? In fact, after years attending church, and later in the ministry, I finally concluded that there was nothing in the rewards category that much interested me at all. The heaven that is on the minds of modern pew-sitters has no appeal for me whatsoever. "Ah, but you get to live forever with Christ!" they croon in obvious delight. Yeah. Up there with all the cherubim, the seraphim, the putti, and the zygotes of unborn fetuses swimming around in a sea of divine glory. Lucky us. Sounds delightful.

The serious problem I face when contemplating an eternity of bliss in a Christian heaven is the inhabitants. The only people up there are all the same. There is simply no diversity at all. Everyone in the Evangelical paradise-to-come is a born-again, Fundamentalist Protestant Christian. These are the very people I ran away from years ago! The idea of spending my forever with the likes of many whom I have met, interacted with, and even worked with is an incubus that I have no stomach for at all.

Actually, in retrospect, I would have to say that I learned more from some 1950s and 60s television than from the pulpit. One of my true heroes of the faith was a humble fellow named Jed Clampett. He was a simple man, content with his lot in life as a poor mountaineer out shootin' at some food. He was likewise content in his wealth when providence smiled down on him and he became a millionaire. He was always doing good—often without thinking about it—giving away freely of his abundance to any he saw in need—much to the chagrin of his banker, Milburn Drysdale, the corporate climber and megachurch attendee. I think Jed is more of the ideal that Jesus must have had in mind way back there when he gave us the beatitudes. (Blessed are the poor among you.) Remember those?

And then there was Granny, the rip-roarin' paranoid Fundamentalist. Everything to her was black-and-white, right and wrong. I recall a particular episode when she was totally pissed off about something or other. Something had gotten her dander up, and she was stormin' out to set things straight, complete with her NRA shotgun in hand. A perfect metaphor for the Fightin' Fundie folk, Republican politicians, and Fox News pundit types like Pat Buchanan, Newt Gingrich, and Ann Coulter. They can't see themselves in her, but that's who they are—Granny.

It was Jed who tried to reason with her—to appeal to her better nature, her inner Christ. Well, that fell flat. She would have none of it. But, true philosopher and theologian that he was, he pulled out his trump card to deal with her mania and righteous indignation. Do you remember how he appealed to her to stop acting like a moron and to let the true love of Jesus shine through? He appealed to her greed. "You'll get another star in your crown!" Jed said softly. That did the trick. It worked then and is still working as well to this day! Ah, yes. The reward-driven life.

Well, the Grannies of this world are a dying breed. Of course, they are really the old white guys who run the congress and the congregations. Their attitudes toward anything new and different are predictable and negative. In fact, they see their job as protecting the tribe. They are the patriarchs—the wise old men, the elders, the chieftains. They are the last of the Mohicans . . . the Chingachgooks. The world is changing around them and they are "holding the fort." I still remember that old fossil song that used to be so popular in Fundamentalist churches around the country: "Hold the fort, for Christ is coming!" Can't you just see the image? All these old duffers— men and women—waving their white handkerchiefs back and forth as banners. Their bunker mentality would be so quaint if it were not so deluded and mean-spirited. These are the people who have made my life as a gay man miserable. They are the Brother Williams, the OCA, and the old time GOP. They are a dying tribe, but they are standing firm and are going down fightin'. They are holding the fort. Even so, come quickly, Lord Jesus!

JESUS IS COMING SOON!

Look busy!

I have noticed that on most of the political TV talk shows (to which I am hopelessly addicted), they are referring to the "culture wars" in the past tense. The old white Christian men of the GOP, and the preachers and televangelists, are really looking old and sounding tired. Well, their message has not changed much, but the world around them has. They are still holding the fort and preaching the same old apocalyptic message: The world is lost, fallen, and doomed. All is shit, woe woe woe. But cheer up . . . sooner or later Jesus is going to appear in the sky and poof . . . All the born-again Protestant Evangelical Fundamentalist Christians will be transported straight up into the sky, "caught up in the clouds" to be with Jesus and his dad, Yahweh, forever and ever. Hallelujah—amen! And the liberals, the fags, the scientists, and the Democrats will all be left behind to fight the war of Armageddon against the Beast and the anti-Christ. Or something like that. Their message is garbled and contradictory. But what do you expect? Consider who we're dealing with here. I do agree that there is a new day a comin'. But it may not be exactly as they envisage it. This is partially true because none of them can agree on what the future holds anyway. Like any of us knows that! LOL. But some among us claim to know, and they influence the fort-holders still.

As I stand here and finish my look back, I am kind of amazed. Wow, a lot has happened to me over the last fifty years, give or take. It has been kind of fun telling you about all the weird and fun things that I have been through (and the bad stuff as well). But I want to wrap this all up with a look now to the future. I will be honest. I don't have a clue what the future will be like. I am no longer a Christian, so I am not in the prognostication biz. I gave that up years ago, as I told you. But there are many who claim to "know" the future. I want to give them a shot. And when someone reads this years from now, we will see just how right they are or are not. Okay? (For the record, I do predict they are not.)

This last chapter is dedicated to the Millennial Generation, aka, "the Millennials." I was born right in the middle of the "Baby Boom," so I have a certain perspective. My son is a Gen-X-er, so he has his own outlook as well. But I am married to a Millennial, so I am having a grand time living with and loving someone of the forward generation. It has its moments. We have so little in common (in many ways)—like music, movies, TV, and clothing; but we do agree on other stuff like men and sex :-) And I will admit really that it is so handy to have someone around all the time helping figure out why my 'puter is acting up, or fixing the TV, or tweaking my cell phone apps. I have beaten my bad karma with machines by marrying somebody who is smarter dealing with them than I am, and who does not let them intimidate him! Totally cool, huh? I'm so happy :-)

We are standing today at a real interesting place. The people in power are older, whiter, and more fucking religious than the rest of the country. All during the ten years that my mom lived at her retirement home and assisted living facility, I watched and observed the "Greatest Generation"—those who fought in the Second World War. They are still the base of the Republican Party. They are dying off rapidly, as my dad (2005) and then my mom (2014) did. Both Protestant and Catholic churches are dwindling, with fewer and fewer congregants . . . who tend to be really old people. Us Boomers seem to be kind of transitional now. When I first started going up to the VA hospital in Portland for various health-related stuff about twenty years ago, I noticed all these old duffers from World War II. They wore their unit baseball hats, with words on them like Iwo Jima and Pearl Harbor. Those people are gone. For ten years or so I saw a lot of vet hats with Korea embroidered on them. Now, when I hobble up there with my arthritic hip to do PT (physical therapy), I see the more familiar words like Da Nang, Saigon, and Nha Trang. Ah, Viet Nam. It seems just like yesterday. Did I tell you about the time when I used to go to the Pentecostal Servicemen's Center? Oh yeah. Guess I did. Sorry, I repeat myself—repeat myself. Sigh.

But, unlike former generations, some of us boomers are not really nostalgically tied to the past. Oh, well, I still listen to the Beatles on *YouTube*, and sing along with Petula Clark . . . *Downtown*. I was lucky to have a Gen-X-er (Dale) as my first boyfriend, so I really love Madonna and the Bangles (and can *Walk like an Egyptian*). That still makes me smile. I am lost in a sea of new music and movies and new stars. But I do know the ones I think are hot, of course. And you know who you are, Eddie, Benedict, Jake, and Bradley! :-) Oh, come on—take a bow. So I am definitely not stuck in the past. However, most of the people in my life who have sought to make my life miserable, have been. They are the Fightin' Fundies—the fossils who harken back to "Bible times" as an ideal society. They believe the Bible verbatim and would bring back the good old days of segregation, Jim Crow, or mandatory school prayer if they could. They are still clinging to the last vestiges of that more "Christian" time when "girls were girls and men were men," of Archie Bunker fame. But the last ten years alone have seen such an erosion of their power and place that they may be fighting their last fight. Still, I have years ahead to fight against them, and I will.

* * * * *

Let me explain something about the rest of this memoir, as it is not like the stuff that you have read so far. It is not really part of the past—recounting events—but a vision of the future. I have been careful to not include names of contemporary personalities for the most part. Any names like Pat Robertson, Lon Mabon, and Scott Lively—who are presently still down here on this Planet—are only referred to as "in the past," because I have known them and worked with (or against) them. Other names from the past, like Tammy Faye Bakker and Jerry Falwell—who have "gone on to be with the Lord"—are likewise part of the past. Nothing in the first nineteen chapters of this book need ever to be changed. It is a record of my life as I remember it. This chapter, however, can be upgraded in a year or two or five, as I don't want to just get stuck here. I may mention some contemporary names of those in the news who will be dead, discredited, or no longer in office in a few years' time, or may replace all or part of this chapter as needed. I want to end with a window open to the future, as I want to dedicate this last chapter to my dear friends, the Millennials! You guys are our hope, so good luck. I live near a major U.S. university so I encounter Millennials every day. The place is crawling with young folks in their twenties and early thirties. And did I mention that I am married to one? Oh yeah, I guess I did :-) Lately, it has been noted in various polls of religious trends that the "NONEs" (persons whose religious affiliations are "NONE of the above") have pushed upward in numbers, acting out all but the Evangelicals so far. Of course, as I mentioned, most of those "Evangelicals" (including the Fightin' Fundies) have seen most of their stunning growth develop from the stealing of Catholic sheep! LOL. They are such rip-off artists. They are crowing about how they are number one now. Well, maybe they are. But instead of preaching the Gospel of love and peace to the "heathen," they will keep on stealing sheep from the disenfranchised papists.

Actually, I will interject here that they may not succeed at all. The new Pope has a very real chance of reversing that trend. He is new, unique, and quite refreshing. Most Catholics seem to adore him . . . his loving and accepting spirit, concern for the poor, and thoughtfulness regarding the environment. And when even atheists like Bill Maher and Sam Harris have a good word for him, he must be doing something right. I am impressed and am giving him a chance.

I might also drop in a historical note here, as you know I am wont to do. When Martin Luther did his thing back in 1517 (kicking off the Protestant Reformation), and the Roman church fractured, it looked like the Mother Church would lose all of Europe north of the Alps (and all points east) to Protestantism. So they launched a lovefest called the Counter Reformation, and wowed the wandering sheep with the glitz and glitter of the Baroque period. Their architecture and statuary are still around as proof. And all those churches, like Lakewood and Saddleback— chock full of namby pamby wandering Catholics—may well be emptied if Pope Frank can just bottle that cool brew that I remember back there in Munich called the "Charismatic Catholic" movement. It was kind of squashed by J2P2 and Ben-the-dick; but Frank might just give it a revival . . . and then let's see what happens in places like the U.S. and Brazil! I am watching with keen anticipation.

Speaking of revivals—that is a word much-loved and cherished by the Fundamentalists. America has seen cyclic periods of high religious zeal and blah disinterest (or downright hostility). After the American Civil War, where we wrenched slavery out of the cold, dead hands of the Right-wing "Christian" Confederacy, there was a period of religious chaos marked by westward expansion and a kind of social free-for-all that Mark Twain relished and wrote about so much. Virginia City, he recalled, "is no place for a Presbyterian!" Gotta love it, huh? Then there was the "Great Awakening" around 1900. It was a super cool time for the Fundies, as it was just to their liking. All sorts of new wild-eyed groups sprang up; and others, like the Mormons and the Pentecostals, really took off. Jerry Hill, who I told you about (with the snake-handling relatives), could trace his religious family history right back to that time. He was embarrassed about it. And now that I look back, I can't blame him.

That time of wild outdoor revival meetings in tents was big time la-la mojo back until they pushed too far, spawning the temperance movement, which brought about the 18th amendment—Prohibition. And we all know how successful that was. Well, the Mike Huckabees, Rick Santorums, and Ted Cruz dingbats of our day are carbon copies of the still-smashers and booze-bottle-breakers of the 1920s and 30s. And Scott Walker speaks openly of the need for a revival of revivals (old-fashioned tent meetings that is)! OMG, I can just see it all now. Actually, when I was itinerating back in the years gone by, there were still a few tent meetings around. I encountered one the year when I had to attend a summer-long seminar that was required of all Assemblies of God missionaries called "School of Missions." It was, of course, held at the A/G headquarters in lovely, tasteful Springfield, Missouri.

That summer Beth and I had just left the Philippines and had been reassigned to Hong Kong. But we had to do the whole whooptydoo seminar, which lasted way too long but went over all sorts of policies and points of interest, like what would happen if we as missionaries were captured and held as hostages. We were told quite rightly that we had no commercial value, as no missionary-sending agency of any stripe would pay money for mere missionaries—stuff like that. But across town and sponsored by some wing-nut evangelist or other, was an actual old-time tent revival meeting. We called it a "hoot-'n-holler." Great fun. I attended one evening, hoping for snakes. Boo. Shucks. That would have at least made it worth sitting in a hot, crummy, canvas, circus-like tent full of screaming, sweaty Pentecostal Fundies. Such a delight. I emphasize the word hot. And Scott Walker thinks that is going to stem the tide of the "gay agenda?" What a fool! Well, maybe we fags could redo those tacky tents in designer colors or something :-) But enough of that for now. I don't think that idea is really going to catch on. Do you?

Change of subject here, okay? The current batch of stupid Republican and/or Fundies all seem to have their panties in a wad over Iran getting nuclear weapons. The Mullahs probably will at some point, but so will several other countries around the Globe. The Fightin' Fundies are afraid of the upcoming war with Islam, which they are provoking. Their excuse to Bomb bomb bomb Iran is that Teheran would certainly nuke Israel (read: Jerusalem) if we "allowed" them to acquire such devastating weaponry. They won't do that. Why? Well, duh, cuz the Dome of the Rock is in Jerusalem, and is sitting right square on top of the Temple Mount. It is where Muslims believe Mohammed flew off into the sky on his magic horse, and is the third most holy site in all of Muslimdom. So, Lindsey Graham and Donald Trump, the Iranians are not going to bomb it. Forget it. Ain't gonna happen.

Modern Evangelical Christians (as I noted earlier) see themselves as a type of Israel. They are the "true" Jews—not those apostate jerks, the Israelis, who are the current inhabitants of the state of Israel. The Battle of Armageddon is scheduled to take place there in the Megiddo Valley sometime after Jesus comes in the sky (in the twinkling of an eye) to rapture all the born-agains out of this world of woe. The rest of us are going to be totally sorry we didn't listen to guys like Scott Walker, Mike Huckabee, and Rick Santorum. Oh, sorry. Correction. Santorum is a Catholic, so he will be left out of the rapture . . . "left behind." Too bad. Of course, there is still hope. He could just ask Ted Cruz how to get saved. And we all know how exciting eternity in Heaven with Ted Cruz nonstop forever is going to be! LOL. I am peeing my pants in utter anticipation.

I have for years predicted the "doom of the rock," as according to a lot of Evangelical Christian "scholars," Jesus can't return to Earth until that monstrosity sitting in the very center of Jerusalem is destroyed and the new Jewish temple built to take its place. Fat chance. Of course, I remember back in 1972 or so when some deranged Australian Christian weirdo tried to burn it. Hey, it is made out of non-combustible materials, you dummy. Funny—it was an Australian kook also who smashed the Pietà in Rome about that time as well. Weird bunch, those Aussies, huh? Well, their weird, upside-down Fundamentalism is anyway. LOL

But I do predict that some whacked-out American Christian could blow it up with a drone someday. It might happen. As I mentioned, the U.S. military is now chock full of super Right-wing religious warmongers, some of whom have the ability and training to direct a drone strike on the Al Aqsa Mosque and environs easily if they were of a mind to. Think about it. Talk about going rogue! Hah! It is coming. I would suggest being as far away from the Middle East as possible when that happens, however, as it will bring about a response from the Muslim world that could wreck your whole day. Christian television is loaded with Eschatology-related programs. "End Times" predictions for y'all who are unfamiliar with that word. Learn it. You're going to hear it again, I assure you. Our friends, the Fightin' Fundies —with whom I cohabituated and coordinated for years, as I have told you —eat this shit up. Their blessed hope is for the world to end—for them to be whisked out of here, sucked up into the sky to meet Jesus in the stratosphere, and then go on to the big cosmic theater in the sky where they have reserved seats to look down and watch the rest of us deal with all the crap that is described cryptically in their favorite book of the Bible—namely, the Revelation. Ooo. How cool is that? They are all just wetting themselves for that. Even so, come quickly, Lord Jesus!

Well, I am not holding my breath. Actually, I struggled for all those years as a born-again Fundamentalist to really embrace Revelation. Like most (other than OCD Bible expositors like John Hagee of San Antonio's Cornerstone Church) who have it all figured out, I just took the easy way out and said that I would understand it all by and by. But guys like Hagee are apoplectic about the end times, so I feel that I will need to wrap up this screenplay of my life with my take on Revelation.

The Christians I have known over the years all chant the same mantra about the fate of the Earth, and why it is not worth saving. "It is all going to burn anyway!" They are so smug. They have another simpleminded little ditty that they love to quote: "We have read the end of the book, and know how it comes out!" Of course, they are referring to the last book of the Bible, the *Revelation*, which is a total whacked-out pipe dream thought up ostensibly by St. John the Divine. I wrote in my book entitled: *The Biblical Mystery Tour* that I doubt seriously that any such thing is possible. My surmising informs me that it was most likely written by a collection of drunk Italian monks in the late first or early second Century who were intent on playing a joke on the world. Its authorship was so in question that it was nearly dumped all together by the cardinals and bishops at the Council of Nicea in 325-7 CE, when they decided what was and what was not going to be considered inspired scripture. They should have gone with their gut on that and left it out. But lucky us . . . we have it. And modern Christians are both fascinated by it and deathly afraid of it as well. The majority of the Republican Party and their highly qualified candidates for president claim to believe the predictions of Revelation as literal and true. Should any of us really believe them about anything, based on that?

I recall the famous Republican catfight of the 2012 election cycle when there was a bevy of Fundamentalist candidates onstage for what was advertised as a debate. Of course, it was no such thing, as there was nothing to debate. They were all swimming in the same pool of Biblical literalism, and parroting replies that their staffs had prepared for them to appease the Fightin' Fundies—their "base" of old, white, Southern folks in retirement facilities and assisted living. Fewer of those fossils around these days, but they keep preaching to please them. Go figure. I recall a particular question posed to the group, which included at the time my very favorite whack-a-doodle dummy of all time, Michelle Bachmann. The question was this: Who among you believes in the theory of evolution? Poison question. Of course, not a single participant raised his or her hand, save for one—the Mormon, John Huntsman . . . remember him? I didn't think so. He got it wrong. Too bad.

At the time I thought to myself: "What a dumb question." Of course, half the U.S. population does not believe that we humans evolved from more primitive life forms, but that instead we were created in one fell swoop in the Garden of Eden (on the sixth day). Duh. So the candidates don't have to pay any price at all for their stupid, boneheaded replies. The question that the moderator should ask is: Did the sun stand still . . . in the sky for twenty-four hours while Joshua fought the battle against the Amorites et. al. as recorded in the Book of Joshua chapter ten? Yes or no? Now that would require the would-be world leaders to line up against pure science and not "just a theory." I guarantee that would not only be harder to answer, but way harder to defend against guys like Bill Nye and Neil DeGrasse Tyson, and the general public as well, for that matter. In my experience, even the most ardent Fundamentalist inerrantist squirms in his pew over that one. We all know that they really don't believe that as fact. But, like I did, they have to pretend that they do. It makes the believer really look like the stupid fool that he or she is, if they try to pull that over on the GP. I doubt that any of the Millennials or the NONEs would buy such an obviously false answer. Of course, the "DONEs" (those of us who are done with all religion) would feel the same way, for sure.

So why do we still allow the fossils to dictate our politics? I realize that a few of our current batch of crazies really do (somewhere in their empty skulls) believe that the sun can stand still if God commands it. But, in that case, should guys like Ted Cruz, Mike Huckabee, and Ben Carson really have their finger on the red button? Should anybody who is that out of touch with the 21st Century be the "leader of the Free World?" I don't think so! But I don't think it really makes much difference anyway, as it really matters little on an eschatological level whether or not there is a born-again in the White House.

After all, we did have a totally committed Christian Fundie there for eight years already (G.W.), and that produced nothing for the Evangelicals. Of course, they were pissed that George couldn't wave his magic staff (like Moses) and call down the death angel to go into every gay home in the country and kill them all as Yahweh did to the firstborn of all the Egyptians back in the book of Exodus. Wow, now that would have been really awesome, huh? No, George was kind of a flop in the Fundie mind. He didn't even manage to get rid of abortion. They don't get that the executive branch of government does not make laws or levy taxes. Damn, why not?

Take that up with Madison and Jefferson, I guess. But he did manage to get us into two endless wars and fucked up the economy to boot. But they keep trying. "If we only had a real Christian President," they moan. Well, wah waah. Good luck with that. It would serve them right to get a Ben Carson, or better, a Ted Cruz. Now those guys are some serious Christians! Hallelujah.

Okay, enough political prognosticating. We will just have to watch everything unfold according to Yahweh's divine plan and Jesus' travel schedule. I want to come full circle and end Tom's terribly terrific, top telepathic treatise. I've told you all about my past, so what is in store for me now? The way I see it, it's a toss-up. Why? I find myself in a theological situation as I contemplate my twilight years and my ultimate demise and departure from this planet. I will really miss me when I'm gone.

I'm facing a very basic theological impasse. It is called "eternal security." Don't know what that is? Well, let me tell you. When I was saved—repenting of my sin, and asking Jesus to come into my heart and become my Lord and savior—I was redeemed from "the pit" and assured an eternal life in Heaven, the Christians-only paradise-to-come. I was thrilled. I was twitterpated with delight. I was wowed. I was so taken with the promise of salvation that I went forth for years telling everybody I could find about it. I made the most important decision of my life—but I did it in a Baptist Church. So what? Well, until that hot humid night in Saigon when I spoke in tongues and went Pentecostal, I was technically a Baptist (attending only Baptist churches, being baptized, or "immersed," likewise, and having BAPTIST stamped on my metal military dog-tags in case I died in combat).

The most Fundie of all Fundies, the Baptists, have a particular doctrine that figures greatly into my future in the afterlife. The doctrine of eternal security is basically referred to as "once saved, always saved," and states emphatically that once a person accepts Christ as his or her personal savior and commits his or her life to Jesus forever—all sins are forgiven and he or she is destined to go to Heaven no matter what. "You cannot lose your salvation" is their so-oft-quoted mantra. Of course, this begs the question: Well, what if one falls away from Christ? . . .Commits murder? . . . Or worse, comes out as a fag? OMG! Not that! But, according to Baptist teaching, that does not matter. If a soul is saved and bound to Christ, it is forever and eternal, and cannot be changed.

Oh shit. Do you see the problem? For Christ, for the Church, for me? I am therefore destined to be raptured with the saved millions when Jesus comes back and returns in the clouds. I am destined to go up and live eternally with the putti—the millions of unborn and stillborn baby souls fluttering around the mercy seat of Christ and God (and Mother Mary). I am destined to spend my forever with dear Brother William from VC, Lon Mabon from the OCA, and all those wonderful born-again Christians belonging to the Westboro Baptist Church and elsewhere in Christendom who hate my fag guts forever. Sounds fun. Huh? And there is no appeal. I can't just tell Yahweh that I don't want my salvation ticket after all. I don't want to live forever in a place populated only by Fundiemonsters. And I don't want to sit up in my ringside seat, watching all my friends and family—and all humanity—frizzle and fry forever in a literal burning Christian hell. Hell no, I won't go!

Well, I may have to if the Baptists have anything to say about it. Of course, when a Baptist proclaims that he is a DONE, and quits the safe haven of the likes of the Southern Baptist Convention, he gets the "left foot of fellowship" and is unceremoniously kicked out with the proclamation that: "Well you were never a real Christian anyway!" So there. Take that! And that way they can shout "go to Hell!" and mean it. But I have spoken to many Baptist clergy who are not so sure. My vision of their Heaven is rather gooey and unappealing. And their concept of Hell is no picnic either. It is not well-defined in the Bible; but a lot has been made up about it for eons, based on nothing but speculation.

When I was studying ancient literature at PSU, I read Dante for the first time. His *Divine Comedy* is well-known as one of the foundational writings of Western Civilization, as it kind of painted a picture for mankind of what Heaven, Hell, and Purgatory are like. Actually, the author had no more to go on than we do. Jesus talks of Hell in a metaphorical way in Matthew chapter eighteen: **If your eye causes you to stumble, gouge it out and throw it away. It is better for you to enter life with one eye than to have two eyes and be thrown into the fire of hell.** (Mt. 18:9). And also in chapter five: **If your right hand causes you to stumble, cut it off and throw it away. It is better for you to lose one part of your body than for your whole body to go into hell.** (Mt. 5: 30).

So there! That's it. Dante Alighieri invents Hell for us in his famous book entitled: *Inferno*. He makes the whole thing up, and both the Catholics throughout the centuries and Fundamentalist Protestants today buy the whole thing lock, stock, and barrel as if it were actually part of scripture itself. Why? Well, cuz it is so convenient—so perfect for them to use as a tool—a weapon against everybody they don't like. "You're going straight to Hell!" is a common taunt that our modern Fundie friends dish out at us sinners on a daily basis. Ooo, we are supposed to be scared—so scared in fact that we will reform our behavior to come more in-line with their prejudices, biases, intolerance, and bigotry. But the notion of Hell is really rather vague in the Bible. Of course, another famous verse in Revelation gets a lot of play on the Fundamentalist broken record as well. It's called the Lake of Fire, and just like dear 'Ol Dante, the modern preachers, teachers, expositors, and televangelists just make this shit up to rattle the rabble.

In Revelation chapter 20, verse 10, we are informed that the Lake of Fire is where the Devil is cast down along with the Beast and the False Prophet. Well, good. They deserve it. Bye. But then comes another of the Fundie's favorites: Revelation 21:8 (Tells it like it is!): **The fearful, and unbelieving, and the abominable** (fags?), **and murderers, and whore mongers, and sorcerers, and idolaters, and all liars, shall have their part in the lake which burneth with fire and brimstone.** Ooo, how awesome . . . I mean, awful.

I have heard a gazillion sermons over the years using this verse as proof of Hell and the terrible fate that awaits those whose names are not written in the *"Lamb's Book of Life"* (Rev. 20: 15). But it isn't really very clear, is it? One time I asked a Fundamentalist minister at a town hall meeting back in the OCA days if I would be allowed to skinny-dip in the Lake of Fire or if I would have to keep my street clothes on for all eternity. He was not amused and accused me of being flippant about a thing of such importance (which I was :-). Haha. Actually I was thinking that it might be cool to just swim over and converse with people long-dead whom I have always wished I could talk to, like Thomas Jefferson, Mark Twain, or even Dante Alighieri himself as this is all his creation. The minister informed me that I would be able to do no such thing, since nobody would be able to swim anywhere in the lake because it is impossible to swim in sulfur, or some other such idiocy that he was obviously just making up on the spot. Of course, I just asked him how he knew and where he got that information. Like he had an answer. Oh sure. He had just pulled it out of his ass.

So, all liars (including those who lie on their visa applications, proclaiming falsely to be teachers when they are not) will be there in the dreaded lake as well. It says ALL liars. So I expect a lot of surprise company actually. Come on in. The fire's fine! But the saved—with or without me—get to live in a way cooler place called "The City Built Foursquare." It is a huge cube floating in the starless sky. It glows with the glory of God himself. I really hope the Baptists are wrong, and I am not required to go there for eternity to live with them and the rest of the born-agains for all time. Hell—the lake of fire—sounds so much better to me. But I just couldn't wrap up my screenplay without doing a little missionary work in the end. I feel it is my duty—my obligation—to entice you with the promise of eternal life in Heaven . . . in the City, "the New Jerusalem." It is such a groovy place. You still have a chance to make a reservation. Jesus is coming. Get ready! Buy a ticket.

Let's face it. At this point (no matter how it was done), Revelation says that the Earth is total toast. But just leaving everything like that would be a real downer, wouldn't it? What a bummer ending. But wait . . . There's more! From his heavenly throne, Jesus proclaims: **"I am making everything new!"** (Rev. 21: 5). Of course, it is all over for the trashed Earth and everybody except the born-again, spirit-filled, Bible-believing Protestant Fundamentalist Evangelical Christians. This is their new home and they have it all to themselves. Yeah! Then—pure *deus ex machina*—a holy city, "the new Jerusalem," glides slowly down out of the empty sky. And is it ever an awesome place! It is brilliant like crystal— just like the Crystal Cathedral :-) It has twelve gates with the names of the twelve tribes of Israel inscribed on them. It is 1400 miles square, with walls 200 feet thick. Wow. The walls are made of jasper and the city is made of gold. The foundations are made of sapphire, emeralds, sardonyx, carnelian, chrysolite, beryl, and all those awesome shiny things. Don't you just want to drop everything and go there right now?

Nobody but Fundies gets to enter. The rest—and I mean everybody else—is shit out of luck. Hop in the lake, Jake. Meanwhile, all the Chreeestians get to walk right into the foursquare "City" on the streets "of purest" gold. The Bible says so. But, hey, nothing impure will ever enter the place. And that's a good thing. For the first time in the lives of our friends, the Fightin' Fundies, they will finally get to live in a "fag-free environment" (forever). Hallelujah! Amen.

EPILOGUE: WHERE TO FROM HERE?

The first time I visited Berlin, the Cold War was totally frozen over. I was still in the U.S. military, and could only stand on the west side of the wall and look over into the "Worker's Paradise" in what was then the DDR—East Germany. I wasn't impressed then, nor a few years later when I did actually cross over the barrier and took a walk on the wild side. It was depressing and dull, and rather scary. My experience with Evangelical Christianity is so similar. I will admit that I embraced my newfound religion with relish at first. But years later, when leaving the religion biz behind, I was (and still am) repelled by American Right-wing Fundamentalist religion. I have been out of it for all these years, and I keep telling myself that I have mellowed. A quick visit to almost any news program assures me that I made the right decision to escape all those years ago. But now and then I catch a whiff of a change in Christian behavior. Well, it is just a whiff, mind you.

The other day I received a phone call from an old friend who met me when I was in the ministry. He and his wife are what I would characterize as "faithful laborers in God's vineyard." Like so many friends from my past, they keep in touch with me, considering me to be "one of Jesus' lost and wandering sheep." Like the parable in Matthew's Gospel, where the shepherd leaves the entire flock to seek the one lost lamb out of a hundred, and rejoices when it is found, they pray for my eternal soul.

Friends like that give me hope for the Evangelicals. They're unlike so many we see on television or hear on religious radio programs while driving across endless miles of desert, surfing the paltry fare for anything but a loudmouth, pulpit-pounding preacher screaming for money. These friends are genuine in their faith. I feel relieved knowing that there are actually folks out there in Jesusland who are trying their best to stay true to their spiritual callings.

I still interact with some of my old friends in the missionary world too. So many are genuine, and I still love them and know that they love me too. I keep telling them that living outside the sociopolitical world of the United States keeps them immune from most of the diseases of Fundamentalism that take root and thrive in this hideous (American) environment so easily.

I never thought the Berlin Wall would come down, but it did! . . . and in a most rapid and amazing way. So, do I hold out any hope for the Fightin' Fundies? Sometimes I do. I never thought I would see marriage equality in the USA. It came in a rather similar way—amazingly fast and enthusiastically received by millions. Of course, the fossils keep hanging on; but I honestly believe that their days are numbered. We watch as Islam drags itself and millions back into the muck and mire of the past. Can the Christian Taliban, the Evangelicals, drag us all back down in like fashion? I can't say for sure, but I know full well that they will keep trying. The ongoing war between the Fundies and the fags is far from over. But—take it from me—I'm just getting warmed up for the next round! Ding!